Promising Practices for Fathers' Involvement in Children's Education

A Volume in
Family-School-Community Partnership Issues

Series Editor:
Diana B. Hiatt-Michael
Pepperdine University

Family-School-Community Partnership Issues

Diana B. Hiatt-Michael, Editor

Promising Practices for Family Involvement in Schools (2001)
edited by Diana Hiatt-Michael

Promising Practices to Connect Schools With the Community (2003)
edited by Diana Hiatt-Michael

*Promising Practices Connecting Schools to Families
of Children With Special Needs* (2004)
edited by Diana Hiatt-Michael

*Promising Practices for Family Involvement
in Schooling Across the Continents* (2005)
edited by Diana Hiatt-Michael

*Promising Practices for Teachers to Engage
With Families of English Language Learners* (2007)
edited by Diana Hiatt-Michael

Promising Practices for Partnering With Families in the Early Years (2008)
edited by Mary M. Cornish

*Promising Practices for Family
and Community Involvement During High School* (2009)
edited by Lee Shumow

Promising Practices to Support Family Involvement in Schools (2010)
edited by Diana Hiatt-Michael

Promising Practices for Family Engagements in Out-of-School Time (2011)
edited by Holly Kreider and Helen Westmoreland

Promising Practices for Fathers' Involvement in Children's Education (2012)
edited by Hsiu-Zu Ho and Diana B. Hiatt-Michael

Promising Practices for Fathers' Involvement in Children's Education

Edited by

Hsiu-Zu Ho
University of California-Santa Barbara

and

Diana B. Hiatt-Michael
Pepperdine University

Information Age Publishing, Inc.
Charlotte, North Carolina • www.infoagepub.com

Library of Congress Cataloging-in-Publication Data

Promising practices for fathers' involvement in children's education /
edited by Hsiu-Zu Ho and Diana B. Hiatt-Michael.
    p. cm. — (Family-school-community partnership issues)
    Includes bibliographical references.
    ISBN 978-1-61735-950-7 (paperback) — ISBN 978-1-61735-951-4 (hardcover)
    — ISBN 978-1-61735-952-1 (ebook) 1. Education—Parent participation. 2.
Father and child. 3. Fathers—Psychology. 4. Home and school. I. Ho, Hsiu-Zu.
    II. Hiatt-Michael, Diana B.
    LB1048.5.P766 2012
    371.19'2—dc23

                                    2012024420

Printed in the United States of America

CONTENTS

FOREWORD

Diana B. Hiatt-Michael

The Family-School-Community Partnership Issues series was initiated in 2000 as a vehicle to connect the latest research with practitioners in the field. In 2004, the American Educational Research Association awarded the Outstanding Contribution Relating Theory to Practice: Interpretive Scholarship Category for the first three volumes in this series. We have attempted to maintain that same high quality in subsequent years. The intent is to connect the latest research from various sources to school and classroom practice so that knowledge of best practices based on sound research can be more quickly transmitted to and applied in schools for children as well as in educator preparation. The researchers in the American Educational Research Association, European Network of Research on Parent Education, and other professional groups have contributed throughout the years and to this present volume.

During the recent conference of European Network of Research on Parent Education in Milan, Italy, a small group of researchers shared concerns that parent involvement in many studies appears to be maternal involvement. These researchers wondered about the role of fathers in their children's education and why fathers' involvement appeared to be eclipsed by mothers. Such wondering so strongly engaged Hsiu-Zu Ho and me that we agreed to join forces as coeditors. At that time, researchers from Canada, Spain, Turkey, Taiwan, and United States agreed to serve as chapter authors. Our mission was to locate additional authors and research that focused on father involvement in education across the globe.

Promising Practices for Fathers' Involvement in Children's Education
pp. vii–ix
Copyright © 2012 by Information Age Publishing

The result of our search across continents and burrowing into the Internet lies in your hands. As noted in these chapters, although, a large number of researchers have focused on the roles of fathers in the lives of their children, surprisingly few studies have been completed on fathers' involvement in their children's education. This volume addresses these limited studies within the context of the cultures in which the studies have taken place.

The volume commences with Marsiglio's thoughtful discussion on the role of fathers for the creation and sharing of social capital that can benefit children's education. He has developed a conceptual model of the father-child education bond, befitting the complexities of contemporary families. The remaining chapters add thoughtfully gathered and interpreted information from various cultures and geographic areas that add specific contributions to his model. Their contributions from preschool to career decision making and accessibility to their children's education are covered in eight chapters, focusing on in-depth research from Canada to Argentina and Korea to Africa. The final chapter concludes with a close look at father-child relationships between fathers and their sons or daughters as related to education.

Surprisingly, a set of themes appeared across chapters and cultures. These broad themes describe the general or prevalent norms but, as a caveat, not necessarily norms accepted throughout a geographic region or culture. First, fathers perceive their role in their child's education as primary financial supporter. The studies indicate that fathers take this role very seriously. Second, fathers highly value education for their children and set educational expectations for their children. These expectations include their children's school attendance, doing well at school, and preparing for their careers. Third, in many areas of the world, fathers are beginning to assume other school-related tasks in the family regarding education, such as homework. Fourth, fathers and teachers express challenges in open and clear communication with each other. Teachers remark that fathers are not involved because so many fathers do not attend school activities, including meetings with the teachers. Because fathers' commitment and support for their children's education may not be visible at the school site, schools consider that these fathers are not involved. Fifth, other fathers and men, termed *social fathers*, are assuming paternal involvement with children—those other than their own, and assisting in their education. Lastly, programs focused on father involvement are emerging, and authors encourage their support, expansion, and research on their benefits to children's education.

All chapters and submissions in this monograph have been peer reviewed. Hsiu-Zu and I extend our deepest appreciation to Martha Axellsaht-Snider, Kelly Carrero, Haiqin Chen, Mary Cornish, Jolene

Gash, Dana Griffin, Valerie Janesick, Barbara Jentleson, Holly Kreider, Ugo Nwokeji, Mavis Sanders, Steven Sheldon, Lee Shumow, Helen Westmoreland, and Frances Van Voorhis. Their thoughtful comments were invaluable, and their suggestions led to revisions, additions, and rejections.

Hsiu-Zu and I are ever grateful to our respective husbands, Bill Below and John Michael, whose love and understanding support our ability to devote sufficient time and energy to the creation of this volume. Hsiu-Zu also appreciates the assistance of her doctoral student Connie Tran for editorial help, particularly, keeping chapters in line with the latest American Psychological Association format. Lastly, my deepest gratitude to our publisher George Johnson for his continued support of this monograph series and the dedicated work of Family School Community Partnership researchers throughout the world.

CHAPTER 1

AMERICAN FATHERS, CHILDREN, AND THEIR EDUCATIONAL EXPERIENCE

Qualitative Reflections on Promoting Social Capital

William Marsiglio and Justin J. Hendricks

Scholars, school personnel, and others continue to explore options to help American fathers play a more meaningful role in supporting their children's education. Much of this research targets fathers of young children in early childhood programs, especially in families eligible to participate in the Early Head Start and Head Start programs (Palm & Fagan, 2008, see also Fitzpatrick, 2011). Survey research also examines how children's educational aspirations and academic performance are correlated with fathers' personal attributes, demographic characteristics, and family circumstances (McBride, Schoppe-Sullivan, & Ho, 2005). Overall, these efforts assume that under the right set of circumstances sufficiently motivated fathers (and mothers) can enhance how well their children adjust to school settings and perform academically (Kreider, Caspe, Kennedy, & Weiss, 2007; Tsikalas, Lee, & Newkirk, 2007; Walker, Hover-Dempsey, Whetsel, & Green, 2004).

Promising Practices for Fathers' Involvement in Children's Education
pp. 1–16

We draw attention to several significant issues relevant to this area by integrating literature streams pertaining to fathering, coparenting, youth studies, and social capital. As sociologists, we foreground fathering as a social arrangement because it is affected by different types of family circumstances and coparenting styles, social class and community resources, and organizational norms and policies (Doherty, Kouneski, & Erikson, 1998; Marsiglio & Roy, 2012). By focusing on this larger context we generate insights about conditions that influence fathers' perceptions of the value of education for their children as well as the diverse ways fathers can be involved with and contribute to their children's educational development. As such, we consider fathers' approach to their children's education as it relates to activities that occur in formal learning environments as well as in places away from school-based settings. We are interested in the full range of experiences Epstein (1996) conceptualizes as relevant to parental involvement (see bolded box in Figure 1.1): school helping with parenting skills, school communicating about events, volunteering at school, learning academic lessons from school at home, families involved in school decision making and governance, and collaborating with community agencies to strengthen school programs.

Figure 1.1 illustrates how we frame our discussion conceptually. We adopt Marsiglio and Roy's (2012) broad view of policymaking by noting that diverse stakeholders can affect fathers' involvement in children's education. These stakeholders use different platforms to initiate social change—federal and state agencies, local community-based groups, grassroots advocacy networks, nonprofit organizations (including schools), media, state clearinghouses, and courtrooms. Social initiatives relevant to fathers' and children's education may be anchored in specific platforms or tied to multiple platforms while focusing on individual families, categories of fathers in distinctive settings like nonresident or incarcerated fathers, fathers living in particular communities or states, as well as fathers in general.

Social initiatives can influence children's school activities, academic performance, and learning orientation by affecting fathers' personal attributes as well the contexts in which fathers interact with their children. For some fathers, a current or former romantic partner may be the most immediate source that shapes fathers' contributions to their children's education. In addition, initiatives can alter the resources and communication patterns that involve schools and communities.

Thus, we highlight strategies for fostering productive partnerships between fathers and family members (most notably mothers/partners), fathers and schools, and schools and other community organizations with the intent of promoting fathers' commitment to their children's education. We discuss the value of creating and mobilizing social capital in

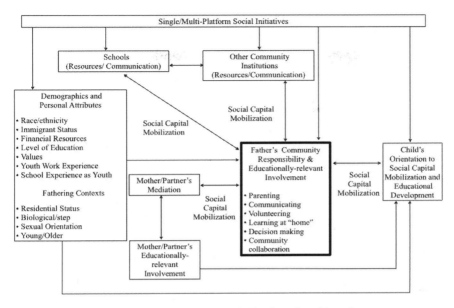

Figure 1.1.   Conceptual model of father-child educational bond.

these different types of partnerships. Social initiatives designed to enhance how much and how well fathers are involved in their children's education are most likely to succeed when social class and gender are taken into account. Understanding how fathers—as men embedded in family, peer, and work networks—perceive and respond to school culture and their children's learning is critical. Toward this end, we discuss several initiatives and qualitative research projects that can provide the foundation for fathers to play a more active role in their children's education.

COMMUNITY RESPONSIBILITY AND SOCIAL CAPITAL

In the fatherhood literature, numerous scholars have explored how father involvement transcends what takes place in home environments (Marsiglio, 2008; Marsiglio & Roy, 2012). Terms such as "community responsibility" (Doucet, 2006) and "parental community social capital" (Pleck, 2010) convey the notion that fathers have the capacity to link households to each other and connect families to other child-based institutions. When fathers reach out in productive ways to coordinate information and resources with youth workers (e.g., teachers, coaches, day care workers),

Help generate
Social capital

fathers have the capacity to establish social capital for their children. Increasing men's involvement can prove vital both because they represent additional supportive adults in children's lives, and as men, they can reinforce for some the value of education for boys as well as girls. That said, circumstances such as not having the privilege of flexible family leave, being subjected to staff members' discomfort with men's participation in school activities, or living away from children as nonresident fathers can constrain some fathers from being more actively involved in supporting their children's activities.

We highlight the significance of studying the processes associated with creating and sharing social capital that can benefit children. In recent decades, theorists have articulated alternative interpretations of social capital as a concept and theory (Bassani, 2007; Bourdieu, 1986; Coleman, 1990; Lin, 2001; Schaefer-McDaniel, 2004). Here we highlight the three dimensions Schaefer-McDaniel (2004) describes as being rooted in previous theorizing: social networks/sociability, trust/reciprocity, and the sense of belonging/place attachment. We also organize our discussion by highlighting community-based and family-based social capital as well as focusing on what has been termed "mobilization" (Bassani, 2007) and "activation" (Lareau & Horvat, 1999)—how resources including cultural capital are utilized to create social capital.

Sociability represents individuals' ability to maintain and access their social networks knowingly in ways that generate social capital (Bourdieu, 1986). We largely accept this interpretation for fathers even though some fathers will be much more strategic in their attempt to achieve certain outcomes by developing and using their networks in specific ways.

According to Coleman (1990), social capital represents "any kind of social relationship that is a resource to the person" (p. 35). As such, individuals' expression of reciprocity and trust helps reinforce the values and norms that define the obligations that make social capital viable. These processes help to solidify various types of interpersonal bonds that involve some combination of youth, family, friends, teachers/mentors, and other caregivers. We view both the quantity and quality of exchanges as important when considering fathers' relations that implicate their children's educational development and outcomes.

Schaefer-McDaniel (2004) underscores the importance of paying attention to youths' sense of belonging and attachment to some sort of social environment or community. This view is consistent with the situated fathering perspective, which suggests that place, including aspects of the physical and cultural context, influences how men develop and express their identities as fathers (Marsiglio, Roy, & Fox, 2005). In particular, the meanings youth and fathers associate with school sites and other learning environments can influence how comfortable they feel in those places and

children connect
fathers to social
capital.

with the people involved. These issues are highly salient for those fathers who have bad memories of their childhood experiences with schools; many are disadvantaged fathers who dropped out. Additionally, some will be troubled by what they perceive to be the feminine culture of schools (Finders & Lewis, 1994; Mead, 2006).

Scholars differentiate between community-based and family-based relations that comprise social capital (Furstenberg, 2005; Marsiglio & Cohan, 2000). For our purposes, the former type of relations generally hinge on fathers' connections with other adults and organizations, most notably schools, in their neighborhoods and communities. These ties enable fathers to "expose their children to healthy dyadic interaction processes, bring about closure in their children's social networks [adults' communicating with one another to monitor and nurture a child], and act as a liaison to valuable community resources for their children" (Marsiglio & Cohan, 2000, p. 85).

Family-based processes involving social capital include fathers' coparenting and kinwork activities and communication (Marsiglio & Roy, 2012). To what extent do fathers sustain relationships with family members anchored in mutual values, expectations, trust, and loyalty? When fathers and other caregivers share similar and responsible childrearing philosophies and conflict resolution strategies, fathers indirectly offer their children a valuable asset. In sum, "social capital indirectly influences youths' well-being because it mobilizes financial, human, cultural, and physical resources into capital" (Bassani, 2007, p. 22).

Furstenberg (2005, p. 814) explains that children "provide critical links to the community, although they may do so differently, depending on social class, ethnicity, age, and gender." Thus, as depicted in Figure 1.1, it is vital to consider children's attributes, especially temperament, when determining how children may react to perceived and real resources and whether or not they will mobilize those assets, and by doing so involve parents in the community, including father (and mother) involvement in the classroom. For example, while teachers may encourage parents to volunteer in the classroom or other learning activities, some children may be adverse to parent involvement and subsequently discourage their parents from participating.

Recently, theorists in the field of youth studies have attempted to synthesize and extend the social capital theory to youth by paying attention to young people's own perceptions of their relationships and networks (Bassani, 2007; Morrow, 1999; Schaefer-McDaniel, 2004). These approaches underscore young peoples' agency while noting how critical it is to incorporate children's own perceptions of their social relationships and networks. Children can be said to mobilize or activate resources in order to acquire social capital (Schaefer-McDaniel, 2004). Viewed in this way, fathers are facilitators of social capital production rather than mere sources. In other words, fathers place children in schools, buy them educational materials, send them to educational camps, expose them to teachers and tutors, introduce them to peers, and so forth, but these resources may or may not materialize into social capital.

In addition, the composition of relationship networks as well as the nature of the interaction between participants can affect how resources are mobilized into social capital (Bassani, 2007). Although scholars continue to debate how this process works, social capital seems to be created as part of an interplay between the composition of networks, the nature of interaction between the members, and the agency of the individual—which in a child's case may differ from an adult. Viewed from the eyes of adults or children, fathers have opportunities to develop their own and their children's networks by bridging family and community contexts. Fathers can contribute by affecting the composition of networks and by the way they interact and communicate with others, including children. Furthermore, longitudinal research with a national sample that does not differentiate between fathers and mothers indicates that the emotional tone of the parent-adolescent relationship influences adolescents' academic achievement (Crosnoe, 2004). This finding, which was weaker among African Americans, suggests that fathers might be able to be more consequential if they worked on improving the emotional aspects of their relationships with their adolescent children.

FATHERS' DEMOGRAPHICS, ATTRIBUTES, AND CONTEXTS

As Figure 1.1 illustrates, all sorts of demographic conditions, personal attributes, and fathering contexts can alter the processes by which family- and community-based social capital are created and shared in ways that can help children succeed academically. These include circumstances associated with race/ethnicity, financial resources, educational background, values, and previous school experience, to name only several. In addition, nonnormative family arrangements represented by single and nonresident parent households as well as stepfamilies and gay fathers can constrain fathers from building social capital via school personnel and other youth workers in the community.

Poor fathers who work multiple jobs to cobble together enough money to meet family needs may have little time to discuss family matters with their wives/partners—the mothers of their children. These time constraints may hinder fathers' opportunities to nurture a cooperative coparenting style that is grounded in shared values. In practical terms, poor working fathers may not have the luxury of altering their schedules to skip work or to leave early to attend their child's school functions. Unfortunately, many poor fathers tend to have less than desirable experiences with the school system. Compared to middle-income fathers, poor fathers are significantly more likely to harbor insecurities about the school environment (Finders & Lewis, 1994). Poor academic performance and delinquent behavior as youths may leave poor fathers feeling isolated from the world of formal education.

Nonresident fathers often complain that they are denied easy access to their children and do not learn about their children's activities in a timely manner if at all (Crowley, 2008). Such claims may implicate resident mothers as well as school teachers and personnel who do not make it their policy to send information directly to resident as well as nonresident parents—the latter most likely being fathers.

Gay fathers can face hurdles when teachers and school personnel are uncomfortable with gay, lesbian, bi, and transgender people. These fathers may be shortchanged in the types of information they receive about their children or they may be given fewer opportunities to participate in school-based functions. Gay "step"fathers—those partnered with a legal gay father—can find themselves in a compromised position relative to schools because they do not have formal parental rights. In states where only one gay man can legally assume paternity, the partner may have no official standing with school personnel, especially if the romantic relationship ends.

Being a father who falls outside the stereotypical borders of the ideal middle-class father means that fathers will have to overcome structural impediments to work with the child's mother to established trust and a shared understanding of how the child should be raised. Young men, challenged because they are nonresident fathers and have limited economic standing, may be shunned by resident mothers and their families who are inclined to avoid the hassles of involving the child's father. Similarly, incarcerated fathers may be at the mother's mercy as to whether they will be permitted to play a role in their children's lives.

PROMOTING MORE EDUCATIONALLY RESPONSIVE FATHER INVOLVEMENT

The types of multilayered partnerships Marsiglio and Roy (2012) discussed as a way to help men become more nurturing dads can also support fathers' efforts to promote their children's educational well-being. First, stronger ties between fathers and other family members can lead to more effective communication channels that enable fathers to be better informed, more committed to passing on their human, cultural, and physical capital to their children, and in a more desirable position to influence their children's educational outlook and outcomes. Front and center are initiatives to improve relationships and communication between coparents. Mediation and other programs need to be sensitive to how some mothers play a gatekeeping role that hinders fathers' participation. In contrast, school personnel can develop strategies to use mothers as the gateway to maximize fathers' involvement. Early Head Start and Head Start programs have found that fathers are more likely to get involved if the program is designed to address the entire family (Palm & Fagan, 2008).

Second, training programs are needed that help improve school personnel's willingness to reach out to fathers in supportive ways. McBride and Rane (1997) suggest that the lack of father involvement in education is due to the idea that fathers, especially in disadvantaged situations, are relatively uninvolved, which has led to policies and teachers/administrators' actions that alienate fathers. As a result, it is important to include fathers/men in initiatives that aim to spur parent involvement in education. Initiatives need to be particularly sensitive to fathers' experiences as men and their sense of belonging in school settings. As is generally true with other fatherhood programs (Marsiglio & Roy, 2012), initiatives to promote fathers' commitment to their children's education are likely to be more successful if they incorporate men as father advocates. In short, men need to hold other men accountable for their involvement in their children's educational development.

Additionally, considering that a sense of belonging is important to building social capital, fathers need to be reasonably comfortable with educational or child-centered contexts. Fathers who have a history of working with youth in community settings (e.g., Boys & Girls Club, Boy Scouts, religious youth groups) may be sensitized to these kinds of contexts, and they will be better prepared to navigate relationships with children (Marsiglio, 2008). Additionally, these men may have a greater understanding of what children in the classroom need and how to interact with children who have difficult or slow-to-warm-up temperaments. Men with these kinds of experiences may also be able to help children who come from situations with complicated family dynamics and thereby enhance in the process of mobilizing resources. Marsiglio (2008) suggests that children who belong to minority groups or disadvantaged groups may benefit the most by their exposure to successful, supportive men who reflect similar backgrounds.

Much has been said about the gendered classroom and some have even suggested that boys, especially boys of color, are in the midst of an education crisis (for review, see Marsiglio, 2008, pp. 285-289). This can be explained in a variety of ways, including arguments that stress the paucity of male elementary school teachers or young males' perceptions of school as a passive, feminine domain. However, regardless of the explanation, it seems that gender plays a role in the education of young people. With relatively few male teachers in the elementary school grades, fathers typically must interact with female teachers and are likely to confront a physical and cultural setting that they deem as feminine. Although it has proven difficult to accomplish, if male teachers were successfully recruited into the elementary school system in significantly greater numbers, some fathers might feel more at ease with participating in school activities. In turn, if fathers were more involved in schools they might challenge some of the gendered perceptions that shape these places. For instance, greater father involvement might encourage more girls to get involved in science and math while helping more boys see education and formal learning as positive. For this to happen, more men from all sorts of backgrounds would have to see schools and learning as positive and this might require them to confront their personal inadequacies in educational contexts.

Third, stakeholders in different organizations can identify creative ways to coordinate their efforts to encourage and enable fathers to be more involved with their children's education both in and away from school. For instance, the grassroots organization Ecodads was recently launched to encourage fathers to find ways to combine their generative spirit with their environmental activism as a vehicle to bond with their children (see Ecodads, 2012, for an overview). Middle and high school social science teachers can partner with local leaders in the Ecodads movement to develop school-based projects that provide fathers opportunities to mentor their own and other children while building community-based social capital. These types of arrangements could foster unique interorganizational commitments that ultimately lead more fathers to play a constructive role in their children's educational development.

Other community groups associated with recreation, child care, public health, churches, jails/prisons, and so forth can be pulled into collaborative initiatives that encourage men's participation in their children's education. "Virtual visitation" programs in jails and prisons can be tailored to help fathers reach out to their children and reinforce literacy efforts while reinforcing father-child emotional bonds (Marsiglio & Roy, 2012). Officials in some correctional facilities have promoted literacy as well as parent-child bonds by using computer technology. For instance, the Reading Family Ties program in Florida enables fathers to read stories to their children using live video via the Internet. In addition to enhancing family ties this program appears to improve literacy for both parents and children (see Holt, 2012). Modern technologies have enabled states to expand perhaps the most popular program—fathers reading books to their children recorded on tape or CD, or videoconferenced live to children (see Davis & Hutt, 2012). Such innovations might inspire other projects that would make it easier for children with fathers who do not live with them because of imprisonment, military deployment, work-related travel, or a relationship breakup to play a more active role in supporting their educational growth.

At least six states have passed legislation that enables judges to award virtual visitation between children and noncustodial parents—most often fathers. Fathers can overcome some of the challenges of place-based visitation because the services are supported in private homes as well as visitation centers and community agencies (Welsh, 2009). Collaborations between family courts and schools could lead to successful efforts that provide nonresident fathers with valuable opportunities to participate more actively in their children's schooling.

Other examples of community partnerships involving schools can enlist support from nonprofits like Big Brothers and Sisters of America as well as businesses which are prepared to adopt schools with high proportions of disadvantaged students. These partnerships can encourage fathers (and adults more generally) to volunteer their time to mentor youth in school-based programs. As has been suggested elsewhere, programs could foster opportunities for fathers and their children to co-mentor younger children (Marsiglio, 2008; Marsiglio & Roy, 2012). Such programs could help fathers reinforce the value of learning and teaching with their own children in the course of assisting other youth.

Creative community partnerships are often necessary to motivate immigrant fathers to be more involved in their children's education. Unfortunately, research on immigrant fathers and their children's education is sparse (Moreno & Chuang, 2012); most research focuses on parent involvement more generally. As Lucas, Henze, and Donato (1990) noted more than 20 years ago, because of immigrant families' unique needs the promotion of minority students' school success is a complex process. In addition, many immigrant families give up everything to seek a new life—including social and cultural capital tied to vast networks of extended family—to immigrate to the United States (Carreón, Drake, & Barton, 2005). Thus stakeholders (e.g., teachers, representatives of child and social welfare agencies, church leaders, public health professionals) must coordinate their efforts to help immigrant children and families rebuild the social and cultural capital necessary to thrive.

An example of this type of partnership could involve religious institutions because they play a prominent role in many Latino cultures. Churches could sponsor groups where immigrant fathers met in a supportive environment to familiarize themselves with the American educational experience and learn English alongside their children. These groups could help fathers create social networks and, potentially, social capital by inviting local school officials to give presentations about the positive ways Latino fathers can interact with teachers and administrators.

In general, social initiatives must be sensitive to immigrant families' needs, including parents' fears that teachers do not understand them, their children, or their culture. Several studies suggest that immigrant parents feel disconnected from schools, but with some support (e.g., including interpreters, teacher training on cultural sensitivity) these parents are willing to share ideas and appear prepared to participate fully in their children's education under the right circumstances (Huerta, 2011; Carreón, Drake, & Barton, 2005). Initiatives should increase communication and understanding between teachers and immigrant parents. For example, teachers could encourage parents to come to school and talk about their cultural celebrations and traditions.

Immigrant fathers are among those who can benefit directly from initiatives encouraging participation in schools. Fathers' involvement in schools can extend their networks and increase their social capital. So too, many immigrant fathers begin to feel a loss of authorship in their children's lives as the children become more proficient in the dominant culture and language (Carreon, Drake, & Barton, 2005). Similar to the programs that target native speaking fathers in fragile families that include children typically born to unmarried low-income parents, immigrant fathers may become more self-confident from reading programs that encourage them to read with their son/daughter while supporting their child's school success.

As stakeholders in children's education consider ways to engage immigrant fathers they should be attentive to the potentially gendered ways these fathers navigate their new standing in the community and family. Their potential loss of financial capital and status as the household head may prompt these men to struggle with their masculine identities and avoid exposing their "failings" in a foreign school environment. Accordingly, the culture of masculinity may cause some men to struggle with being involved, especially in spaces that may be considered feminine (i.e., schools); however, it is incorrect to assume that fathers do not care—especially Latino fathers (Moreno & Chuang, 2012).

FUTURE RESEARCH

Because little research focuses on fathers' involvement with their children's educational development, much can be gained by exploring fathers' experiences in this area. Although our conceptual model emphasizes the social capital concept, it has historically been a difficult concept to operationalize and measure (Bassani, 2007; Furstenberg, 2005;

Morrow, 1999). Morrow (1999) criticizes past researchers for using family structure or size as measures of social capital in families. As a result, Furstenberg (2005) suggests, and we agree, that "without better qualitative studies … we may go astray and reach unwarranted conclusions about the utility of this theory before we can give it due consideration" (p. 819).

Consequently, we restrict our recommendations to qualitative and mixed-methods projects relevant to our conceptual model's main themes and a broad interpretation of fathers' involvement in children's education. Although we are interested in fathers generally, we primarily address those who face the most pressing constraints. Our suggestions highlight the larger ecological context that provides fathers opportunities to influence their children's education. Because fathers (and mothers) can influence their children's school experience and educational development in varied ways, researchers should consider the full gamut of activities Epstein (1996) identifies which include interactions between families, children, schools, and other community agencies.

From a narrow lens, we need to know more about fathers' orientation to community responsibility as it relates to their child's education. In-depth interviews can explore fathers' life histories as they pertain to their formal and informal education. How do men in a narrative form reconstruct their school experiences during their youth? What types of sentiments and memories do they represent? What noteworthy conditions and social forces do men identify as shaping their past and current involvement? In particular, how do men with below average educational attainment make sense of their limited educational resources?

Men's recent experiences with wives/partners are also likely to be influential in one way or another. Coparental processes may be particularly decisive in shaping fathers' involvement when fathers and mothers live apart. Developing a better understanding of the dyad's interpersonal expectations and parenting dynamics can inform efforts designed to support coparental relations as they pertain to children's education.

In addition, researchers should adopt a broader lens to examine the circumstances surrounding men's specific strategies for employing capital on behalf of their children. This analysis should consider how staff's and children's views and reactions come into play. Similar to Lareau and Horvat's (1999) approach, interviews with teachers and other school staff can improve understanding of the social capital activation processes. These interviews should take into account the staff's explicit and implicit rules of interaction which can either foster or hinder fathers' involvement. Being sensitive to the intersection of race, class, and gender should contextualize fathers' involvement not just as parents but as certain types of men who are deciding if and how they should be involved in their children's educational lives. What are men's perceptions of school, their potential involvement with specific academic sites, and school personnel? Developing a deeper appreciation for how children perceive and respond to fathers' efforts may also enhance understanding about the ways social capital is activated (Bassani, 2007; Lin, 2001). How do fathers (and mothers) change the dynamics of the classroom by their involvement and how does this shift influence the child's ability to mobilize resources? In some cases children may cling to parents, which may prevent children from expanding their social networks, whereas in other cases parents may help to facilitate the building of children's social networks. Similarly, we need to consider how fathers come to see themselves through their children's eyes, especially when it comes to matters related to learning, knowledge, and school.

Mixed-methods approaches that incorporate in-depth interviews and focus groups into experimental designs that emphasize program evaluation could help shed light on the strengths and weaknesses of programs that focus on fathers in prisons, the military, and other nonresident contexts. These inquiries should seek to evaluate the extent to which and how creative initiatives reinforce fathers' commitments to their children's education while fostering better educational outcomes for children. In addition, efforts should also consider when and how fathers' participation in particular programs influence their own self-confidence and ability to coparent effectively. From a developmental perspective, questions abound about the extent to which and how men identify their involvement with their children's education as personally transformative in that they see themselves in a new light as fathers, coparents, and men.

Research on fathers' influence in their children's schooling is an ideal topic for a participatory action research approach that involves researchers collaborating closely with community stakeholders invested in children's education. Although it did not deal significantly with the connection between schools and fathering, the Canadian Fatherhood Initiative Research Alliance provides an excellent example of how a participatory action approach can foster university-community partnerships that produce useful results (Ball & Daly, in press). Interdisciplinary teams that draw on the complementary expertise found in disciplines like education, sociology, anthropology, gender studies, psychology, and child and family studies might be well-positioned to secure support from local school systems to assess prevailing patterns and introduce demonstration projects involving fathers.

Given public concerns about American youths' educational competitiveness in a global market, stakeholders need to explore vigorously opportunities that can enhance young people's educational development. We underscore the value of developing a better qualitative understanding of the larger ecological context in which fathers create and mobilize social capital to produce a holistic educational experience for children. On a more practical level, we call for creative collaborations across social change platforms to help fathers from diverse backgrounds and family circumstances develop social capital to assist their children. Ultimately, fathers need to be incorporated more effectively into a wide range of productive partnerships that involve family, schools, and other child-oriented organizations.

REFERENCES

Ball, J. & Daly, K. (in press). *Father involvement in Canada: Contested terrain.* Vancouver, British Columbia, Canada: University of British Columbia Press.

Bassani, C. (2007). Five dimensions of social capital theory as they pertain to youth studies. *Journal of Youth Studies, 10*(1), 17-34. doi:10.1080/13676260701196087

Bourdieu, P. (1986). The forms of capital. In J. Richardson (Ed.), *Handbook of theory and research for the sociology of education* (pp. 241–258). New York, NY: Greenwood Press.

Carreón, G. P., Drake, C., & Barton, A. C. (2005). The importance of presence: Immigrant parents' school engagement experiences. American Educational *Research Journal, 42*(3), 465-498. doi:10.3102/00028312042003465

Coleman, J. (1990). *Foundations of social theory.* Cambridge, MA: The Belknap Press of Harvard University Press.

Crosnoe, R. (2004). Social capital and the interplay of families and schools. *Journal of Marriage and Family, 66,* 267-280.

Crowley, J. E. (2008). *Defiant dads: Fathers' rights activists in America.* Ithaca, NY: Cornell University Press.

Davis, P., & Hutt, K. (2012). How to (and why) do a storybook project. Retrieved from http://www.fcnetwork.org/storybook.pdf

Doherty, W. J., Kouneski, E. F., & Erickson, M. F. (1998). Responsible fathering: An overview and conceptual framework. *Journal of Marriage and Family, 60*(2), 277–292.

Doucet, A. (2006). *Do men mother?* Toronto, Ontario, Canada: University of Toronto Press.

Ecodads. (2012). Ecodads overview. Retrieved from http://docs.ecodads.org/ecodadsoverview.pdf

Epstein, J. L. (1996). Advances in family, community, and school partnerships. *New Schools, New Communities, 12*(3), 5–13.

Finders, M., & Lewis, C. (1994). Why some parents don't come to school. *Educational Leadership, 51*(8), 50–54.

Fitzpatrick, T. (2011). *Father involvement in early childhood programs.* Plymouth, MN: Minnesota Fathers & Families Network. Retrieved from http://www.mnfathers.org/pdf/ChildWelfareAnalysisEarlyChildhood2011.pdf

Furstenberg, F. F. (2005). Banking on families: How families generate and distribute social capital. *Journal of Marriage and Family, 67,* 809–821.

Holt, A. W. (2012). Reading family ties for men: Program for incarcerated fathers. Retrieved from http://www.fcnetwork.org/fatherhood/holt.html

Huerta, T. M. (2011). Humanizing pedagogy: Beliefs and practices on the teaching of Latino children. *Bilingual Research Journal, 34*(1), 38–57.

Kreider, H., Caspe, M., Kennedy, S., & Weiss, H. (2007). Family involvement in middle and high school students' education. *Family Involvement Makes a Difference, 3*, Retrieved from http://www.hfrp.org/publications-resources/publications-series/family-involvement-makes-a-difference/family-involvement-in-middle-and-high-school-students-education

Lareau, A., & Horvat, E. M. (1999). Moments of social inclusion and exclusion race, class, and cultural capital in family-school relationships. *Sociology of Education, 72*(1), 37–53.

Lin, N. (2001). *Social capital: A theory of social structure and action.* Cambridge, England: Cambridge University Press.

Lucas, T., Henze, R., & Donato, R. (1990). Promoting the success of Latino language minority students: An exploratory study of six high schools. *Harvard Educational Review, 60*(3), 315–340.

Marsiglio, W. (2008). *Men on a mission: Valuing youth work in our communities.* Baltimore, MD: Johns Hopkins University Press.

Marsiglio, W., & Cohan, M. (2000). Conceptualizing father involvement and paternal influence: Sociological and qualitative themes. *Marriage and Family Review, 29*, 75–95.

Marsiglio, W., & Roy, K. (2012). *Nurturing dads: Social initiatives for contemporary fatherhood.* New York, NY: Russell Sage Foundation.

Marsiglio, W., Roy, K., & Fox, G. L. (Eds.). (2005). *Situated fathering: A focus on physical and social spaces.* Lanham, MD: Rowman & Littlefield.

McBride, B. A., & Rane, T. R. (1997). Father/male involvement in early childhood programs: Issues and challenges. *Early Childhood Education Journal, 25*(1), 11–15.

McBride, B. A., Schoppe-Sullivan, S. J., & Ho, M. (2005). The role of father involvement in schools in mediating contextual influences on student achievement. *Journal of Applied Developmental Psychology, 26*, 201–216.

Mead, S. (2006). *The evidence suggests otherwise: The truth about boys and girls.* Washington, DC: Education Sector.

Moreno, R. P., & Chuang, S. S. (2012). Latino fathers and their involvement in their children's schooling. In H-Z. Ho & D. B. Hiatt-Michael (Eds.), *Promising practices for fathers' involvement in children's education* (pp. 59-77). Charlotte, NC: Information Age.

Morrow, V. (1999). Conceptualising social capital in relation to the well-being of children and young people: A critical review. *The Sociological Review, 47*(4), 744–765.

Palm, G., & Fagan, J. (2008). Father involvement in early childhood programs: Review of the literature. *Early Child Development & Care, 178*(7), 745–759.

Pleck, J. H. (2010). Paternal involvement: Revised conceptualization and theoretical linkages with child outcomes. In M. E. Lamb (Ed.), *The role of the father in child development* (5th ed., pp. 58-93). Hoboken, NJ: Wiley.

Schaefer-McDaniel, N. (2004). Conceptualizing social capital among young people: Towards a new theory. *Children, Youth and Environments,14*(1), 140–150.

Tsikalas, K. E., Lee, J., & Newkirk, C. (2007, July). *Home computing, student engagement and academic achievement.* Paper presented at the Council of Chief State School Officers National Conference on Large Scale Assessment, Nashville, TN. Retrieved from http://www.hfrp.org/publications-resources/publications-series/family-involvement-research-digests

Walker, J. M. T., Hover-Dempsey, K. V., Whetsel, D. R., & Green, C. L. (2004). *Parental involvement in homework: A review of current research and its implications for teachers, after school program staff, and parent leaders.* Retrieved from www.gse.harvard.edu/hfrp/projects/fine/resources/research/homework.html

Welsh, D. (2009). Virtual parents: How virtual visitation legislation is shaping the future of custody law. *Journal of Law and Family Studies, 11*(1), 215–225.

CHAPTER 2

FATHER INVOLVEMENT IN CANADA

Rollande Deslandes

OVERVIEW OF CANADIAN RESEARCH

For decades, many educational scholars, practitioners, and media have been decrying the high rate of school dropout in industrialized countries. In order to counter this problem and that of low academic achievement, Canadian educators are encouraging fathers as well as mothers to be more involved in the schooling of their children and particularly that of their sons. The benefits of paternal involvement have been documented over the years. Studies conducted in numerous countries, notably Canada, the United Kingdom, and the United States, have demonstrated the contribution of the father's positive involvement on the child (e.g., Allen & Daly, 2007; Lamb & Tamis-LeMonda, 2004; Palkovitz, 2002). For instance, Allen and Daly, two Canadian researchers associated with the Father Involvement Research Alliance,[1] published reviews in 2002, then in 2007, on the subject of national and international research examining the impact of the fathers' involvement on children's developmental outcomes. Paternal involvement was found to be positively associated with children's and teenagers' school performance and motivation, school attendance, and positive attitudes toward school. The children and teenagers of involved fathers also show high levels of social maturity and more highly developed social skills.

On the whole, fathers' involvement with their children has increased in recent years. Pacaut (2011), from the Quebec Ministry of Families, Seniors and the Status of Women, examined the case of 1,000 families drawn from the longitudinal study on child development in Québec. The findings show that fathers perform better with children during playtime, bedtime, and when driving to sports activities, that is, during socialization activities. Compared with mothers, however, they are much less invested in planning and preparing meals, caring for sick children and providing help with homework (Leduc, 2011). As it can be observed, equal distribution of tasks has not yet been achieved. At the same time, many mothers and fathers insist, loud and clear, that they have "a crazy schedule" and difficulty balancing work and family (Galipeau, 2011). They work long hours, and performance requirements are high. Greater flexibility and more accommodations are required in the workplace to avoid excessive demands in terms of time and energy.

Across the provinces, Canada has promoted family engagement in schools in a number of governmental acts and programs (Deslandes, 2006). Dubeau (2002) conducted a review of over 80 relevant articles written by Canadian researchers. The purpose of this review was to provide an overview of the state of research on fathers in Canada for the national forum entitled Father Involvement in Canada: The Creation of a Community-Research Partnership held in Toronto in March, 2002. The articles highlighted were mainly by authors in the provinces of British Columbia, Ontario, and Quebec. Research topics were grouped into four categories:

1. studies comparing families based on the father's presence or absence;
2. studies comparing various groups of fathers;
3. studies having a systemic perspective of the family and analyzing the influence of family subsystems; and
4. studies focused on the differences between maternal and paternal behaviors.

Those reported in this chapter fall into the last category—differences between maternal and paternal behavior. These studies, conducted since the early 2000s, examined the involvement of fathers in comparison to that of mothers. The measures adopted for these studies adhere to a family perspective. These family-centered studies rest upon the belief that the father's role is equal or similar to that of the mother. Thus, the research focused on both parents; however, for the purpose of the topic of this book, the paternal findings will be highlighted.

FOUR STUDIES ON THE ROLES
OF FATHER AND MOTHER INVOLVEMENT

Research Design

This author conducted four recent research studies on the role of Canadian fathers and mothers. The data collection for the four studies was conducted on 872 primarily White adolescents across 3 years on the influence of parenting and parental involvement practices on academic achievement at the secondary level (1998-2001[2]). These studies were in continuity with a previous study with 525 adolescents (Deslandes, 1996; Deslandes, Royer, Turcotte, & Bertrand, 1997).These adolescents completed a questionnaire that was based on instruments developed by Steinberg, Lamborn, Dornbusch, and Darling (1992) and Epstein, Connors, and Salinas (1993). They were both adapted in the Quebec context (Deslandes, Bertrand, Royer, & Turcotte, 1995). Prior studies had indicated that student reports possessed validity equal or better than observers (Schwarz, Barton-Henry & Pruzinsky, 1985). For each reported study, Table 2.1 summarizes the research objectives and design, the sample size and characteristics, and the measures and the analyses that were conducted.

Subscales for this questionnaire included items that asked student's perceptions of parental warmth, supervision and psychological autonomy granting as well as affective support (one of the five dimensions of parental involvement along with communication with the teachers, parent-adolescent interactions based on daily school matters, parent-school communication and parent-adolescent communication) were found to contribute most significantly to school achievement. In addition, items were added to ascertain family characteristics like family structure, parent gender and adolescent gender and evolution of parents' involvement through the years of secondary schools. School achievement was represented by the year-end point averages as they appeared in the official school records (see Table 2.2).

Besides school achievement, the study addressed adolescents' autonomy. Studies show that adolescents who achieved high level of autonomy perform better in school than their peers do (Deslandes, Potvin, & Leclerc, 2000; Greenberg, 1982; Steinberg, Elmen, & Mounts, 1989). These studies underline parents' contribution to the development of autonomy. Based on Greenberger's works (1982, Greenberger, Josselson,

Table 2.1.   Characteristics of our Studies Included in the Review

Authors	Objectives/Questions	Design, Sample	Measures	Analyses
Deslandes (2003)	To investigate parent gender differences and changes in fathers' and mothers' parenting and involvement in schooling practices	Cross-sectional and longitudinal study (3-years); participants: 542 adolescents of 14.4 years at Time 1 (eighth grade), French-speaking, White population; nontraditional families (25%); diverse SES	Student report of parenting style (Steinberg, Elmen, & Mounts, 1989; Steinberg, Lamborn, Dornbusch & Darling, 1992) student report of parent involvement (Epstein et al., 1993, Q-1)	T tests at each time of the study on fathers' and mothers' scores; Paired-samples and independent samples T tests and GLM repeated measures analyses
Deslandes (2000)	To compare fathers' and mothers' involvement in schooling practices	One-year study; participants: 872 of Grade 8 students, girls = 53.7%, boys = 46.3%	Student report of parent involvement (Epstein et al., 1993, Q-1) student achievement: year-end point averages from report card; student gender fathers' and mothers' education levels; Student report of autonomy (Greenberger, Josselson, Knerr, & Knerr, 1975)	Paired T tests, MANOVAs, and ANOVAs
Deslandes & Cloutier (2000)	To examine fathers' and mothers' predictive models of girls' and boys' school achievement To examine fathers' and mothers' predictive models of girls' and boys' work orientation			Multiple regression analysis (enter); Block 1: family structure, fathers' and mothers' education level; fathers' or mothers' involvement in schooling
Deslandes & Cloutier (2005)	To compare fathers' and mothers' parenting style and parental involvement with boys and girls from traditional/nontraditional families	Cross-sectional, data from a 3-year study; participants during the 3 years: 518 adolescents (girls = 54.3%, boys = 41.7%), Grades 8, 9, and 10	Student report of parenting style; student report of parent involvement; student gender family Structure: traditional, non-traditional	MANOVAs and ANOVAs

Table 2.2. Parenting and Parental Involvement Subscales

Instruments	Subscales	Sample Items
Parenting (Steinberg et al., 1989, 1992; adaptation Deslandes et al., 1995)	Warmth/acceptance, 10 items, $\alpha = 0.86$	I can count on my father/mother to help me out, if I have some kind of problem
	Supervision, 6 items, $\alpha = 0.80$	My father/mother really knows what I do with my free time
	Psychological autonomy-granting, 8 items, $\alpha = 0.80$	My father/mother answers my arguments by saying something like "You'll know better when you grow up" (reverse code)
Parent involvement (Epstein et al., 1993; adaptation by Deslandes et al., 1995)	Affective support, 6 items, $\alpha = 0.82$	My father/mother gives me encouragement about school
	Communication with the teachers, 4 items, $\alpha = 0.73$	My father/ mother talks with my teachers on the phone
	Parent-adolescent interactions based on daily school matters, 4 items, $\alpha = 0.80$	My father/mother asks if I did my homework
	Parent-school communication, 3 items, $\alpha = 0.59$	My father/mother goes to a meeting for parents at the school
	Parent-adolescent communication, 3 items, $\alpha = 0.65$	My father/mother discusses with me about my future (work, studies)
Autonomy scale (Greenberger et al., 1975; adaptation, Deslandes, Potvin, & Leclerc, 1999). It includes three subscales: work-orientation, self-reliance, and identity	Self-reliance, 9 items, $\alpha = 0.71$	The main reason I'm not more successful is that I have bad luck from this (reverse score)
	Identity, 10 items, $\alpha = 0.83$	I can't really say what my interests are (reverse score)
	Work orientation, 10 items, $\alpha = 0.85$	I tend to go from one thing to another before finishing any one of them (reverse scored)

Knerr, & Knerr, 1975), autonomy development referred to the capacity to function effectively (individual adequacy), part of the concept of psychosocial maturity, along with interpersonal adequacy and social adequacy. Autonomy based on Greenberger (1982, see also Deslandes, Potvin, & Leclerc, 1999) is conceptualized along three dimensions:

1. Self-reliance-corresponds to a sense of self-control and self-initiative;

2. Work orientation refers to the adolescent's work skills, aspirations for competent work performance, and capacity to experience pleasure in work; and

3. Identity measures the adolescent's sense of self-esteem, concern with life goals, internalization of values and concern with life goals.

Autonomy and more specifically, a healthy psychological work orientation seems to partly mediate the links between parenting practices and school achievement (Deslandes et al., 2000; Steinberg et al., 1989).

Summary of Findings

Parenting Practices. The following findings are from a comparison of fathers and mothers across the 3 years of the study (Deslandes, 2003). Adolescents perceive their fathers as being less loving and responsive (warmth) and less knowledgeable of their whereabouts after school at night and on weekends (supervision) than their mothers across Grades 8, 9, and 10 levels (equivalent to middle years, freshman and sophomore years in the United States). They also perceive their fathers, compared to their mothers, as encouraging them at a higher degree to express their individuality within the family at least during Grades 8 and 9 (psychological autonomy granting). However, in Grade 10 (16 years of age), fathers and mothers are perceived to be alike in their levels of psychological autonomy granting, meaning that mothers become more and more willing to promote adolescents' autonomy as they mature.

Parental Involvement Practices. As expected, over the 3 years of the study, fathers remain the least involved in the adolescents' schooling with one exception in Grades 9 and 10, in relation with father-adolescent communication. It seems that, when adolescents turn 15 and 16 years old, fathers and mothers discuss with them at a similar frequency about current events, future work or study. They equally provide help in planning time for homework, chores and other responsibilities. In general, mothers, more than fathers, provide encouragement and praise about school, attend activities at school that the adolescent is in, or talk with him/her about courses he/she can choose (affective support), talk with the teachers (communication with the teachers), ask the adolescent about school, about grades and whether he/she did homework (daily interactions about school matters), go to a meeting for parents at the school or talk about school with the parents of their youngsters' friends (parent-school communication). These findings appear to reflect fathers' and mothers' traditional ways of becoming involved with their adolescents, the academics being the mothers' responsibilities more than the fathers'. Furthermore, as mentioned by Rice and Mulkeen (1995), it is not surprising that adolescents see themselves closer to their mother than their father, the latter one having fewer interactions with them and being less involved academically.

Interestingly, when teenagers' gender is taken into account (Deslandes & Cloutier, 2000), the findings of the first-year study reveal that the fathers of boys attend school meetings more often and talk more with other parents than the fathers of girls. Furthermore, fathers discuss their children's future projects and current events more with their sons than with their daughters. In terms of practice, these results suggest that the adolescents' school, work and career aspirations could be a promising avenue to work with fathers, especially regarding boys. Fathers of boys tend to contact teachers more often than fathers of girls. The mothers of boys are more likely to contact teachers than the mothers of girls. It is well known that boys have more learning and behavior problems than girls do.

Changes Across 3 Years. On a 3-year longitudinal basis, results regarding parenting practices indicate decreases in levels of fathers' and mothers' warmth but increases in their psychological autonomy granting practices, fathers' scores being higher than mothers'. No difference was observed in their supervision levels. As for parent involvement practices, findings showed a decline in both fathers' and mothers' affective support, communication with the teachers, daily interactions on school matters, and parent-school communication. The father-adolescent communication scores, contrary to the mother's, rose from Grade 8 to Grade 9 (Deslandes, 2003).

PARENTING AND PARENTAL INVOLVEMENT PRACTICES WITH BOYS AND GIRLS IN TRADITIONAL AND NONTRADITIONAL FAMILIES

The data was further analyzed to compare traditional families—defined as two biological-parent families—and nontraditional families—defined as single-parent and reconstituted families and others (Deslandes & Cloutier, 2005). These findings are presented under the following two factors.

General Parental Practices

For Grade 8, findings show that fathers in nontraditional families encourage greater psychological autonomy, that is, greater expression of the adolescents' individuality within the family. However, fathers offer less structure (i.e., supervision) than fathers in traditional families, and this is true regardless of teenagers' gender. As for mothers, the effects of family structure and the teenager's gender are in no way significant. A year later, in Secondary 3 (Grade 9), the findings highlight a single effect linked to family structure: fathers in nontraditional families encourage autonomy more but supervise their teenager less, again regardless of gender. As for mothers, teenagers report that the mothers in nontraditional families demonstrate less warmth and supervise them less than mothers in traditional families. In the same line of thought, mothers are perceived as showing more warmth and encouraging greater psychological autonomy to girls than to boys. The results are similar in Secondary 4 (Grade 10), whereas fathers in nontraditional families encourage autonomy more, but tend to supervise less than those in traditional families.

Parental Educational Involvement Practices

For all the grades examined, young people judge that fathers and mothers in nontraditional families offer less affective support, communicate less with teachers, interact less with them on a daily basis, and attend parent-teacher meetings less often. No difference was observed regarding father-teenager communication.

Lessons Learned

In terms of parenting practices, fathers, compared to mothers, are perceived as granting greater psychological autonomy regardless of their teenager's gender, which suggests a more permissive parenting style that is even more prevalent in nontraditional fathers. Indeed, the latter encourage autonomy more and supervise less than fathers in traditional families. Consistent with previous studies (Nord, Brimhall, & West, 1997; Paulson & Sputa, 1996; Shumow & Miller, 1999), fathers are less involved in schooling than mothers except for discussions about current events and future projects as well as for guidance in time management, with the level being higher in eighth- and ninth-grade teenagers. Regarding these issues, fathers in nontraditional families communicate with their teenager as much as fathers in traditional families. It appears that fathers find it easier to talk to their teenager about subjects not related to school. Plausibly, by dealing in this way with social development, they are able to transmit family values about the importance of education (Wentzel & Battle, 2001).

In the next two studies, the author explores paternal involvement statistical models predictive of girls' and boys' school achievement and work orientation level.

FATHERS' AND MOTHERS' PREDICTIVE MODELS OF GIRLS' AND BOYS' SCHOOL ACHIEVEMENT

Paternal Involvement Model

The analyses of the findings from the first-year study of Grade 8 teenagers revealed a paternal involvement model with three variables, accounting for close to 6% of the variance in school achievement for boys and close to 13% for girls (Deslandes & Cloutier, 2000). For both girls and boys, affective support comes first, followed by interactions based on daily school activities between father and sons and between father and daughters indicating a negative relation. For girls, another variable helps predict school achievement: father-daughter communication (negative relation).

Maternal Involvement Model

For its part, the mothers' predictive model of school achievement regarding boys includes two variables explaining 9% of the variance—namely affective support in first place and mother-son interactions based on daily school activities (negative relation) in second (Deslandes & Cloutier, 2000). The predictive model of school achievement for girls comprises five variables, which account for 14% of the variance: emotional support, mother-daughter interactions based on daily school activities (negative relation), mother's communication with teachers, mother-daughter communication (negative relation), and mother-school communication. Three of these variables demonstrate a negative relation with school achievement.

Lessons Learned

Just like mothers, fathers' affective support contributes to boys' and girls' achievement scores and more importantly to the latter ones. In case of low grades with boys and girls, they then interact more often on daily school matters and they communicate more often with girls. Fathers' involvement, like mothers', was more associated with girls' school achievement than with boys'. The paternal model predictive of school achievement was twice as important for girls than for boys, which tends to show that educational support practices have a more significant impact on girls. Yet, it may be possible that boys' perceptions do not accurately portray their parents' involvement. Instead, their perceptions may act more as a filter reflecting the expression of social desirability, insensitivity to the reality of their parents' actions, the exclusively personal attribution of school achievement, etc. Another explanation refers us to the contextual model of parental style and participation developed by Darling and Steinberg (1993). According to the authors, the child's receptivity to parental influence appears to increase the effectiveness of a parental practice. It's possible that girls, eager to please their parents, are more receptive than boys to parents' interventions, and even to their influence. It may also be the case that boys, seeking to forge their identity, resist the influence of their parents—particularly that of the same-sex parent—at least with respect to school achievement (Darling & Steinberg, 1993).

FATHERS' AND MOTHERS' PREDICTIVE MODELS OF GIRLS' WORK ORIENTATION

Paternal Parenting and Involvement Models

Fathers' parenting practices account for 11% of the variance in a boy's work orientation (supervision, encouragement of psychological autonomy, and affective support) and 4% in a girl's work orientation (encouragement of psychological autonomy, and warmth). Fathers' parental involvement practices explain 8% of the variance for boys with father-son communication in first place and affective support in second. Regarding girls, the father's involvement explains 6% of the variance (affective support: positive relation) and interactions based on daily school matters (negative relation) (Deslandes, 2000).

Maternal Parenting and Involvement Models

Mothers' parenting practices explain 14% of the variance in the boys' work orientation level (warmth, supervision, and psychological autonomy granting) and 7% of the variance in the girls' work orientation level (warmth and psychological autonomy granting). Mothers' involvement practices regarding boys explain 11% of the variance with first, mother-son communication followed by affective support. With respect to girls, the maternal involvement practices account for 13% of the variance (affective support: positive relation) and interactions based on daily school matters (negative relation).

Lessons Learned

Fathers' and mothers' parenting practices affect their children's work orientation. Noteworthy, fathers' and mothers' parenting practices promote work orientation in their sons—that is, effort, interest in work well done, and ability to complete a task affect boys almost three times more than in their daughters. In other words, through their warmth, supervision, and psychological autonomy granting, both fathers and mothers, contribute to the boys' work orientation development. Just as the preceding study demonstrated boys' lesser receptivity to family influence regarding school achievement, this latter study is equally significant where work orientation is concerned. Regarding involvement practices, fathers, similarly to mothers, contribute to predict boys' work orientation through communication with adolescents and affective support. However, for girls, fathers' involvement practices are twice less important than mothers. A possible explanation for the mothers' strong influence on their daughters is that the mother acts as a same gender model for her daughter.

Limits of These Studies' Findings and Conclusions

The main limits of these research studies obviously involve their exploratory nature and the use of teenagers' perceptions for measuring parenting and involvement practices. Moreover, as little research has been done on fathers' parenting and involvement practices during their child's teenage years, these studies fill a gap. Fathers seem to play a major role in the development of a teenager's autonomy as well as in decision making regarding future projects (studies and work). It's hardly surprising that fathers are less involved in their teenagers' schooling. Up to now, it was implicitly assumed that help with homework was a maternal duty. However, certain authors speak of the gatekeeping role of mothers in this respect (e.g., Allen & Daly, 2007). Overall, there is reason to speak of the complementary of the paternal and maternal roles, which would be a definite advantage for young people. Moreover, the observation that fathers in nontraditional families appear more permissive than those in traditional families demands our attention. A possible explanation may be that mothers often gain custody of their children during a separation and that fathers see them less frequently. Regarding methodology, it is important to pursue cross-sectional studies since longitudinal studies often show a loss of participants over the years. Now, as we have seen, fathers tend to become more involved in school activities when they have a son. As for the predictive models of school achievement and work orientation, the roles of fathers and mothers appear to be similar, with a greater predictive power for perseverance and interest regarding work well done by boys. Complementarity and similarity in the roles of fathers and mothers are the order of the day for teenagers.

FATHERS' AND MOTHERS' INVOLVEMENT IN HOMEWORK

In a context of larger numbers of women working outside the home and larger numbers of men gaining custody of their children, we chose to focus on the involvement of fathers of primary school children with regard to homework. Although several studies have been conducted on homework and its usefulness in Canada (Canadian Council on Learning, 2009; Deslandes, 2009), it appears that few such studies included fathers along with mothers in their samples. In this section, we aim to identify differences between fathers' and mothers in terms of beliefs regarding homework functions, their responsibilities, and involvement practices in homework.[3]

Homework Research Participants

The participants of this research program are part of a 3-year research conducted on homework (2004-2007) in 20 different Quebec schools. Fathers' and mothers' profiles are illustrated in Table 2.3. Because of our particular interest in fathers, we'll report only on their sociodemographic characteristics. Fewer fathers participated in the studies in Grades 1 and 3 (9-10% of the sample) compared to those who did in Grades 4 and 6 (14 to 15% of the sample). Those numbers correspond to the proportion of males that have been participating in our previous studies (Deslandes & Bertrand, 2004). In the lower grades, fewer of them, (between 55.6% and 66.7%), were from traditional families as opposed to 73% in higher grades. However, fathers of lower grades were more highly educated than those of higher grades and they responded thinking more about their daughters (around 57%) than about their sons (about 42.5%). At higher grades, fathers responded regarding mainly their sons (70.6% and 65.4%).

Major Findings

There were few differences between fathers and mothers in the lower grades (see Table 2.4). Fathers who answered the questionnaires for Grade 3 believed more than mothers that homework helps their child to learn and develop work skills. In Grade 4, fathers believed more than mothers

**Table 2.3. Demographic Characteristics
of the Samples (in Percentages)**

		First Grade	Third Grade	Fourth Grade	Sixth Grade
Participant gender	Female	181 (91%)	109 (90%)	205 (85.8%)	140 (84.3%)
	Male	18 (9%)	12 (10%)	34 (14.2%)	26 (15.7%)
Family structure	**Female**				
	Traditional	72.2	73.4	60	65
	Nontraditional	27.8	26.6	40	35
	Male				
	Traditional	55.6	66.7	72.7	73.1
	Nontraditional	44.4	33.3	27.3	26.9
Education level	**Female**				
	Secondary or lower	26.8	17.8	36	31.2
	College (Cegep)	39.7	43.9	34	37
	University	33.5	38.3	30	31.9
	Male				
	Secondary or lower	44.4	25	41.2	26.9
	College (Cegep)		16.7	29.4	19.2
	University	55.6	58.3	29.4	26.9
Student gender	**Female**				
	Girls	56.4	57.8	47.3	45
	Boys	43.6	42.8	52.7	55
	Male				
	Girls	55.6	58.3	29.4	34.6
	Boys	44.4	41.7	70.6	65.4
Student achievement	**Female**				
	Learning difficulties	39.8	25.9	36	36
	Succeeds well	28.7	34.3	31	29.5
	Succeeds very well	31.5	39.8	33	34.5
	Male				
	Learning difficulties	22.2	33.3	20.6	36
	Succeeds well	38.9	8.3	44.1	40
	Succeeds very well	38.9	58.3	35.3	24

that homework promotes success in school. Fathers, to a greater extent than mothers, felt it was part of their responsibility to sit down with their child during homework (Grade 4) and make sure it was completed. Grade 6 fathers, more than mothers, asked the child to do homework over when it was not done correctly and review homework with a view to correcting

Table 2.4. Means and Standard Deviations and T Tests of Fathers' and Mothers' Measures

	Grade 1					Grade 3					Grade 4					Grade 6				
	F[1]		M[2]			F		M			F		M			F		M		
Items	M	SD	M	SD	p	M	SD	M	SD	p	M	SD	M	SD	p	M	SD	M	SD	p
Homework helps my child learn						2.24	.598	2.58	.515	*										
helps my child develop work skills						2.12	.542	2.50	.522	*										
promotes success in school											2.12	.735	2.47	.563	***					
Sit down with my child during homework	2.66	.498	2.39	.608	*						1.91	.723	2.24	.654	**					
Make sure my child's homework is done											2.46	.546	2.65	.485	*					
When my child's homework is not done correctly, I ask him/her to do it over again																1.59	1.03	2.04	1.13	*
I ask my child to review homework to correct mistakes																1.56	.074	1.96	.774	*
I tell my child he/she is doing his/her homework well											2.35	.571	2.12	.686	*					
I inform my child when homework has not been done correctly						2.58	.712	2.92	.289	**						1.56	.940	1.96	.846	*
I know what kind of help to give my child with homework						2.35	.612	2.67	.492	*										

Note: [1]F = females (mothers). [2]M = males (fathers). ***$< p$ .001. **$< p$ .01. *$< p$ .05.

30

mistakes. Grade 3 fathers said that they knew exactly how to help their child with homework. The fathers' education level was above the norm. All in all, fathers who participated in the studies seemed to demonstrate a more authoritarian style, one that involved greater supervision, like sitting down with the child and making sure that homework was done, and strict strategies, such as starting over and correcting mistakes. The findings also highlight a more positive perception of the usefulness of homework for fathers than for mothers.

Limits of the Study

One of the limits of our study concerns the size and composition of the sample of fathers. The reason for the limited size of the sample is the difficulty of recruiting fathers for a study of this nature. Thus, it's not possible to extrapolate the findings to represent all the fathers of elementary school children in Quebec. For now we can only speak of tendencies, and the topic will have to be explored in greater depth.

FATHER INVOLVEMENT BY SUBGROUPS

In Québec, the group ProsPère,[4] a pillar of the team GRAVE-ARDEC,[5] founded in 1993 and connected with Father Involvement Research Alliance, has accomplished outstanding work over the last 15 years regarding the acquisition and promotion of innovative practices in the area of paternity (Chamberland, 2009). The promotion of paternal involvement, support for community initiatives that foster its emergence and studies with fathers in contexts of vulnerability are only a few of ProsPère's many achievements. Regarding this issue, we must mention some of their studies using a qualitative approach.

Fathers Living in Poverty

The objective of the study conducted by Allard, Binet, Bergeron, Lindsay, and Lacharité (2002) was to explore how the 15 interviewed unemployed fathers living in poverty and insecurity were involved with their children under 3 years (Allard et al., 2002). Results indicate that low social status does not necessarily result in irresponsible fathers. Although the majority is doing well, many are experiencing difficulties regarding bath taking or diaper change, anxiety over their fears of reproducing the models they have known or at the exercise of discipline. Participants are aware of the strengths they can rely on as they perceive fatherhood as a project, the fun playing with their children, and sharing household chores with their wives.

Paternal Involvement in the Birth Process and Early Childhood

Lacharité (2009) notes that over the years, fathers have become objects of knowledge and a target for intervention during the period surrounding the birth of the child. Social and institutional attention is given to them. It is thus less possible for a father to be in the back scene at the birth of a child. His presence is qualified and negotiated according to the expectations of other actors involved in the situation. In their study, Baker, Miron, and de Montigny (2009) analyzed 23 midwives' representations of fathers of infants and of their relationship with them. The practice of midwifery has been legalized in Quebec since 1999. Midwives practice in the "maisons de la naissance" (birth homes), parents' home, and in some hospitals with which they have a local agreement. Findings indicate that midwives strive to create special areas with fathers during pregnancy, childbirth and postnatal period. They help to support early father involvement.

Paternal Involvement of Migrant Fathers

Gervais, de Montigny, Azaroual, and Courtois (2009) conducted a study based on semistructured interviews with 12 fathers from North Africa in a context of immigration (Gervais et al., 2009). The objective was to describe fathers' involvement and the influence of immigration on the development of their paternal identities. Results put into evidence the involvement of immigrant fathers like playing with and bathing their child. Immigrant fathers perceive paternity primarily as a responsibility and a commitment. Interestingly, the migration context can make possible the expression of their paternal identity allowing a greater commitment to their child compared to what it would have been in their home country. For instance, in Maghreb societies, the paternal role is often limited by the presence of the extended family. Study findings also reveal that the immigration period and services provided by the host country can have an impact on the representation of fathering and father involvement. Compared to second generation immigrant fathers, first generation immigrant fathers seemed to develop paternal identities in opposition to their culture and family representations of their paternal role. Second generation immigration seemed to be more ambivalent between their own father's role model as a provider and a figure of authority and their desire to become closer to their child.

Paternal Involvement of Incarcerated Fathers

Children of judiciary controlled fathers represent a significant proportion of youngsters in Quebec youth centers. According to a study with 850 young people in various youth centers, between 12.1% and 32.1% of children have a parent who would have known or been suspected of criminal activities (Pauzé et al., 2000, cited in Dubeau, Barrette, & Lafortune, 2009). However, incarceration affects the father in his parental role in several aspects: legal (difficulty maintaining her parental rights), economic (increasing economic dependence), social (isolated in captivity), psychological (low self-esteem, anxiety), and relational (separation). Because several incarcerated fathers do not maintain conjugal relationships with the mothers of their children, the father-child contacts are difficult. Researchers conducted an action research entitled *Growing up well with an incarcerated father* in order to set up services to imprisoned fathers and their families (Dubeau, Barrette, & Lafortune, 2009). These services are structured around two axes, intervention and prevention. The first aims to improve the fathers' parenting skills and the second is to prevent child adjustment problems.

PRACTICES TO SUPPORT FATHER INVOLVEMENT

Legal Provisions Concerning Paternity Leave

On January 1, 2006, the Quebec Government put into effect provisions for a paternity leave under the Quebec Parental Insurance Plan. As stipulated in sections 79.1 and 79.8 of the Act Respecting Labour Standards in Quebec, the biological father who has met certain requirements can benefit of a paternity leave starting on the week on which the child is born. The father can either choose to receive 70% of his gross weekly income over 5 weeks or to receive 75% of his gross weekly income over 3 weeks. The paternity leave aims at facilitating fathers' involvement and engagement with the newborn and the new mother.

Intervention Practices

A crucial intervention practice is to sensitize the general population, especially fathers, to the importance of their role regarding the upbringing and education of their young children and teenagers. Educators, social and health practitioners need to persuade mothers to make more room for fathers. The goal is certainly not to incite rivalry between feminist groups and those working with men. On the contrary, the issue involves the sharing and the complementarity of roles within the family. One of ProsPère's experiments is particularly inspiring. "Draw me a Dad" involves asking young children to draw a picture of how they perceive the paternal role, and their drawings are then exhibited in public places (Turcotte & Ouellet, 2009). This example leads us to envision the possibility of discussion groups or perhaps a school assignment asking students to describe the role of fathers or how they would like fathers to act. Another inspiring example is that of participatory theater to educate decision makers and all parties involved regarding the importance of the father's role with his children (Forget, 2009).

Practitioners and educators should consider activities that emphasize fathers' participation in interactions with their children as, for example, during the neighborhood celebrations (family weekend festivals) that often take place in August in Quebec or during organized school activities (shows, sports competitions, cultural activities, etc.) or in the child's classroom. Within the same school context, teachers could be encouraged to send personalized invitations to fathers, as well as mothers, in traditional and nontraditional families with a view to strengthening relations with them and conveying the message that their contribution to their child's schooling is important. The agenda of such meetings could include exchanges, discussions, and demonstrations (i.e., modeling) of certain strategies in the form of encouragement, teaching, and reinforcement likely to facilitate the parents' and particularly the fathers' task with their children and teenagers, for example, during homework.

As for paternal parenting practices aimed at promoting the development of children and teenagers and their school achievement, educational support and self-help groups are now offered to fathers in Quebec at the Health and Social Service Centers or in community organizations such as the *Maisons de la Famille* and others. Obviously, these primary interventions are to be pursued as well as those offered to groups of more vulnerable fathers who must be supported in their parenting competencies and given the opportunity to develop new knowledge. Another very relevant idea is to envision primary prevention groups for fathers and mothers that allow the role of each to be negotiated. Such intervention activities would be designed to ensure complementarity rather than adversity in the parents' respective actions. In the same vein, we might consider father-child groups that offer opportunities for interaction.

Finally, with the support of philanthropic organizations, training could be offered to teachers, social and health practitioners and involved parties in order to foster an improved understanding of the importance of paternal participation and to convey information about the learning, technical and interpersonal skills required to enhance the image of fathers and to conduct effective actions WITH fathers.

NOTES

1. Father Involvement Research Alliance, situated at the Centre for Families, Work & Well-Being at the University of Guelph in the province of Ontario was created back in 2002 during a national forum held in Toronto. For more information, visit http://www.fira.ca
2. Autonomy level and parents-adolescent interactions linked to school achievement. A 3-year longitudinal study supported by a grant from the Centre for Research in Social Sciences and Humanities (SSHRC 1998-2001) awarded to Deslandes.
3. A longitudinal and cross-sectional study on homework at the primary and secondary levels. This study was made possible by a grant from the Centre for Research in Social Sciences and Humanities (SSHRC 2004-2008) awarded to Deslandes (project leader) and Rousseau.
4. GRAVE-ARDEC is a research and action group on the victimization of children and a research alliance on the development of children in their community. For a description, see http://www.graveardec.uqam.ca/
5. Groupe ProsPère is a research team developed thanks to the initiative of Camil Bouchard, who assumed responsibility for the document "Un Québec fou de ses enfants" (A Quebec crazy about its children). This team aims to encourage the involvement of fathers, particularly in low-income areas. See, http://www.graveardec.uqam.ca/prospere

REFERENCES

Allard, F., Binet, L., Bergeron, M., Lindsay, J., & Lacharité, C. (2002). Devenir père en situation de pauvreté [Becoming a father in poverty]. In C. Lacharité & G. Pronovost et E. Coutu (Eds.), *Actes du 6e symposium québécois de recherche sur la famille* [Proceedings of the 6th Symposium Quebec Family Research] (pp. 77-101). Québec, Canada: Presses de l'Université du Québec.

Allen, S., & Daly, K. (2007). The effects of father involvement: An updated research summary of the evidence. Ontario, CA: University of Guelph. Retrieved from http://www.fira.ca/cms/documents/29/Effects_of_Father_Involvement.pdf

Baker, M., Miron, J. -M., & de Montigny, F. (2009). Entre la sage-femme et le père, des espaces coconstruits: Étude exploratoire [Between the midwife and the father, coconstructed spaces: Exploratory study]. *Enfance, Familles, Générations 11*. Retrieved from http://www.efg.inrs.ca/presentation.html

Canadian Council of Learning. (2009). A systematic review of literature examining the impact of homework on academic achievement. Ottawa, Ontario, Canada: Canadian Council of Learning. Retrieved from http://www.ccl-cca.ca/ccl/Reports/SystematicReviews/Homework.html

Chamberland, C. (2009). ProsPère et le transfert des connaissances [Prosper and knowledge transfer]. In D. Dubeau, A. Devault, & G. Forget (Eds.), *La paternité au XXIe siècle* [Fatherhood in the 21st century] (pp. 365-370). Québec City, Québec, Canada: Presses de l'Université Laval.

Darling, N., & Steinberg, L. (1993). Parenting style as context: An integrative model. *Psychological Bulletin, 113*(3), 487-496.

Deslandes, R. (1996). *Collaboration entre l'école et les familles: Influence du style parental et de la participation parentale sur la réussite scolaire au secondaire* [Collaboration between schools and families: Influence of parenting style and parental involvement on academic achievement in high school] (Doctoral dissertation). Educational Psychology, Quebec City, Québec, Canada: Laval University.

Deslandes, R. (2000). Liens entre l'orientation vers le travail de l'adolescent et l'accompagnement parental pour une meilleure réussite scolaire des adolescents [Links between the adolescent's work orientation and parental support for higher academic achievement of adolescents]. *Scientia Pardagogica Experimentalis, 38*(2), 199-217.

Deslandes, R. (2003). Evolution of parenting and parent involvement in schooling practices and Canadian adolescents' autonomy over a three-year span. In S. Castelli, M. Mendel, & B. Ravns (Eds.), *School, family, and community partnerships in a world of differences and change* (pp. 89-104). Gdansk, Poland: Gdansk University.

Deslandes, R. (2006). La problématique école-famille-communauté dans la formation des futurs enseignants [School-family-community issue in pre-service teachers' training]. In J. Loiselle, L. Lafortune, & N. Rousseau (Eds.), *L'innovation en formation à l'enseignement* [Innovation in teacher training] (pp. 184-204). Québec City, Québec, Canada: PUQ.

Deslandes, R. (Ed.). (2009). *International perspective on student outcomes and homework: Family-school-community partnerships.* New York, NY: Routledge.

Deslandes, R., & Bertrand, R. (2004). Motivation des parents à participer au suivi scolaire de leur enfant au primaire [Parents' motivation to participate in their elementary children's schooling]. *Revue des sciences de l'éducation, 30*(2), 411-434.

Deslandes, R., Bertrand, R., Royer, É., & Turcotte, D. (1995). Validation d'instruments de mesure du style parental et de la participation parentale dans le suivi scolaire [Validation of measurement scales of parenting style and parental involvement in schooling]. *Measure et évaluation en éducation, 18*(2), 63-79.

Deslandes, R., & Cloutier, R. (2000). Engagement parental dans l'accompagnement scolaire et réussite des adolescents à l'école [Parental involvement in schooling and adolescents' success in school]. *Bulletin de Psychologie Scolaire et d'Orientation, 2*, 53-72.

Deslandes, R., & Cloutier, R. (2005). Pratiques parentales et réussite scolaire en fonction de la structure familiale et du genre des adolescents [Parenting and academic achievement based to family structure and adolescents' gender]. *Revue Française de Pédagogie, 151,* 61-74.

Deslandes, R., Potvin, P., & Leclerc, D. (1999). Validation québécoise de l'Échelle de l'autonomie de l'adolescent [Validation of the Quebec French version of the adolescent autonomy scale]. *Science et Comportement, 27*(3), 37-51.

Deslandes, R., Potvin, P., & Leclerc, D. (2000). Les liens entre l'autonomie de l'adolescent, la collaboration parentale et la réussite scolaire [Relation between adolescent's autonomy, parenting and parental involvement practices and school achievement]. *Canadian Journal of Behavioural Science, 32*(4), 208-217.

Deslandes, R., Royer, É., Turcotte, D., & Bertrand, R. (1997). School achievement at the secondary level: Influence of parenting style and parent involvement in schooling. *McGill Journal of Education 32*(3), 191-208.

Dubeau, D. (2002). État de la recherche portant sur les pères au Canada [State of research on fathers in Canada]. Retrieved from http://www.graveardec .uqam.ca/prospere/pages/pdf/rapportdiane_dubeau.pdf

Dubeau, D., Barrette, M., & Lafortune, D. (2009). Grandir sainement avec un père détenu [Growing up well with an incarcerated father]. In D. Dubeau, A. Devault, & G. Forget (Eds.), *La paternité au XXIe siècle* [Fatherhood in the 21st century] (pp. 305-330). Québec City, Québec, Canada: PUL.

Epstein, J. L., Connors, L. J., & Salinas, K. C. (1993). *High school and family partnerships: Questionnaires for teachers, parents, and students'.* Baltimore, MD: Johns Hopkins University: Center on Families, Communities, Schools and Children's Learning.

Forget, G. (2009). Le transfert des connaissances: Un enjeu important de la recherche. In D. Dubeau, A. Devault, & G. Forget (Eds.), *La paternité au XXIe siècle* [Fatherhood in the 21st Century] (pp. 371-399). Québec City, Québec, Canada: PUL.

Galipeau, S. (2011, September 16). Conciliation famille-travail. Ils ne savent pas comment ils font. [Work-family balance. They do not know how they do it] *La Presse. Vivre*, pp. 1-3.

Gervais, C., de Montigny, F., Azaroual, S., & Courtois, A. (2009). La paternité en contexte migratoire: Étude comparative de l'expérience d'engagement paternelle et de la construction de l'identité paternelle d'immigrants [Fatherhood in the context of migration: A comparative study of the experience of father involvement and immigrants' paternal identity construction]. *Enfance Familles Générations, 11.* Retrieved from http://www.efg.inrs.ca/presentation.html

Greenberger, E. (1982). Education and the acquisition of psychosocial maturity. In D. McClelland (Ed.), *The development of social maturity* (pp. 155-189). New York, NY: Irvington.

Greenberger, E., Josselson, R., Knerr, C., & Knerr, B. (1975). The measurement and structure of psychosocial maturity. *Journal of Youth and Adolescence, 4*(2), 127-143.

Lacharité, C. (2009) L'expérience paternelle entourant la naissance d'un enfant : contextes sociaux et pratiques professionnelles [Paternal experience surrounding the birth of a child: Social contexts and work practices]. *Enfance,*

Familles, Générations 11. Retrieved from http://www.efg.inrs.ca/presentation .html

Lamb, M. E., & Tamis-LeMonda, C. S. (Eds.). (2004). The role of the father. In *The role of the father in child development* (4th ed., pp. 1-31). New York, NY: Wiley.

Leduc, L. (2011, May 9). Papa, qu'est-ce qu'on mange? [Dad, What's for dinner?] *La Presse*, p. A14.

Nord, C. -W, Brimhall, D., & West, J. (1997). *Fathers' involvement in their children's schools* (NCES 98-091). Washington, DC: U.S. Department of Education, National Center for Education Statistics. (ED 409 125).

Pacaut, P. (2011). *La part des pères québécois dans les tâches liées aux soins et à l'éducation des enfants* [The share of Quebec fathers in tasks related to the care and education of children]. Seminar presented at the INRS Institute. Retrieved from http://partenariat-familles.inrs-ucs.uquebec.ca/DocsPDF/ ResumeConfmidi20avril2011.pdf

Palkovitz, R. (2002). Involved fathering and child development: Advancing our understanding of good fathering. In C. S. Tamis-LeMonda & N. Cabrera (Eds.), *Handbook of father involvement: Multidisciplinary perspectives* (pp. 119-140). Mahwah, NJ: Erlbaum.

Paulson, S. E., & Sputa, C. L. (1996). Patterns of parenting during adolescence: Perceptions of adolescents and parents. *Adolescence, 31*(122), 369-381.

Pauzé, R., Toupin, J., Déry, M., Mercier, H., Cyr, M., Cyr, F., & Frappier, J.-Y. (2000). *Portrait des jeunes inscrits à la prise en charge des Centres jeunes du Québec. Description des services reçus au cours des premiers mois* [Portrait of youngsters enrolled in Quebec Youth Centers. Description of services received during the first months] (Research report). Ottawa, Ontario, Canada: Health Canada.

Quebec Government. (2006). Paternal leave and Parental Insurance Plan. Retrieved from http://www.educaloi.qc.ca/en/loi/parents/374 and http://www .rqap.gouv.qc.ca/a_propos_regime/information_generale/historique_en.asp

Rice, K., & Mulkeen, P. (1995). Relationships with parents and peers: A longitudinal study of adolescent intimacy. *Journal of Adolescent Research, 10*, 338-357.

Schwarz, J., Barton-Henry, M., & Pruzinsky, T. (1985). Assessing child-rearing behaviors: A comparison of ratings made by mother, father, child and sibling on the CRPBI. *Child Development 56*, 462-479.

Shumow, L., & Miller, J. D. (2001). Parents' at-home and at-school academic involvement with young adolescents. *Journal of Early Adolescence 21*(1), 68-91.

Steinberg, L., Elmen, J. D., & Mounts, N. S. (1989). Authoritative parenting, psychosocial maturity, and academic success among adolescents. *Child Development 60*, 1424-1436.

Steinberg, L., Lamborn, S. D., Darling, N., Mounts, N. S., & Dornbusch, S. M. (1994). Over-time changes in adjustment and competence among adolescents from authoritative, authoritarian, indulgent, and neglectful families. *Child Development, 65*, 754-770.

Steinberg, L., Lamborn, S. D., Dornbusch, S. M., & Darling, N. (1992). Impact of parenting practices on adolescent achievement: Authoritative parenting, school involvement, and encouragement to succeed. *Child Development 63*, 1266-1281.

Turcotte, G., & Ouellet, F. (2009). Une experience de mobilization autour de l'engagement paternal dans deux communautés vulnérable du Québec. [A mobilization experience around paternal involvement in two vulnerable communities in Quebec]. In D. Dubeau, A. Devault, & G. Forget (Eds.), *La paternité au XXIe siècle* [Fatherhood in the 21st century] (pp. 153-173). Québec City, Québec, Canada: PUL.

Wentzel, K. R., & Battle, A. A. (2001). Social relationships and school adjustment. In T. Urdan & F. Pajares (Eds.), *Adolescence and education. General issues in the education of adolescents* (pp. 93-118), Greenwich, CT: Information Age.

CHAPTER 3

FATHER INVOLVEMENT IN STUDENTS' EDUCATION IN TAIWAN

Hsiu-Zu Ho, Kuang-Hui Yeh, Chih-Wen Wu, Connie N. Tran, and Wei-Wen Chen

In recent decades Taiwan's dynamic socioeconomic growth and political transformation have brought changes to a number of traditions, including gender equality and gender roles (Beckert, Strom, Strom, & Yang, 2006).[1] Along with these new developments related to gender roles, a small but growing body of research on parent involvement has begun to focus on the role and participation of fathers in contemporary Taiwanese society (Chern, 2005; Chiang, Huang, & Lin, 2005; Ho, Chen, Tran, & Ko, 2010; Hsu, Zhang, Kwok, Li, & Ju, 2010; Huang & Wang, 2007).

Traditionally, the childcare and household responsibilities fell solely upon the mother; however, with more women currently entering the workforce, it is becoming more difficult for women to fulfill the role of full-time motherhood (F. L. Chen, Yang, & Wang, 2010). Consequently, many women are choosing to delay marriage and parenthood. In their study, Chen and colleagues (2010) found: more women (than men) to advocate the sharing of housework in dual-income households; younger generations to be less supportive of marriage and more open to divorce; and younger generations to prefer fewer children. The authors pointed to

Promising Practices for Fathers' Involvement in Children's Education
pp. 41–57
Copyright © 2012 by Information Age Publishing

the increasing number of women in the workforce and lack of government support for childcare as likely sources of such findings. According to a report by the Directorate General of Budget, Accounting, and Statistics, (DGBAS, 2011), as of 2009, the percentage of women as economic household heads (i.e., person with the largest income in the household and main provider) since 1999 had increased by 8% across all income groups, suggesting women in Taiwan are becoming more financially independent. The gender gap in the labor participation rate has steadily decreased in the last several decades and the female share in employment increased from 38% in 1989 to 44% in 2009 (DGBAS, 2011). In addition, the birthrate in Taiwan has dropped by about 37% since 2000 and the fertility rate as of 2010 was 1.1, among the lowest in the world. The decrease in the number of children may in part be a result of women's higher educational attainment, meaning a delay in marriage and therefore, childbearing (DGBAS, 2011). While policies are varied across provinces/cities, the government is taking a number of measures to increase the birthrate. For example, since January 1, 2011, Taipei City Government's Department of Health has implemented a "Wish You a Good Pregnancy" project, such that free prepregnancy health examinations are provided for married couples. Furthermore, every couple with a newborn will receive NT$20,000,[2] and parents with a child younger than 5 years old will receive a NT$2,500 child-rearing subsidy per month (Department of Health, 2011). Kindergarten fees (NT$12,543) are waived for 5-year-olds (http://born.igd.tw/policy.php). In addition, more public day care centers are being established, and the Ministry of Education is attempting to help with the cost of education (K. Liu, 2011). Economic and sociocultural changes in Taiwan have also led to changes in family structure, with a growing number of nuclear households accompanied by declining multigenerational households. Currently, while many grandparents do not live in the same household with their grandchildren, grandparents still play important roles in their grandchildren's lives, including picking them up from school, staying with them when their parents are away, and assisting with their educational costs. With an increasing number of dual-income and nuclear families, the traditional views held by fathers and mothers toward parenting roles are being challenged.

REVIEW OF STUDIES ABOUT FATHER INVOLVEMENT IN TAIWAN

Research on father involvement in Taiwan is relatively new, considering the fact that most prior research has focused on mother involvement or parent involvement, without distinguishing between the differential effects of mothers and fathers on the lives of their children. One explanation for the lack of research on father involvement is that in Taiwan, a father's role has traditionally been considered as the breadwinner. Studies on mother and father involvement in Taiwan have found that, generally, mothers are more likely than fathers to be engaged and educationally involved with their children (Hsu et al., 2011; Ho et al., 2010; Hung, 2005). Even representations in the Taiwanese media, such as in the form of television commercials, show that more mothers than fathers are targeted for domestic and child-related products; women are depicted more often than men performing and being successful at household chores, caring for children, and being involved in educational activities with their children (Tsai, 2010). While fathers are not seen in primary roles, Tsai (2010) found they are more likely to be viewed playing with their children or in supportive roles. However, in the few cases where fathers are viewed taking on primary roles, they are depicted as emotionally involved and engaged in their parenting roles, suggesting that progressive parenting roles are occurring in Taiwan. Similarly, in a study that sought evidence of progressive media representation of father involvement in Taiwan, Ho, Ko, Tran, Philips, and Chen (in press) found portrayals of fathers as co-parents with their wives and engaged in household chores and childcare in children's storybooks (e.g., *The Chu Family, Red Rooster*), primary-school textbooks, and television commercials. In a qualitative study of voices of Taiwanese fathers (Ho et al., 2011), paternal roles beyond that of the "breadwinner" were identified in a thematic analysis that include: disciplinarian, emotional supporter, caregiver, decision maker, chauffeur, handyman, and companion of outdoor activities/sports.

REVIEW OF STUDIES ON FATHER INVOLVEMENT AND ACADEMIC ACHIEVEMENT IN TAIWAN

In addition to studies that have examined the roles of Taiwanese fathers, a few studies have focused on the influence of father involvement on their children's academic achievement. In a 2005 study, Chern found that primary school students whose fathers were highly engaged (and who also discussed career development with their children) had high levels of academic achievement (Chern, 2005). In their study of Taiwanese fathers of children ages 10 to 14, Beckert and his colleagues found a significant relationship between father involvement and student academic achievement. Furthermore, children's perceptions of their fathers' involvement varied by gender and child's achievement status (Beckert et al., 2006). More favorable ratings of father involvement (with regard to ability to teach, handling frustration, managing time) were found for sons and daughters who performed above average in school. However, the directionality of that relationship is unclear. For example, Beckert and his colleagues found that fathers of younger children who spent more time with their sons with above-average grades also rated themselves significantly higher in their ability to teach, while daughters with above-average grades who spent more time with their fathers gave their fathers significantly higher scores on ability to teach.

In a study examining the impact of father-mother involvement on student academic achievement using the large-scale longitudinal Taiwan Education Panel Survey (TEPS), results showed that mother involvement has positive effects on seventh-grade students' academic achievement, whereas father involvement does not (Hsu et al., 2010). Although this study distinguished fathers from mothers and focused on an adolescent population, it only used seventh-grade data and was not longitudinal. Furthermore, while Hsu and his colleagues (2011) examined the direct effect of father and mother involvement on adolescent academic achievement, they did not take into account the mediating process by which parental involvement influences student academic outcomes. Hence, it is important to uncover the process by which parent involvement leads to achievement. Although Hsu and colleagues (2011) did not find a direct effect of father involvement, it is possible that father involvement has an indirect effect on student achievement. For example, students' educational aspirations may be a possible mediator between involvement and achievement (see Hong & Ho, 2005, for a study on U.S. eighth-12th graders, providing evidence for student educational aspiration as a significant mediator). That is, father and mother involvement influences adolescents' expectations, which subsequently influences their academic performance.

In a study on the effects of Taiwanese parenting practices on students' educational aspirations and aspirations, Kan and Tsai (2005) found that parenting practices of reinforcement in the form of encouragement from both father and mother had a positive effect (mothers greater than fathers) on children's educational aspirations. Although the study did not include fathers' educational involvement, Kan and Tsai still demonstrated positive mother/father effects on educational expectations and aspirations. In a study using the Taiwan Education Panel Survey, K.-S. Liu, Cheng, Chen, and Wu (2009) found students' educational expectations to predict initial academic achievement as well as achievement growth; for example, higher levels of educational expectation were associated with higher learning-growth rates. These studies show that students' educational aspirations can be an important mediator between father/mother involvement and student achievement outcomes.

PRESENT STUDY USING TEPS

The present study extends the research by Hsu et al. (2011) in the following ways: (1) The inclusion of indirect/mediating effects, specifically student educational aspiration, as a mediator linking the effects of parental involvement on student academic outcomes; (2) The inclusion of four types of parent-child dyads (father-son, father-daughter, mother-son, and mother-daughter) as possibly moderating the mediating process mentioned above; (3) The inclusion of a longitudinal design to examine the indirect effects of father/mother involvement on academic outcomes 2 years later.

Participants

The present study utilized data from the large-scale longitudinal TEPS, which was funded and collected by Academic Sinica, the Ministry of Education, and the National Science Council in Taiwan. TEPS is a long-term panel study with four waves included. The present study utilized the data from the first two waves: the first-wave data was collected in 2001 from seventh graders; the second wave was assessed in 2003 from ninth graders. There are three categories of variables in the dataset: students' self-reported data; data answered by parents; data answered by teachers. The present study used data from students and parents, as well as students' academic performance. The first-wave data in 2001 included 13,979 seventh graders, and 12,566 of them finished the second assessment in 2003. There were 6,364 male students (50.64%), and the average age during the first wave was 12.39 year olds ($SD = .55$).

Measures

Father/Mother Involvement. Based on Hsu et al. (2011), the present study used the following items completed by students from the first wave to measure father/mother involvement: (1) How often does your father discuss with you about obtaining employment or advancing your education (career plan discussion)? (2) How often does your father listen to you discuss your thinking (listening to adolescent thinking)? (3) How often does your father check your homework and tests and understand your achievements (monitoring behavior)? (4) How often does your father participate in school activities (participation in school)? Replacing "father" with "mother," the same questions were adopted to measure mother involvement. A four-point Likert scale was used for the four questions

(1 = *never*, 2 = *sometimes*, 3 = *often*, 4 = *always*). In the present study the mean was 9.30 (*SD* = 2.73) for father involvement and 11.21 (*SD* = 2.79) for mother involvement.

Students' Own Educational Aspirations. The item regarding students' educational aspirations was completed by the students from the first wave. The responses to the question, "What educational level do you expect to reach?" include four levels of educational aspirations: 1 = *no expectations*; 2 = *high school or lower*; 3 = *college education*; 4 = *graduate school*. The mean score was 2.76 (*SD* = 1.03).

Academic Achievement. TEPS constructed a standardized assessment tool to assess adolescents' curriculum-free academic performance, which includes performance in general analytic ability, reading, mathematics, and science. The present study adopted the item response theory scores on the standardized test obtained from the publicly released file of the TEPS to measure academic achievement in the second-wave assessment. The mean score was 0.84 (*SD* = 1.21).

Covariates. According to past literature, the following variables are related to adolescents' academic performance: family socioeconomic status, father's and mother's educational levels, and parents' educational expectations/aspirations (e.g., Jeynes, 2007; Mullis, Rathge, & Mullis, 2003; Yan & Lin, 2005). Therefore the following variables were treated as control variables in our analysis.

Family Socioeconomic Status. Six levels were created according to a family's monthly income (Taiwan Dollars, TWD), and circled by parents during the first wave assessment. The six levels were: 1 = less than 19,999 TWD; 2 = 20,000 – 49,999; 3 = 50,000 – 99,999; 4 = 100,000 – 149,999; 5 = 150,000 – 199,999; 6 = more than 200,000 (*M* = 2.68; *SD* = 1.00).

Father/Mother Educational Level. Parents reported their educational level during the first-wave assessment. Four levels were included: 1 = junior high school or lower; 2 = senior high school; 3 = college education; 4 = graduate school. The average educational level was 2.13 for fathers (*SD* = 1.08) and 1.93 for mothers (*SD* = .93).

Father's/Mother's Educational Aspiration for His/Her Children. The question, "What educational level do you expect your child to reach?" was administered to parents during the first-wave. Four levels were included: 1 = no expectation; 2 = high school or lower; 3 = college education; 4 = graduate school. The mean score was 2.99 (*SD* = 0.87).

Data Analysis

The present study utilized structural equation modeling to analyze the data. Structural equation modeling is able to simultaneously examine multiple causal paths and to compare whether path parameters are equal among multiple sample groups in the same model through testing differences in Chi-square values.

The present study used LISREL software to analyze the data. χ^2, NNFI, CFI, RMSEA, and SRMR were selected as indicators of goodness-of-fit. The cut-off points for the indicators χ^2 and the degree of freedom ratio are between 2 to 3. CFI and NNFI larger than 0.90 (Bentler, 1990; Bentler & Bonett, 1980), RMSEA less than 0.06 (Hu & Bentler, 1999; Kaplan, 2000), and SRMR less than 0.08 (Hu & Bentler, 1999) are acceptable fit.

RESULTS AND DISCUSSION OF STUDY

Descriptive Statistics and Correlations

Table 3.1 presents the correlation matrix regarding relevant variables in the present study. Note that regardless of adolescents' gender, mothers have a higher mean level of involvement than fathers. For both adolescent boys and girls, student academic achievement was significantly and positively correlated with family income, both fathers' and mothers' educational levels, parents' educational aspirations, father/mother involvement, and students' own educational aspirations.

Results for the Hypothesized Structural Model

The structural model is shown in Figure 3.1. Based on Hsu et al. (2011), four items measuring father involvement and four items measuring mother involvement were set up as freely-estimated parameters in order to improve the degree of the overall model's goodness-of-fit. Although the chi-square value ($\chi^2(114) = 764.50$; $\chi^2/df = 6.71$) was much larger than the traditional cut-off-point, all other goodness-of-fit indexes were within the traditionally accepted cut-off-points (RMSEA = .03; NNFI = .98; CFI = .99; SRMR = .03). The poor goodness-of-fit of Chi-square value can be explained by its instability due to the large sample size (Bollen & Long, 1993).

Results of the structural equation modeling analysis indicated that regardless of adolescents' gender, both father and mother involvement had significant effects on student's educational aspiration ($\gamma_{\text{Father-Son}} = .18$, $\gamma_{\text{Father-Daughter}} = .08$, $\gamma_{\text{Mother-Son}} = .10$, $\gamma_{\text{Mother-Daughter}} = .14$, all $p < .05$). Student's educational aspiration also had a significant effect on their actual academic achievement ($\beta_{\text{Sons}} = .16$, $\beta_{\text{Daughters}} = .17$, both $p < .01$).

Table 3.1. Correlation Matrix Among Variables Examined for Both Boys and Girls

	1	2	3	4	5	6	7	8	9	M	SD
Household income		.480*	.479*	-.025*	.279*	.133*	.139*	.171*	.315*	2.690	1.000
Father education level	.474*		.696*	-.028*	.308*	.197*	.144*	.207*	.395*	2.120	1.092
Mother education level	.479*	.696*		-.056*	.295*	.164*	.189*	.201*	.394*	1.930	.928
Age	-.039*	-.062*	-.057*		-.013	.020	.019	.040*	.017	12.380	.523
Parental educational aspiration	.314*	.345*	.339*	-.014		.163*	.190*	.266*	.310*	2.970	.854
Father's involvement	.133*	.190*	.152*	-.001	.187*		.481*	.180*	.151*	9.192	2.742
Mother's involvement	.124*	.139*	.176*	-.001	.183*	.542*		.203*	.192*	11.476	2.720
Student's educational aspiration	.147*	.205*	.201*	-.018	.240*	.236*	.217*		.304*	2.810	.992
Academic achievement	.301*	.376*	.356*	-.052*	.358*	.128*	.159*	.279*		.910	1.153

Note: The statistics for boys are below the diagonal and those for girls are above the diagonal. $*p < .01$ (2-tailed).

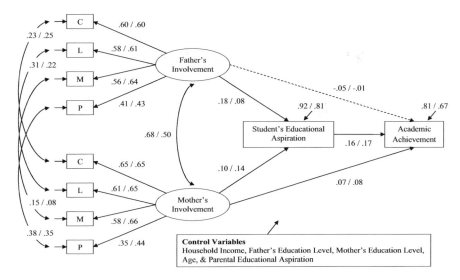

Notes: C = career plan discussion; L = listening to adolescent thinking; M = monitoring behavior; P = school participation. $\chi^2(114) = 764.50$, $p < .001$; comparative fit index (CFI) = .99; RMSEA = .030; SRMR = .030. All paths are statistically significant at a= .05 level except for dashed path from father's involvement to academic achievement. The first coefficient refers to son's data, the second to daughter's data; the original coefficients of direct effect in the parenthesis.

Figure 3.1.   Final structural model with standardized solution.

When further examining the mediating relations (father/mother involve-ment–student's educational aspiration–student academic achievement) using the Sobel Test, the results demonstrated that the mediating effects were significant for all four types of parent-child relationships (Sobel_Father-Son = 6.65, Sobel_Mother-Son = 4.82, Sobel_Father-Daughter = 4.08, Sobel_Mother-Daughter = 6.26, all $p < .01$). Hence, when considering students' educational aspirations as the mediator, father and mother involvement both have significant indirect effects on students' academic achievement. The relation between parental involvement and students' academic achievement can be understood as an internalization process of a culturally transmitted set of values from parents to children (Marchant, Paulson, & Rothlisberg, 2001). Due to filial duty and the close-knit par-ent-child relationship in the Chinese cultural context, educational beliefs, including importance of education and high parental expectations embedded in parental involvement, may transfer into students' own edu-cational aspirations, which subsequently improve students' academic achievement (W.-W. Chen & Ho, in press).

Further analysis of Chi-square differences was conducted to examine whether there were differences in path parameters between sons and daughters or between different dyads. No significant difference was found between sons (β_{Son} = .16) and daughters ($\beta_{Daughter}$ = .17) in the path from students' educational aspirations and academic achievement. However, when considering the gender effect of parents and students on the relation between parental involvement and students' educational aspirations (father-son, father-daughter, mother-son, and mother-daughter), the father-son dyads ($\gamma_{Father-Son}$ = .18) are significantly stronger than either father-daughter dyads ($\gamma_{Father-Daughter}$ = .08) ($p < .05$) or mother-son dyads ($\gamma_{Mother-Son}$ = .10) ($p < .05$). In addition, the mother-daughter dyads ($\gamma_{Mother-Daughter}$ = .14) are significantly stronger than the mother-son dyads ($\gamma_{Mother-Son}$ = .10) ($p < .05$) and father-daughter dyads ($\gamma_{Father-Daughter}$ = .08) ($p < .05$).

According to social learning theory (e.g., Bandura & Walters, 1959), the role modeling effect is strengthened by gender identification during the socialization process (Maccaby, 2000). Parents tend to have stronger effects on same-sex than opposite-sex children—they feel greater responsibility for the socialization of same-sex children and exert closer control over them (Chang, Schwartz, Dodge, & McBride-Change, 2003; Huston, 1983; Power & Shanks, 1989). Given prevalent gender separation in social roles in the Chinese cultural context, duties of socializing children are also traditionally assumed by their same-sex parents. Due to the common interests between fathers and sons in daily activities, research also suggests that Chinese fathers might spend more time with their sons than their daughters, and have more opportunities to monitor and control their sons' behaviors (X. Chen, Liu, & Li, 2000). Such intensive father-son interactions may facilitate their sons' internationalization processes and exert more influence on their sons' educational beliefs, and the same argument holds for the Chinese mother-daughter relationship.

Lastly, it is noteworthy that the present study replicated findings from Hsu et al. (2011) with respect to direct effects of mother/father involvement on students' academic achievement. That is, when considering the impact of father and mother involvement alone on student academic achievement (with relevant control variables), father involvement had no significant direct effect on student academic achievement ($\gamma_{Father-Son}$ = $-.02$, $\gamma_{Father-Daughter}$ = $-.00$), while mother involvement does directly impact student academic outcomes ($\gamma_{Mother-Son}$ = .09, $\gamma_{Mother-Daughter}$ = .10). Moreover, utilizing the ninth-grade data as the criterion of academic achievement in the present study, the findings with regard to direct effects were similar to those for seventh-grade academic achievement. Therefore, this further improved the predictive validity of the findings of Hsu and her colleagues. In other words, mother involvement influenced not only children's academic achievement on the concurrent year, but also their academic achievement 2 years later.

PROMISING PRACTICES/CURRENT GOVERNMENT AND WORK POLICIES

Taiwan's government, corporations/industries, and schools have undertaken a number of steps towards promising practices related to the important roles working parents have in their children's lives.

Government Policies

Recent policies in Taiwan regarding parental leaves may also impact father involvement. The Gender Equality in Employment Act of 2002 requires that companies must allow employees, both mothers and fathers, up to 2 years of unpaid parental leave per child, until that child reaches the age of 3 (Executive Yuan Taiwan R.O.C., 2008). The Employment Insurance Act of 2009 allows employees who ask for parental leave and who have paid into Taiwan's basic labor insurance program for at least 1 year to be eligible for 60% of their salary for up to 6 months (Council of Labor Affairs, Executive Yuan Taiwan, R.O.C., 2009). While originally intended for mothers, the policy has been expanded to fathers as well. Since the introduction of the subsidy program, the minister of the Council of Labor Affairs has reported that 37,000 employees have received approval to take part in the plan, with men comprising 20% ("Parental Leave," 2010). Furthermore, according to the Council of Labor Affairs, those employers who fail to offer employees these privileges are subject to fines up to NT$60,000 ("Parental Leave," 2010). For example, a father who recently took paternity leave found himself demoted when he returned to work. One promising outcome of this incident is that the company was fined NT$50,000 by Taipei's Department of Labor for violating the Gender Equality in Employment Act (Lin, 2011). Implementation of parental leave varies among corporations. Some may grant fathers paid leave for 1 year while others explicitly state if they take leave, they may not be hired back or may not be hired back at the same level. Hence, one of the reluctances of taking parental leaves, as expressed by working parents, is the threat of losing one's job or being demoted in one's position. While these policy changes indicate a recognition of the need for supporting father and mother involvement, they have not been widely implemented.

Corporations

A number of corporations in Taiwan have instituted programs, activities, and practices that accommodate and promote father involvement. For example, in 2009, the Taiwan Semiconductor Manufacturing Company Limited opened a day-care center with 9 teachers and 7 classrooms to serve children ages 2-8 ("Good Welfare," 2009) with hours of the center accommodating the working schedule of the parents ("Lucky," 2009). In another example, employees at the Hermes-Epitek workplace have formed parent groups that meet at the worksite to share childrearing experiences and learn parenting skills. Hermes-Epitek provides subsidies for the parent group to purchase various types of educational materials on parenting and childrearing (Bin, 2009).

According to the Gender Equity Law, enterprises hiring more than 250 laborers should establish or provide childcare services in Taiwan. While one third of such enterprises are distributed in the Taipei area (758 enterprises), over 85% of them in August, 2011, have set up day care-related measures or provided day care services (Department of Labor, Taipei City Government, 2011). For example, Weichuan Corporation contracts with day care centers in the neighborhood to provide a discount on day care services of their employees' children. Fully equipped nursery rooms are offered in the office. The Department of Law, Taipei City Government, also organized "Guidance and Assistance Groups of Friendly Daycares in Workplaces" to encourage the other 15% of enterprises to attend to the policy as soon as possible in order to offer more friendly working environments and lessen working parents' burdens.

Schools

Gender Equity in School Curriculum. Instituted in 2004, the Gender Equity Education Act was established to "promote substantive gender equality, eliminate gender discrimination, uphold human dignity, and improve and establish educational resources and an environment of gender equality" (Ministry of Education, Taiwan, 2004). The act stipulated that all schools have a gender equity education committee whose tasks include "promoting curricula, teaching, and assessments on gender equity education." Examples of gender equity curricula are seen in the curricular domains of language arts, life education, social studies, and health and physical education in lessons for elementary grade levels.

Since September, 2011, the Department of Education, Taipei City Government expanded the implementation of after-school services in order to satisfy the needs of childcare in dual-income families. Requested by parents, schools, including 141 elementary schools and 133 public kindergartens in Taipei, will open "after-school care classes" to take care of students by school teachers or people in schools until seven o'clock at night for elementary school students and six o'clock at night for kindergarteners (Department of Education, Taipei City Government , 2011).

The Taipei City Government integrated day-care centers, nursery schools, and women center resources to establish 35 "friendly childcare gardens" in communities for parents to provide nearby childcare resources and temporary day-care services. Facilities, including parent-child game houses, toy libraries, and centers for parent-child story books, as well as activities including child development screening, parenting courses, and parent-child reading together, are free and open to the public, in order to promote parental involvement. While activities and services mentioned above are assumed to target both mothers and fathers, it is still unclear how they specifically enhance father's and men's involvement. What roles of fathers are explicitly addressed in these services as well as how fathers view these resources merit further investigation.

Initiatives to Promote Father Involvement. Traditionally in Taiwan, parent involvement in schools was viewed as interference with teachers' authority and expertise. Hence, parent participation in schools is a relatively new practice within Taiwanese culture. The Ministry of Education Taiwan R.O.C. enacted the "Regulations for Parental Involvement in Compulsory Education School Affairs" in 2006 that requires parent involvement programs in elementary and junior high schools. Such programs promote parent involvement in schools, for example, through workshops, parent associations, parent-teacher conferences, and parents as volunteers in schools; and also promote communication with teachers and administrators. The policy also encourages parents, particularly in the elementary grade levels, to supervise children's learning activities, which model learning activities for the home. As of 2009, the government had constructed 25 family education centers to promote "parent-child study-together-programs" or "parent-child outdoor activities" (Ministry of Education, 2009).

A number of community associations or clubs in Taiwan sponsor activities that may enhance father participation. Such activities include hiking, biking, bird watching, butterfly observations, and Taiwanese cultural activities (e.g., visiting temples, historical sites, community ecological resources).

A community-based program, "Parents-Children Read Together," helps to promote Taiwanese fathers and mothers reading with their children. These regularly held reading events are open to the public. For example, an elementary school in Taoyuan developed a reading project where families are provided a suggested booklist and encouraged to set aside a reading hour in their homes. A worksheet developed for each book is given to the parents and children to complete and prizes are awarded to families that complete 12 books (Taoyuan Hsingkuo Elementary School, 2009).

One study by Wu (2005) indicated that factors influencing father involvement in schools include fathers' willingness to participate, the type of activity, and the way that the schools implement the activities. One common practice in Taiwanese elementary schools is to invite fathers to the classroom to discuss their chosen profession. For example, the father who is a bicycle shop owner might illustrate how to ride a bicycle, how to use protective gear, and what kind of bicycle features to look for. Fathers are more likely to attend events relevant to academics (e.g., a lecture by experts/scholars on "How to improve the academic achievement of your child") compared to other topics. Because fathers are most interested in activities related to their children's academic success, it is most helpful if the activities they are asked to participate in are perceived as being beneficial to their children's learning (Wang, 2000). While subject matter is of primary importance, other factors such as place, duration of event, and day of the week are also crucial considerations to promote father involvement.

Although a number of policies in government, corporations and schools are in place to promote father involvement, cultural change throughout every faction of society is necessary to support fathers. Positive attitudes and supportive actions of employers, spouses, teachers, and school administrators are needed in order for fathers to participate in the education of their sons and daughters.

NOTES

1. Taiwan has grown from an agrarian to an information-technology-based economy and from an authoritarian to democratic political system.
2. The currency symbol for New Dollars in Taiwan is NT$ and the currency code is TWD.

REFERENCES

Bandura, A., & Walters, R. H. (1959). *A study of the influence of child rearing practices and family interrelationships.* New York, NY: Ronald Press.

Beckert, T. E., Strom, R. D., Strom, P. S., & Yang, C. (2006). The success of Taiwanese fathers in guiding adolescents. *Adolescence, 41*(163), 493-509.

Bentler, P. M. (1990). Comparative fit indexes in structural models. *Psychological Bulletin, 107*(2), 238-246.

Bentler, P. M., & Bonett, D. G. (1980). Significance tests and goodness of fit in the analysis of covariance structures. *Psychological Bulletin, 88*(3), 588-606.

Bin, C.-H. (2009). What could enterprise do to be more friendly to family? *Education, Parenting, Family Lifestyle, 7*, 156-158.

Bollen, K. A., & Long, J. S. (1993). *Testing structural equation models.* Newbury Park, CA: SAGE.

Chang, L., Schwartz, D., Dodge, K. A., & McBride-Chang, C. (2003). Harsh parenting in relation to child emotion regulation and aggression. *Journal of Family Psychology, 17*(4), 598-606.

Chen, F.-L., Yang, P., & Wang, L. L. (2010). The changing profile of the Taiwanese family and governmental response. *Journal of Asian Public Policy, 3*(2), 135-145.

Chen, W.-W., & Ho, H.-Z. (in press). The relation between perceived parental involvement and academic achievement: The roles of Taiwanese students' academic beliefs and filial piety. *International Journal of Psychology.*

Chen, X., Liu, M., & Li, D. (2000). Parental warmth, control, and indulgence and their relations to adjustment in Chinese children: A longitudinal study. *Journal of Family Psychology, 14*, 401-419.

Chern, J.-F. (2005). *A relevant study on fatherhood involvement in academic achievements and peer interactions for 5th grade students: An example of the primary school in Kaohsiung* (Unpublished master's thesis). National Kaohsiung Normal University, Kaohsiung, Taiwan. Retrieved May 10, 2010, from http://etds.ncl.edu.tw/theabs/site/sh/detail_result.jsp?id=093NKNU0332079

Chiang, M.-Y., Huang, E., & Lin, C.-Y. (2005). The gender differences of parents' involvement in elementary school: The example of Kaohsiung. *Research on Education and Society, 8*(1), 81-114.

Council of Labor Affairs, Executive Yuan Taiwan, R.O.C. (2009). *The employment insurance act.* Retrieved from http://www.cla.gov.tw/cgi-bin/SM_theme?page=49d330a7

Department of Education, Taipei City Government. (2011). After-school care services. Retrieved from http://www.edunet.taipei.gov.tw/ct.asp?xItem=1190451&ctNode=33656&mp=104001

Department of Health, Taipei City Government. (2011). Wish you good pregnancy. Retrieved from http://born.igd.tw/index.php

Department of Labor, Taipei City Government. (2011). Daycares in enterprises. Retrieved from http://www.bola.taipei.gov.tw/ct.asp?xItem=663953&ctNode=20634&mp=116001

Directorate General of Budget, Accounting and Statistics, Executive Yuan, Republic of China. (2011). Women and men in R.O.C. (Taiwan) Facts and Figures. Retrieved from http://eng.stat.gov.tw/public/data/dgbas03/bs2/gender/2011GenderImages%28Eng%29.pdf

Executive Yuan Taiwan R.O.C. (2008). Gender Equality in Employment Act (2002). Retrieved from http://laws.cla.gov.tw/Eng/FLAW/FLAWDAT01.asp?lsid=FL015149

Good welfare! The TSMC opens the third day care center, the acceptance rate accelerated to 60%. (2009, July 27) *Now News.* Retrieved from http://www.nownews.com/2009/07/27/91-2484093.htm

Lucky! The TSMC built a five-star day care center. Two hundred million dollars bonus provided in July. (2009, July 27) *EENEWS*. Retrieved from http://ee342342.pixnet.net/blog/post/26978781

Ho, H-Z., Chen, W-W., Tran, C. N., & Ko, C-T. (2010). Parental involvement in Taiwanese families: Father-mother differences. *Childhood Education, 86*(6), 312-317.

Ho, H-Z., Ko, C-T., Tran, C. N., Phillips, J. M., & Chen, W-W. (in press). Father involvement in Taiwan: A progressive perspective in the cultural media. In J. Pattnaik (Ed.), *Father/male involvement in young children's lives: An international analysis*. New York, NY: Springer.

Ho, H-Z., Tran, C. N., Ko, C-T., Phillips, J. M., Boutin-Martinez, A., Dixon, C. N., & Chen, W-W. (2011). Parent involvement: Voices of Taiwanese fathers. *International Journal about Parents in Education, 5*(2), 35-42.

Hong, S. & Ho, H-Z. (2005). Direct and indirect longitudinal effects of parental involvement on student achievement: Second-order latent growth modeling across ethnic groups. *Journal of Educational Psychology, 97*(1), 32-42.

Hsu, H-Y., Zhang, D., Kwok, O-M., Li, Y., & Ju, S. (2011). Distinguishing the influences of father's and mother's involvement on adolescent academic achievement: Analyses of Taiwan Education Panel Survey data. *Journal of Early Adolescence, 31*(5), 694-713.

Hu, L., & Bentler, P. M. (1999). Cutoff criteria for fit indexes in covariance structure analysis: Conventional criteria versus new alternatives. *Structural Equation Modeling, 6*(1),1-55.

Huang, Y-C., & Wang, K-T. (2007, October). *A linear structure analysis of male participation in parenting*. Paper presented at Seminar on Family and Work: A Transitional Phenomenon and Multiple Imagination, Kaohsiung, Taiwan.

Hung, C-L. (2005). Family background, parental involvement and environmental influences on Taiwanese children. *The Alberta Journal of Educational Research, 51*(3), 261-276.

Huston, A. C. (1983). Sex-typing. In E. M. Hetherington (Ed.), *Handbook of child psychology: Socialization, personality, and social development* (pp. 388-467). New York, NY: Wiley.

Jeynes, W. H. (2007). The relationship between parental involvement and urban secondary school student academic achievement: A meta-analysis. *Urban Education,42*(1), 82-110.

Kan, K., & Tsai, W-D. (2005). Parenting practices and children's education outcomes. *Economics of Education Review, 24*, 29-43.

Kaplan, D. (2000). *Structural equation modeling: Foundation and extensions*. Thousand Oaks, CA: SAGE.

Lin, L. (2011, October 1). Foundation fined NT$50,000 after man was demoted for taking paternity leave. *The China Post*. Retrieved from http://www.chinapost.com.tw/taiwan/national/national-news/2011/10/01/318430/Foundation-fined.htm

Liu, K. (2011, May 13). MOE minister lays out education reform policy. *Taiwan Today*. Retrieved from http://taiwantoday.tw/ct.asp?xItem=163871&CtNode=427

Liu, K-S., Cheng, Y-Y., Chen, Y-L., & Wu, Y-Y. (2009). Longitudinal effects of educational expectations and achievement attributions on adolescents' academic achievements. *Adolescence, 44*(176), 911-924.

Maccoby, E. E. (2000). *The two sexes: Growing up apart, coming together.* Cambridge, MA: Harvard University Press.

Marchant, G. J., Paulson, S. E., & Rothlisberg, B. A. (2001). Relations of middle school students' perceptions of family and school contexts with academic-achievement. *Psychology in the Schools, 38*(6), 505-519.

Ministry of Education, Taiwan R.O.C. (2004). *Gender equity education act.* Retrieved from http://www.gender.edu.tw/upload/LaswNRules/GENDER%20EQUITY %20EDUCATION%20ACT.DOC

Ministry of Education, Taiwan R.O.C. (2006). *Parent involvement regulation.* Retrieved from http://140.111.34.179/parent_1-1.php

Ministry of Education. (2009). *Minister of Education family education net.* Retrieved from http://moe.familyedu.moe.gov.tw/front/bin/ptdetail .phtml?Part=map_a

Mullis, R. L., Rathge, R., & Mullis, A. K. (2003). Predictors of academic performance during early adolescence: A contextual view. *International Journal of Behavioral Development, 26*, 541-548.

Parental leave program popular with dads as well. (2010, May 8) *Taipei Times.* Retrieved from http://www.taipeitimes.com/News/taiwan/archives/2010/05/08/ 2003472478

Power, T. G., & Shanks, J. A. (1989). Parents as socializers: Maternal and paternal views. *Journal of Youth and Adolescence, 18*, 203-220.

Taoyuan Hsingkuo Elementary School. (2009). Family reading plan in 2009. Retrieved from http://tw.class.urlifelinks.com/class/?csid=css000000087548 &id=model3&cl=1252459007-9860-187&mode=con&m3k=1252459062- 6164-7011&_ulinktreeid=

Tsai, W. S. (2010). Family man in advertising? A content analysis of male domesticity and fatherhood in Taiwanese commercials. *Asian Journal of Communication, 20*(40), 423-439.

Wang, C-K. (2000). An exploratory study on the formation of child-rearing fatherhood. *Research in Applied Psychology, 6*, 1-40.

Wu, T-C. (2005). *A study of parental education needs and attending willingness for fathers in Kaohsiung city public kindergartens* (Unpublished master's thesis). Kaohsiung Normal University, Kaohsiung City, Taiwan.

Yan, W., & Lin, Q. (2005). Parental involvement and mathematics achievement: Contrast across racial and ethnic groups. *The Journal of Education Research, 99*(2), 116-127.

CHAPTER 4

LATINO FATHERS AND THEIR INVOLVEMENT IN THEIR CHILDREN'S SCHOOLING

Robert P. Moreno and Susan S. Chuang

Although there is a significant amount of research that demonstrates that fathers play an important role in their children's lives (Lamb, 2004), there still is less attention on ethnic and racial minority fathers in North America (Chuang & Tamis-LeMonda, 2009; Downer, Campos, McWayne, & Gartner, 2008). This is particularly the case for Latino families (see Campos, 2008; Chuang & Moreno, 2008). This is unfortunate given that Latinos are the largest and fastest growing ethnic minority group in the in the United States. For example, between 2000 and 2009, the U.S. population increased by approximately 9% as compared to 37% for the Latino population.

At the same time, Latinos, which includes Latino fathers, have the lowest level of education of any racial and ethnic group (Saenz, 2010). Moreover, much of the existing research portrays Latino fathers as "absent," "abusive," and overly "macho" (see Mirandé, 2008). Fortunately, recent research has taken a more balanced view, which better understands Latino fathers as breadwinners, nurturers, and child caretakers (e.g., Mirandé;

Promising Practices for Fathers' Involvement in Children's Education
pp. 59–77

Tamis-LeMonda, Kahana Kalman, & Yoshikawa, 2009). With respect to education, fathers appear to influence their children's perceptions of their own academic confidence and place a greater importance on their children's academics, when compared to mothers (Palkovitz, 2002). However, fathering researchers have not taken advantage of the education literature on parental involvement, thus creating a disconnect between the two fields. To address the issue of Latino fathers' roles in their children's academic lives, this chapter will draw upon both literatures to gain a more comprehensive and accurate understanding of Latino families.

CONCEPTUALIZATIONS OF PARENTAL INVOLVEMENT IN SCHOOL

Although parent involvement has been conceptualized numerous ways (see Olivos, Ochoa, & Jiménez-Castellanos, 2011), many studies have reported significant associations between parental involvement activities (e.g., monitoring of homework, regularly reading with children, holding high expectations of student's academic success, supportive home environment, attending and participating in school functions) and measures of student academic achievement (Fan & Chen, 2001; Jeynes, 2005). One of the most prominent and influential models was developed by Epstein and her colleagues (Epstein & Simon, 2001). At the core of Epstein's model are six types of involvement—namely parenting, communicating, volunteering, learning at home, decision making, and collaborating with the community. This framework of involvement has been useful in understanding how parental involvement was associated with decreasing truancy issues, reducing behavioral and discipline problems, and increasing academic scores as well as family and community involvement (Epstein, 2005; Epstein & Jansorn, 2004; Epstein & Sheldon, 2002; Sheldon & Epstein, 2005).

However, the utility of this model may be limited, particularly as it pertains to ethnic/racial minority and immigrant populations (Moreno & Chuang, 2011). For example, Ingram, Wolfe, and Lieberman (2007) studied three public schools that reported high levels of poverty, high minority populations, as well as high scores on standardized achievement exams. The researchers focused on examining the specific ways the schools involved parents to construct a model that would increase parent involvement and overall school effectiveness. The findings indicated that only two of six types of involvement (parenting and learning at home) were relevant. The participants focused on specific parenting practices that promoted learning and acceptable behavior while at school, and parents were consistently involved in learning activities with their child. Ingram et al. suggest that improving academic achievement for high risk populations is a result of effective parenting strategies and learning-at-home activities. The remaining involvement types (communicating, volunteering, decision making, and collaborating with the community) play a relatively minor role in parents' involvement activity. For example, parents indicated that although they always felt encouraged to volunteer by teachers and administrators, they were rarely able to do so (e.g., unable to take time off work). In addition, they seldom communicated with their children's teachers, helped with classroom activities, and rarely collaborated in community activities (Ingram et al.). These findings are consistent with previous research that indicate Latino parents are primarily engaged in their children's education at home, out of the school's view (Moreno & Lopez, 1999). Thus, important components of the involvement process may be invisible to researchers and educators.

In general, Latinos have been cast in a negative light with respect to education. Specifically, Latinos have been viewed as not valuing education and, as a result, are not involved in their children's schooling (Moreno & Valencia, 2010; Valencia & Black, 2002). Countering this position is research that has indicated that Latina mothers participate in a wide range of parental involvement activities. Their activities range from "basic obligations" to "involvement in school governance." However, the extent of the involvement depends on the type of involvement. For example, Latina mothers tend to be more engaged in home-based activities, as opposed to involvement activities at the school site such as volunteering in classrooms or participating in school governance (Delgado Gaitan, 2004; Moreno, 2004)

In addition, factors such as parents' level of education and acculturation have been linked with Latino parental involvement. For example, researchers found that more educated mothers viewed their participation in their children's school as "part of their job" when compared to their less educated counterparts. However, the role of parental education can be complex when viewed in conjunction with other factors such as parents' acculturation level. For example, Moreno and Lopez (1999) found that Latina mothers who had at least a high school education, but were less acculturated (more oriented to Mexican culture), had the greatest levels of self-efficacy regarding their involvement in their children's schooling. Similarly, less acculturated mothers had higher expectations and higher expected attainment from their children than their more acculturated counterparts. Conversely, less acculturated mothers had less knowledge of school activities than their more acculturated counterparts. In contrast, others have found that more highly acculturated Mexican origin parents were more likely to promote child behaviors that were similar to their culture of origin such as hierarchical parent-child relations, respect, and politeness. These parents also were more likely to defer to teachers and maintain a distance from them (e.g., refrain from questioning teachers' authority). A mismatch between parents' and teachers' perceptions on children's education may contribute to a decrease of parents integrating into the educational experiences of their children (Bradley & McKelvey, 2007). However, others found that more acculturated parents integrated more child-centered attitudes which may be more line with the western culture. More acculturated parents may be more likely to speak English at home and be more responsive and accepting of teachers' expectations for parental involvement in their children's schooling (Fuligni & Fuligni, 2007).

Relatedly, specific barriers have been associated with limited involvement. A lack of accessible information, for example, can inhibit parents' ability to participate in school activities. A lack of information and unfamiliarity with the school system (in the case of immigrants) can contribute to Latino parents' uncertainty as to how, and the degree to which, they should participate (Chrispeels & Rivero, 2001). Thus, the lack of accessible information has been linked to parents' low education level and income, as these parents may have fewer resources to support their children's academic performance (Fuligni & Yoshikawa, 2003).

One reason for the limited utility of Epstein's model with respect to ethnic/racial minorities and immigrants may be its scope. Although the model is comprehensive in addressing the multiple aspects of parents' involvement with schools, it does not tap into broader parenting and family dynamics. These broader processes and practices, despite their more peripheral nature, may influence parents' school involvement. In the case of fathers for example, their participation in their children's schooling may be influenced by their broader conceptions of their role and responsibility as a parent. In addition, researchers have pointed to the importance of the father's relationship with their child's mother as an important consideration to understanding overall paternal involvement (Fagan & Barnett, 2003). Drawing upon the broader research on fathering, we hope to elaborate on Epstein's model allowing us a clearer understanding of the factors associated with Latino fathers' involvement in their children's schooling.

FATHERING AND LATINO FATHER INVOLVEMENT

Over the past 3 decades, there has been tremendous attention to the roles and influence of fathers in families. Although much of the research has focused on non-Hispanic Whites, more researchers have explicitly explored fathering among ethnic and racial families (Chuang & Moreno, 2008). The research on fathering indicates that a number of factors are associated with increased paternal involvement in childrearing (Lamb,

2004). For example, fathers' levels of involvement in childcare activities are influenced by how fathers define their parenting role. As Chuang and Su (2008) reported, native and immigrant Chinese fathers of toddlers viewed their fathering roles as multidimensional, including economic provider, caregiver, responsible for household chores, and playmate to their children. Thus, fathers spent significant amounts of time playing with and caring for their children and engaged in various household chores (see Chuang, Moreno, & Su, in press). Moreover, paternal involvement is also associated with fathers' beliefs about gender roles. Fathers who hold more "traditional" views on family gender roles are less inclined to participate in child rearing. The father's relationship with their child's mother is also an important factor. Fathers who have a more positive relationship with their children's mothers are more likely to be involved (Palkovitz, 2002).

Although researchers have consistently stressed the importance of fathers, there is limited research that has examined the specific ways that fathers are involved in their children's academic lives. Of the existing research, the findings suggest that fathers interact with their children in ways that are distinct from mothers. Fathers afford their children with unique experiences that can facilitate their academic success. Specifically, fathers may engage with their children in ways that challenge their linguistic and self-regulatory capacity, which in turn, may better prepare their children for school (Lamb & Tamis-LeMonda, 2004). In addition, other researchers have found that fathers' monitoring (knowledge of their sons' whereabouts) was associated with their peer relationships and fathers' warmth was particularly relevant for their sons' classroom behavior (Dumka, Gonzales, Bonds & Millsap, 2009).

Despite increased concern with fatherhood and the importance of father involvement in the family, we know surprisingly little about Latino fathers, particularly immigrant fathers (Campos, 2008). This is particularly unfortunate given the demographic trends showing that Latinos are among the fastest growing and largest racial/ethnic group in the United States. For example, according to the U.S. Census, Latinos comprised approximately 14% of the U.S. population (U.S. Census Bureau, 2006).

In addition, early characterizations of Latino families have been rooted in a superficial and stereotypic understanding of Latino family functioning. For example, early descriptions of Latino families describe the family as male dominated where the father is "lord and master," yet absent or minimally involved in the family and peripheral with respect to childrearing (Mirandé, 2008; Taylor & Behnke, 2005). This negative characterization of Latino families and fathers is, in part, rooted in a misunderstanding of machismo. Although machismo is an important construct within the Latino culture, the term has been synonymous with hypermasculinity. However, this view neglects more positive components of machismo such as the fulfillment of familial obligations and responsibilities such as a protector and provider (Mirandé). More recent qualitative and quantitative research has questioned the early characterizations of Latino families and fathers. For example, Latino fathers have been shown to be quite warm, nurturing, and actively involved in childrearing (Mirandé). Researchers have found that Latino fathers exhibited less control and more responsibility for childrearing when compared to non-Hispanic white fathers (Coltrane, Parke, & Adams, 2004; Hofferth, 2003). Others studies have shown that Latino fathers are as, or more, involved in direct interactions and monitoring of their children when compared to White and African American fathers (Adams, Coltrane, & Parke, 2007; Toth & Xu, 1999; Yeung, Sandberg, Davis-Kean, & Hofferth, 2001). With respect to education and schooling, studies found that Latino fathers play an active role. For example, Latino fathers placed a high value on their role as a teacher and role model for their children (Fitzpatrick, Caldera, Pursley, & Wampler, 1999; Lamb, 2004).

DESIGN OF THE STUDY

The following study is an attempt to build upon both the general research on paternal involvement and the educational parental involvement research. The findings from this study should provide a more comprehensive understanding of the factors that are associated with Latino fathers' involvement in their children's schooling. The study addresses two basic questions: (1) What are fathers' beliefs and levels of engagement regarding their children's school involvement?; and (2) What factors are associated with their school involvement practices?

Participants

The sample consisted of 40 Latino fathers of elementary school children from a midsized city in the Northeast. The children (55.0% male, 45.0% female) ranged in grade level from kindergarten to third grade (kindergarten 28.6%, first 34.3%, second 28.6%, and third 8.5%). The average age of fathers was 34.6 years ($SD = 5.97$). Fifty-one percent of the fathers possessed less than high school education, with 35.1% indicating high school education, with the remaining 13.9% possessing baccalaureate degree or greater. Participants also varied in ethnic background (10.0% Cuban, Dominican 2.5%, Mexican origin 17.5%, Puerto Rican 60.0%, Central American 5.0%, South American 5.0%). All fathers were lived within the household with 51.4% married, and the remaining indicating "never married." In general, the sampled paralleled the diversity of the surrounding Latino community.

Procedures

Participants were recruited from an elementary school with a large and diverse Latino student enrolment. Latino fathers were specifically targeted through flyers distributed by school personnel. Upon consent, fathers were administered a questionnaire in both Spanish and English. To ensure equivalence, the questionnaire were translated into Spanish and then back-translated into English by three bilingual Spanish-speaking individuals.

Measures

Sociodemographic Factors. Fathers provided information on their age, marital status, acculturation status, occupational level, length of time in the U.S., number of children and adults in the home, and their educational level.

Parent Involvement Survey. The survey was composed of two subscales, parent involvement beliefs and parent involvement behaviors—based on Epstein's typology: parenting, communication, volunteering, learning at home, decision making, and community. The parent involvement beliefs scale consisted of 20 items, measuring various parental beliefs regarding their involvement in school (e.g., "My job as a father is to teach my child to behave in school."). The parental involvement behavior scale consisted of 25 items which measured various parental behaviors and activities (e.g., "I take my child to the library"). For both scales, the items were on a 4-point Likert scale (1 = *strongly disagree*, 4 = *strongly agree*; Cronbach's α = .94).

Barriers to School Involvement. This measure consisted of 11 items that were designed to assess fathers' perceived barriers to school involvement (Moreno & Lopez, 1999). The items addressed issues of safety, limited communication, unresponsive setting, and limited resources (e.g., "I don't understand materials that are sent home;" "I don't have transportation"). Using a 4-point Likert scale, respondents indicated their level of agreement (1 = *strongly disagree*, 4 = *strongly agree*; Cronbach's α = .86).

Parental Involvement Knowledge. Involvement knowledge consisted of three items designed to assess parents' knowledge of school-related information ("I know what grades my child gets;" "I know useful ways of helping my child learn;" "I know how much homework my child gets."). Using a 4-point Likert scale, respondents indicated their level of agreement (1 = *always*, 4 = *never*; Cronbach's α = .68).

Perceived Self-Efficacy. Perceived efficacy consisted of six items designed to assess fathers' perceived efficacy regarding their school involvement (e.g., "I have the skills I need to help my child learn;" "Getting involved is difficult for me"). Using a 4-point Likert scale, respondents indicated their level of agreement (1= *strongly disagree*, 4 = *strongly agree*; Cronbach's α = .72).

Father's Relationship With Mother. The Network of Relationships Inventory (NRI) was used to assess the father's relationship (quality and power) with their child's mother (30 items; Furman & Buhrmester, 1985). The relationship inventory was divided into 11 subareas. These included companionship, conflict, instrumental aid, antagonism, intimacy, nurturance, affection, admiration, relative power, reliable alliance, and satisfaction (subscale reliabilities ranged from Cronbach's αs = .52 to .85, with an overall Cronbach's α = .94). Example items included: "How good is your relationship with your child's mother?"; "Between the two of you, who tends to be the BOSS in this relationship?"; "How much free time do you spend with your child's mother?"; "How sure are you that your relationship will continue in the years to come?" Using a 5-point Likert scale, respondents indicated their level of agreement (1 = *never*, 5 = *always*).

Father's Role. The Role of the Father Questionnaire (Palkovitz, 1984) is a 15-item survey designed to assess each participant's role as a father (e.g., "It is essential for the child's well-being that fathers spend time interacting and playing with their children"; "Fathers play a central role in the child's personality development"). Using a 5-point Likert scale, respondents were asked to mark the choice that best represents their attitudes regarding their child's care (1 = *strongly agree*, 4 = *strongly disagree*; Cronbach's α = .94).

Parental Monitoring. To index the fathers' general level of responsibility for his child, we utilized a 3-item scale from the Parental Monitoring Assessment (Small & Kerns, 1993). Items were modified to be more consistent with the age of the children (e.g., "I know where my child is after school"; "I know the children my child spends time with."). Using a 5-point Likert scale, respondents indicated their level of agreement (1 = *never*, 5 = *always*; Cronbach's α = .81).

Financial Strain Index. To index the financial situation of the participants' households, we utilized 4 items from Conger, Conger, Elder, and Lorenz's (1992) process model of economic hardship. Example items include: "How often does your household put off buying something you need because you don't have money?"; "How often can your household afford to do things just for fun like going to the movies or eating out?"

Using a 5-point Likert scale, participants indicated their ability to purchase household necessities (1 = *never*; 4 = *all of the time*; Cronbach's α = .73).

Gender Ideology. To examine the father's gender-based attitudes toward child rearing and marital roles, we utilized Hoffman and Kloska's (1995) Gender-Based Attitudes Toward Child Rearing (GBACR) and Gender-Based Attitudes Toward Marital Roles (GATMR) scales (Cronbach's αs = .75, .91 respectively). Example items of GATCR include: "I see nothing wrong with giving a little boy a doll to play with;". Example items on GATMR include: Men should make the really important decisions in the family. Using a 4-point Likert scale, participants indicate their level of agreement (1 = *strongly agree*; 4 = *strongly disagree*).

Acculturation. The Acculturation Rating Scale for Mexican Americans-II (Cuellar, Arnold, & Maldonado, 1995) is designed to assess the participants' level of acculturation in two areas: language and social network (Cronbach's αs = .92, .62, respectively). Language example items included: "In general, what language(s) do you read and speak?"; "What language(s) do you usually speak with your friends?" Using a 5-point Likert scale, participants indicated their level of agreement (1 = *only Spanish*, 5 = *only English*). Social network examples included: "Who are your close friends?"; "What people do you visit or what people visit you?" Using a 5-point Likert scale, participants indicated their level of agreement (1 = *all Latinos/Hispanics*, 5 = *all Americans*).

RESULTS

First, to examine the relation between fathers' involvement beliefs and behavior, a series of t tests and correlations were conducted. The analyses indicated that fathers' involvement behaviors were significantly lower than their beliefs for volunteering, communication, and decision making. However, fathers' behaviors and beliefs were significantly correlated across all categories ($ps < .05$; see Table 4.1).

Intercorrelations among the involvement behavior categories (parenting, communication, etc.) ranged from $rs = .31$ to $.77$ ($ps < .05$). Given the intercollinearity between fathers' beliefs and behavior and that our primary focus was with involvement activities, the remaining analyses utilized father involvement behavior as the dependent variable. The parental involvement behavior items were averaged to create a total involvement behavior score.

In an effort the minimize collinearity and reduce the number of independent variables, principal components analyses were conducted for barriers to school involvement and fathers' relationship with mother.

**Table 4.1.   Means and Correlations for Latino Fathers'
Beliefs and Behaviors Regarding School Involvement Types (N = 40)**

	Beliefs		Behaviors			
	M	SD	M	SD	T	r
Parenting	3.48	0.43	3.47	0.39	0.13	0.52**
Learning at home	3.26	0.48	3.37	0.55	−1.77†	0.73**
Volunteering	2.96	0.59	2.33	0.76	5.95**	0.54**
Communication	3.48	0.43	2.70	0.68	9.40**	0.64**
Decision making	2.79	0.61	1.76	0.82	7.78**	0.35**
Community	2.21	0.43	2.10	0.70	0.22	0.31*

Note: $^†p < .10$. *$p < .05$. **$p < .01$.

First, a principal components analysis with a varimax rotation was performed for the 11-item barriers to school involvement measure. The
results yielded a three-factor solution, which explained 75% of the variance: (1) poor school climate, 45% of the variance, (2) poor communication, 17% of the variance, and (3) school unresponsiveness, 12% of the
variance (see Table 4.2).

The principal components analysis was repeated for the 30-item of the
fathers' relationship with the mother measure. The results yielded a
seven-factor solution that explained 88% of the variance. The first factor
(companionship/intimacy) explained 42% of the variance, the second factor (reliability/satisfaction) 13% of the variance, the third factor (antago-
nism/conflict) 8% of the variance, the fourth factor (affect/approval) 7% of
the variance, the fifth factor (power) 6% of the variance, the sixth factor
(intimacy) 5% of the variance, and the seventh factor (instrumental aid)
4% of the variance.

Next, a series of correlational analyses were conducted to examine the
factors associated with Latino fathers' school involvement practices. First,
correlational analyses were conducted between the demographic variables
and fathers' involvement behavior. The analyses indicated no significant
association between fathers' level of school involvement and their income,
education, age, acculturation level, or child's grade level. However, significant correlations were found between fathers' involvement behavior and
their level of self-efficacy ($r = .45$) and school knowledge ($r = .52$). Significant associations were also found between fathers' level of school involvement and general parent measures such as fathers' paternal role ($r = .31$)
and their level of monitoring ($r = .35$). Thus, fathers who had greater levels of self-efficacy and knowledge, as well as a more positive view
regarding their role as a father, reported greater involvement activity.

Table 4.2. Results for the Hierarchical Regression Analyses of Fathers' School Involvement

Dependent Variable	Model	Independent Variable	R^2	Adjusted R^2	ΔR^2	β	F	F Change	df
School involvement	1	Efficacy	0.38	0.38	.38**	.37*	11.18**	11.18**	37
		School knowledge				.36*			
	2	Efficacy	0.43	0.39	.06†	.35*	9.18**	3.60†	36
		School knowledge				.16			
		Poor school communication				-.31†			
	3	Efficacy	53	0.46	.10*	.34*	7.63**	3.45*	34
		School knowledge				.08			
		Poor school communication				-.40*			
		Parental monitoring				.36*			
		Role of the father				.19			
	4	Efficacy	0.62	0.54	.10*	.30*	7.63**	4.11*	32
		School knowledge				.03			
		Poor school communication				-.39*			
		Parental monitoring				.36**			
		Role of the father				.28†			
		Relationship satisfaction/reliability				.23†			
		Relationship communication				.26*			

With respect to barriers to school involvement, only poor communication was significantly associated with fathers' involvement ($r = -.54$). Significant associations were also revealed between the fathers' relationship with their child's mother (reliability/ satisfaction and communication) and his involvement behavior ($rs = .37, .37$, respectively). Thus, fathers who reported that schools poorly communicated to them were less likely to be involved. However, fathers who reported greater satisfaction and reliability in their relationship with their child's mother, as well as better communication, were more likely to be involved in their child's schooling.

Based on the correlational analyses, a hierarchical multiple regression analysis was conducted to predict fathers' overall school involvement activity. The variables were entered in four blocks. Block one consisted of individual factors related to school involvement (efficacy, knowledge). Block two consisted of parent-school factors (poor school communication). Block three consisted of general parenting factors (parental monitoring, role of the father). Block four consisted of father/mother relationship factors (satisfaction/ reliability, communication). As shown in Table 5, the full model was significant, $F(7, 32) = 7.63, p < .000, R^2 = .62$, with individual factors, parenting factors, and father/mother relationship factors each contributing a significant portion of the variance to the full model. Poor school communication ($\beta = -.39$) was the most influential predictor, followed by parental monitoring ($\beta = .36$.), efficacy ($\beta = .30$), and father/mother communication ($\beta = .26$).

INTERPRETATION OF RESULTS

Our study extends our understanding of Latino fathers' levels of involvement in their children's academic lives. As expected, Latino fathers in this study strongly believed that they were responsible for their children's schooling. Moreover, their beliefs were generally consistent with their reported behaviors. There are, however, important distinctions in the degree to which their beliefs of how they should be involved in various aspects of school with their reported behavior. More specifically, the fathers' beliefs regarding their involvement were highest for more home-based activities such as parenting and learning at home. Fathers believed that they should take an active role in meeting their children's needs and provide an overall positive home environment. Similarly, fathers believed that it was important to communicate with their child's teacher (e.g., be aware of their child's progress and school activities) and provide a learning environment at home (monitor homework, read to their child). Latino fathers, however, were less inclined to believe it was their responsibility to engage in more school-based activities (volunteering, decision making). This pattern parallels the fathers' report of their involvement activities. Fathers reported their highest level of involvement in the area of general parenting and maintaining a learning environment in the home. They were least involved in decision-making activities such as participating in parent-teacher organizations. This home-school involvement distinction is not unique to Latino fathers; similar results were reported for Latina mothers in California and Chinese immigrant parents in Washington, DC whose school site involvement was significantly less than their home-based activities (Ji & Koblinsky, 2009).

Next, the findings revealed an interesting relation between fathers' involvement beliefs and behaviors. Although fathers' beliefs and corresponding behaviors were significantly associated across all involvement types (fathers who had higher beliefs in a particular category were more likely to engage in activities of the same category), overall levels of beliefs and behaviors varied as a function of involvement type. For example, the analyses revealed no significant differences between fathers' beliefs or behaviors in parenting, learning at home, and community involvement, suggesting that fathers acted in accordance with their beliefs. Thus, fathers' limited engagement in community activities or organization in relation to school programs was predicated on their belief that these were not part of their role. In contrast, our findings indicated that fathers engaged in involvement activities to a lesser extent than their beliefs would suggest. This is the case in the areas of home-school communication, assisting classrooms or volunteering for school activities, and participation in school decision making. Thus, although fathers recognize that it is part of their responsibility to engage in these involvement areas, their actual participation does not quite coincide with their beliefs. This is best seen in the area of home-school communication. This may be due, in part, to the ease or difficulty fathers have in communicating with teachers or understanding school materials.

Turning our attention to the factors that predict Latino fathers' involvement, our findings showed that a number of factors are associated with overall involvement activity. As expected, the attitudes and beliefs that were more directly related to school were associated with involvement. Latino fathers who were more efficacious and knowledgeable about school activities were more likely to be involved. Similarly, fathers who had limited resources (transportation and child care) and reported poor home-school communication (did not receive or understand school materials) tended to be less involved in their children's schooling. However, broader parenting beliefs and behaviors were also indicators of school involvement. Fathers who viewed their parenting role as more central to their child's development and monitored their child closely were more likely to be involved in their child's activities. Finally, the findings indicated that the quality of the fathers' relationship with the mothers was also important, specifically, the reliability and intimacy of the relationship.

The subsequent regression analysis was consistent with the initial findings. Factors at various levels remained significant predictors of involvement. For example, not only were more proximal factors to involvement activity important predictors (fathers' self-efficacy regarding involvement, poor school communication), but broader and more distal factors were also significant. For example, general parental activities such as monitoring remained an important predictor, as did the fathers' communication with the child's mother.

Collectively, the findings suggest that Latino paternal involvement in schooling should be viewed from a more nuanced and contextual perspective. It is not the case that Latino fathers simply "don't care" or "don't see it as their responsibility" to be involved in their child's schooling. On the contrary, the findings clearly indicate that Latino fathers believe that it is their responsibility to be involved, however they make distinctions between the types of involvement. These results are consistent with the previous research that also has found that Latina mothers tend to be less engaged in involvement activities at the school (Delgado Gaitan, 2004; Klimes-Dougan, Lopez, Adelman, & Nelson, 1992). Thus, when educators evaluate the level of paternal involvement, it is important to differentiate among the various types of parent involvement. Fathers may be involved in those activities that are least visible to teachers and school administrators, yet these are the most important with respect to student achievement (Jeynes, 2003).

Limitations and Recommendations

Caution must be exercised when interpreting these findings. Although the discussion suggests that greater paternal efficacy, monitoring, and better relationships with the mother lead to greater involvement in school, These findings are based upon correlational analyses. In addition, the relatively small number of participants and composition of Latino fathers limits the statistical power and generalizability of the study (Kraemer & Thiemann, 1987). Despite the limitations, the present study provides some insight and direction for future research on Latino fathers' involvement with their children's schooling.

Given our findings, we suggest that traditional indicators of involvement are necessary but may not be sufficient. Although individual and school level measures are an important consideration in understanding paternal involvement, broader familial factors, such as father-mother communication, may play an important role in facilitating or constraining involvement activities. Thus, maintaining various lines of communication is crucial at multiple levels. Not only is it important for schools to have clear and open communication with fathers (and vice versa), fathers must have clear and open communication with the child's mother. Thus, supportive familial and educational environments, where accessible information is exchanged and roles are negotiated, may be crucial for increased paternal involvement in schooling.

Elsewhere we have argued that it is important to acknowledge that schools are far from neutral institutions and, in many instances, may not be culturally responsive to Latino families. By their selective use of particular languages, curriculum, organization structures, and assumptions about home environments, schools "invite" certain segments of the community and discourage others (Moreno, Lewis-Menchaca, & Rodríguez, 2011). If we are to successfully utilize parent involvement as a vehicle to increase academic achievement across a diversity of families, parent involvement must be re conceptualized to include culturally appropriate practices among diverse families. We suggest parental involvement (which tends to assume a unidirectional relationship) be transformed to a family-school engagement model which is built upon mutual dynamic and bidirectional partnership (Delgado Gaitan, 2004; Moreno et al., 2011). Thus, understanding families in a broader context can complement existing parent involvement models, thereby providing us with a better foundation to incorporate fathers, mothers, and even extended family members in the process of schooling and education.

REFERENCES

Adams, M., Coltrane, S., & Parke, R. D. (2007). Cross-ethnic Applicability of the Gender-based Attitudes Toward Marriage and Child Rearing Scales. *Sex Roles*, 56(5-6), 325-339.

Bradley, R. H., & McKelvey, L. (2007). Managing the differences within: Immigration and early education in the United States. In J. E. Lansford, K. Deater-Deckard, & M. H. Bornstein (Eds.), *Immigrant families in contemporary society* (pp. 157-176). New York, NY: The Guilford Press.

Campos, R. (2008). Considerations for studying father involvement in early childhood among Latino families. *Hispanic Journal of Behavioral Sciences, 302* 133-160. doi:10.1177/0739986308316658

Chrispeels, J. H., & Rivero, E. (2001). Engaging Latino families for student success: How parent education can reshape parents' sense of place in the education of their children. *Peabody Journal of Education, 76*(2), 119-169.

Chuang, S. S., & Moreno, R. P. (Eds.). (2008). *On new shores: Understanding immigrant fathers in North America*. Lanham, MD: Lexington Books.

Chuang, S. S., Moreno, R. P., & Su, Y. (in press). Moving fathers from the "sidelines": An exploration of contemporary Chinese fathers in Canada and China. In K. B. Chan & N. C. Hung (Eds.), *Advances in research in Chinese families: A global perspective*. New York, NH: Springer.

Chuang, S. S., & Su, Y. (2008). Transcending Confucian teachings on fathering: A sign of the times or acculturation? In S. S. Chuang & R. P. Moreno (Eds.), *On new shores: Understanding immigrant fathers in North America* (pp. 129-150). Lanham, MD: Lexington Books.

Chuang, S. S., & Tamis-LeMonda, C. S. (Eds.) (2009). From shore to shore: Understanding fathers, mothers, and children in North America. *Sex Roles, 60* (7/8). doi:10.1007/s11199-009-9601-0

Coltrane, S., Parke, R. D., & Adams, M. (2004). Complexity of father involvement in low-income Mexican American families. *Family Relations, 53,* 179-189.

Conger, R. D., Conger, K. J., Elder, G. H., & Lorenz, F. O. (1992). A family process model of economic hardship and adjustment of early adolescent boys. *Child Development, 63*(3), 526-541. doi:10.2307/1131344

Cuellar, I., Arnold, B., & Maldonado, R. (1995). Acculturation rating scale for Mexican Americans-II: A revision of the original ARSMA scale. *Hispanic Journal of Behavioral Sciences, 17*(3), 275-304. doi:10.1177/07399863950173001

Delgado Gaitan, C. (2004). *Involving Latino families in schools: Raising student achievement through home-school partnerships*. Thousand Oaks, CA: Corwin.

Downer, J., Campos, R., McWayne, C., & Gartner, T. (2008). Father involvement and children's early learning: A critical review of published empirical work from the past 15 years. *Marriage & Family Review, 43*(1-2), 67-108. doi:10.1080/01494920802010264

Dumka, L. E., Gonzales, N. A., Bonds, D. D., & Millsap, R. E. (2009). Academic success of Mexican origin adolescent boys and girls: The role of mothers' and fathers' parenting and cultural orientation. *Sex Roles, 60,* 588-599. doi:10.1007/s11199-008-9518-z

Epstein, J. L. (2005). A case study of the partnership schools Comprehensive School Reform (CSR) Model. *The Elementary School Journal, 106*(2), 151-170. doi:10.1086/499196

Epstein, J. L., & Jansorn, N. R. (2004). School, family and community partnerships link the plan. *Education Digest, 69,* 19-23.

Epstein, J. L., & Sheldon, S. B. (2002). Present and accounted for: Improving student attendance through family and community involvement. *Journal of Educational Research, 95*(5). 308-318. doi:10.1080/00220670209596604

Fan, X., & Chen, M. (2001). Parental involvement and students' academic achievement: A meta-analysis. *Educational Psychology Review, 13,* 1-22.

Fagan, J., & Barnett, M. (2003). The relationship between maternal gatekeeping, paternal competence, mothers' attitudes about the father role, and father involvement. *Journal of Family Issues, 24*(8), 1020-1043. doi:10.1177/0192513X03256397

Fitzpatrick, J., Caldera, Y. M., Pursley, M., & Wampler, K. (1999). Hispanic mother and father perceptions of fathering: A qualitative analysis. *Family and Consumer Sciences Research Journal, 28*(2), 133-166. doi:10.1177/1077727X99282002

Fuligni, A. J., & Fuligni, A. S. (2007). Immigrant families and the educational development of their children. In J. E. Lansford, K. Deater-Deckard, & M. H. Bornstein (Eds.), *Immigrant families in contemporary society* (pp. 231-249). New York, NY: Guilford.

Fuligni, A. J., & Yoshikawa, H. (2003). Socioeconomic re-sources, parenting, and child development among im-migrant families. In M. Bornstein & R. Bradley (Eds.), *SES, parenting, and child development* (pp. 107-124). Mahwah, NJ: Erl-baum.

Furman, W., & Buhrmester, D. (1985). Children's perceptions of the qualities of sibling relationships. *Child Development, 56*(2), 448-461. doi:10.2307/1129733

Hofferth, S. (2003). Race/ethnic differences in father involvement in two-parent families: Culture, context, or economy. *Journal of Family Issues, 24*(2), 185-216.

Hoffman, L. W., & Kloska, D. D. (1995). Parents' gender-based attitudes toward marital roles and child rearing: Development and validation of new measures. *Sex Roles, 32*(5-6), 273-295. doi:10.1007/BF01544598

Ingram, M., Wolfe, R. B., & Lieberman, J. M. (2007). The role of parents in high-achieving schools serving low-income, at-risk populations. *Education and Urban Society, 39*, 479-497.

Jeynes, W. (2003). A meta-analysis: The effects of parental involvement on minority children's academic achievement. *Education and Urban Society, 35*, 202-218.

Jeynes, W. H. (2005) A meta-analysis of the relation of parent involvement to urban elementary school student academic achievement. *Urban Education, 40*, 237-269.

Ji, C. S., & Koblinsky, S. A. (2009). Parent involvement in children's education: An exploratory study of urban, Chinese immigrant families. *Urban Education, 44*, 687-709.

Klimes-Dougan, B., J. A. Lopez, H. S. Adelman, & Nelson, P. (1992). Two studies of low income parents' involvement in schooling. *The Urban Review, 24*(3), 185-202.

Kraemer, H. C., & Thiemann, S. (1987). *How many subjects: Statistical power analysis in research.* Newbury Park, CA: SAGE.

Lamb, M. E. (Ed.). (2004). *The role of the father in child development* (4th ed.). Hoboken, NJ: Wiley.

Lamb, M. E., & Tamis-LeMonda, C. S. (2004). The role of the father: An introduction. In M. E. Lamb (Ed.), *The role of the father in child development* (4th ed., (pp. 1-31). New York, NY: Wiley.

Mirandé, A. (2008). Immigration and Latino fatherhood: A preliminary look at Latino immigrant and non-immigrant fathers. In S. S. Chuang & R. P. Moreno (Eds.), *On new shores: Understanding immigrant fathers in North America* (pp. 217-230). Lanham, MD: Lexington Books.

Moreno, R. P. (2004). Exploring parental involvement among Mexican American and Latina mothers. In R. M. De Anda (Ed.), *Chicanas and Chicanos in contemporary society* (2nd ed., pp. 81-97). Lanham, MD: Rowman & Littlefield.

Moreno, R. P., & Chuang, S. S. (2011). Challenges facing immigrant parents and their involvement in their children's schooling. In S. S. Chuang & R. P. Moreno (Eds.), *Immigrant children: Change, adaptation, and cultural transformation* (pp. 239-254). Lexington, MA: Lexington Books.

Moreno, R. P., Lewis-Menchaca, K., & Rodríguez, J. (2011). Parental involvement: A critical view through a multicultural lens. In E. M. Olivos, A. M. Ochoa, & O. Jiménez-Castellanos (Eds.), *Critical voices in bicultural parent engagement: Operationalizing advocacy and empowerment* (pp. 21-38). Albany, NY: SUNY Press.

Moreno, R. P., & Lopez, J. A. (1999). Latina parent involvement: The role of maternal acculturation and education. *The School Community Journal, 9*(1), 83-101.

Moreno, R. P., & Valencia, R. R. (2011). Chicano families and schools: Challenges for strengthening family-school relations. In R. R. Valencia (Ed.), *Chicano school failure and success: Past, present, and future* (3rd ed., pp. 197-210). New York, NY: Routledge Press.

Olivos, E. M., Ochoa, A. M., & Jiménez-Castellanos, O. (Eds.). (2001). *Critical voices in bicultural parent engagement: Operationalizing advocacy and empowerment.* Albany, NY: SUNY Press.

Palkovitz, R. (1984). Parental attitudes and fathers' interactions with their 5-month-old infants. *Developmental Psychology, 20*(6), 1054-1060. doi:10.1037/0012-1649.20.6.1054

Palkovitz, R. (2002). Involved fathering and child development: advancing our understanding of good father. In C. S. Tamis-LeMonda & N. Cabrera (Eds.), *Handbook of father involvement: multidisciplinary perspectives* (pp.119-140). Mahwah, NJ: Erlbaum.

Saenz, R. (2010). Latinos in the United States 2010. Population bulletin update. Washington, DC: Population Reference Bureau.

Sheldon, S. B., & Epstein, J. L. (2002). Improving student behavior and school discipline with family and community involvement. *Education and Urban Society, 35,* 4-26.

Sheldon, S. B., & Epstein, J. L. (2005). Involvement counts: Family and community partnerships and mathematics achievement. *Journal of Educational Research, 98*(4), 196-206. doi:10.3200/JOER.98.4.196-207

Simon, B. S., & Epstein, J. L. (2001). School, family, and community partnerships: Linking theory to practice. In D. Hiatt-Michaels (Ed.), *Promising practices for family involvement in schools* (pp. 1-24). Greenwich, CT: Information Age.

Small, S. A., & Kerns, D. (1993). Unwanted sexual activity among peers during early and middle adolescence: Incidence and risk factors. *Journal of Marriage & the Family, 55*(4), 941-952. doi:10.2307/352774

Tamis-LeMonda, C. S., Kahana-Kalman, R., & Yoshikawa, H. (2009). Father involvement in immigrant and ethnically diverse families from the prenatal period to the second year: Prediction and mediating mechanisms. *Sex Roles, 60*(7-8), 496-509. doi:10.1007/s11199-009-9593-9

Taylor, B., & Behnke, A. O. (2005). Fathering across the border: Latino fathers in Mexico and the United States. *Fathering: A Journal of Theory, Research, and Practice about Men as Fathers, 3*(2), 99-120.

Toth, J. F., Jr., & Xu, X. (1999). Ethnic and cultural diversity in fathers' involvement. A racial/ethnic comparison of African American, Hispanic, and White fathers. *Youth & Society, 31,* 76-99.

U.S. Census Bureau. (2006, August 15). *Census Bureau data shows key population changes across nation* [Press release]. Washington, DC: Author.

Valencia, R. R., & Black, M. S. (2002). Mexican Americans don't value education!: On the basis of the myth, mythmaking, and debunking. *Journal of Latinos and Education, 1*(2), 81-103. doi:10.1207/S1532771XJLE0102_2

Yeung, W. J., Sandberg, J. F., Davis-Kean, P. E., & Hofferth, S. L. (2001). Children's time with fathers in intact families. *Journal of Marriage and Family, 63*(1), 136-154.

CHAPTER 5

FATHERS' AND TEACHERS' PERCEPTION ABOUT THEIR PARTNERSHIP IN SECONDARY SCHOOLS IN SPAIN

Raquel-Amaya Martínez-González, Beatriz Rodríguez-Ruíz, and María-José Rodrigo-López

INTRODUCTION

Traditionally, fathers and mothers played a differential role regarding family responsibilities and children's education, being the necessary collaboration between families and schools mainly performed by mothers. The gendered distribution of family responsibilities was recognized by the Committee of Experts on Children and Families of the Council of Europe (Day, 2006), when trying to support effective parenting in European countries. This initiative, stated in the Recommendation (2006)/19 of the Council of Europe, includes parental involvement at schools and partnerships as an important measure to be promoted. According to this recommendation, the concept of "positive parenting" centers around parental behavior that is respectful of the child's best interests and rights as articulated by the United Nations Convention on the Rights of the Child and also considering the parents' needs and resources.

Promising Practices for Fathers' Involvement in Children's Education
pp. 79–93
Copyright © 2012 by Information Age Publishing
All rights of reproduction in any form reserved.

This European initiative is based on the fact that at present, the complexity of the current society and the diversity of family typologies and their internal dynamics make it necessary to introduce changes in the traditional roles of fathers and mothers. Accordingly, fathers are expected to be more involved and coresponsible together with the mothers in housework and in children's raising and education. This includes not just caring for them at home but also collaborating with the school along their academic life (Lamb, 2004). This expectation, however, as McBride, Rane, and Bae (2001) pointed out, is still far from been adjusted and performed in many families, where the mother tries to cope with their traditional family duties plus the ones associated to their jobs in the labour market. Regarding getting fathers/men involved both at home and at schools, research show more studies based on young children (Appl, Brown, & Stone, 2008; Karther, 2002; López, 2007; McBride, Brown, Bost, Shin, Vaughn, & Korth, 2005; Ortiz & Stile, 2001) than on compulsory secondary school students; this indicates that fathers' involvement in parenting tasks, still deserves more attention on the part of researchers, policymakers and professionals.

In this paper, fathers' collaboration with compulsory secondary education schools in Spain was explored taking into account both, their own perspective as fathers and that of the teachers; the aim was to catch a closer insight on the kind of activities fathers are more willing or available to attend at school, as well as on the barriers they might encounter to do so. As McBride et al. (2001) suggested, attention must also be directed to teachers, as educators begin exploring the development and implementation of programs to encourage fathers' involvement. Better understanding the latter's behavior and the difficulties they might encounter in this field, could help educators to identify some useful strategies to encourage fathers' involvement in schools and in their children's education.

THE SPANISH EDUCATIONAL CONTEXT
FOR SCHOOL-FAMILY-COMMUNITY PARTNERSHIP

Partnership and Fathers' Involvement

In the last decades, Spanish researchers showed an increasing interest in analyzing factors affecting school-family-community partnerships as a potential predictor of children's behavior and school achievement (see Bazarra, Casanova, & Ugarte, 2007; Comellas, 2009; Forest & García Bacete, 2006; Franco-Martínez, 1989; García-Bacete & Martínez-González, 2006; Gregorio-García, 1990; Kñallinsky, 1999; López-Larrosa, 2009; López-López, 2006, 2008; Martínez-González, Rodríguez-Ruiz,

Pérez-Herrero & Torío-López, 2005; Villalta, Tschorne, & Torrente, 1989). Also, in these last decades, Spain, as other European developed countries (Council of Europe, 2006), experienced important political and social changes. Among them: democratization of the social discourse, equalitarian policies for men and women, women access to the labour market, diversity of family structures and dynamics, immigration, competitiveness in the labour market, integration of information and communication technologies (ICTs) in the broad social life, diversity in job opportunities, et cetera. All affect families', schools' and communities' dynamics and their effects on education.

Some of these effects regarding family dynamics are related to the following: (1) less time devoted to parents-children interaction—especially in monoparental families, (2) parents' strong concerns regarding their children's up-bringing and educational process, (3) more grand-parents involved and holding responsibility in their grand-children's education, and (4) more parents demanding kindergarten and school teachers to take care of their children's development in all areas of competence: behavior, attitudes, values and knowledge. As a result, teachers and schools need to adjust their traditional educational expectations and roles to these new family and social demands. These teachers express concerns that they are expected to assume responsibilities for children's upbringing, which traditionally the family and specially the mothers used to carry out. Nevertheless, neither the schools, the teachers or the educational system is ready to take over such responsibilities. This divergent perception between teachers and parents leads to confrontations between them, especially when the children fail academically at secondary school.

However, the incorporation of ICTs in society and in the educational system has increased the frequency and reduced the time lag during which parents can connect with teachers and the school. The school has developed new technological ways in which parents can regularly connect to the school. This new dependence on ICTs also revealed evidence of the gap among parents, teachers and children in their respective abilities to use ICT. This added a new factor that makes parents' daily involvement in their children's education even more difficult.

Moreover, social risks affecting childhood and adolescence such as drug consumption, teenage pregnancy, ICTs and sexual abuse, dropping-out from school, academic failure, among others, contributed to the awareness of European and Spanish citizens of the need of building bridges and partnesrhips between schools, families and communities (Council of Europe, 2006). This led educational policymakers and leaderships to consider the convenience to formalize training preservice pre-school, primary and secondary school teachers for partnerships with families and community agents. As a result, the current Spanish curriculum for training teachers in higher education, formally includes a compulsory subject on promoting parental involvement and school-family collaboration (Real Decreto 55/2005, January, 21; Real Decreto 1393/2007, October, 29).

Parents' involvement in schools has been legislated in Spain since the 1970s, with the objective of promoting the quality of children's education. The most relevant partnership actions taking place in Spanish schools nowadays are: (1) parents' participation in general meetings held for groups of parents of children attending the same classroom, (2) parent-teacher interviews, (3) meetings and activities performed by parents' associations, and (4) parents' participation in school councils. These are important areas of involvement. But they are not always performed in an effective way in terms of stimulating parents' frequent participation as a preventive measure against pupils' misbehavior, academic failure and dropping out (Epstein, 2011; Hiatt-Michael, 2001; Martínez-González et al., 2000; Martínez-González et al., 2005; Musitu & Cava, 2001; Redding, 2005; Symeou, 2007).

Regarding fathers' involvement both at home and at school, little has been investigated and concluded so far in Spain. What has been made clear through research is that the mothers are the ones who more frequently attend school meetings and other related activities. This applies to all levels of compulsory school—primary and secondary—and at preschool. They also are more willing to participate in parenting programs and in research projects regarding parental involvement (Martínez-González et al., 2005).

NATIONWIDE STUDY ON FATHER-TEACHER PERCEPTIONS OF THEIR PARTNERSHIP

Purpose and Questionnaire

This study was undertaken in two regions of the country to compare fathers' and teachers' perceptions of their partnership in compulsory secondary school grades. In Spain, compulsory secondary schools grades involve youth ages 12-16. The aim of the study was to identify potential factors that both facilitate and hinder fathers' active involvement in their children's school and education. From these results, some strategies to support fathers' participation are suggested.

The study focuses on two dimensions of parental involvement identified by Ho Sui-Chu and Willms (1996) as "school involvement," in contrast to "parents' actions at home"; according to these authors, school involvement includes contact between parents and school personnel and volunteering in school and attending parent-teacher conferences and open-house meetings. Accordingly, the two dimensions analyzed in this research are: (1) *Typology of activities fathers attend at school* and (2) *Difficulties fathers face to participate in school activities.* For dimension one, it was hypothesized that fathers rarely attend school academic activities affecting their children. The specific issues analyzed took into account how often fathers attended: (1) general meetings for parents at the school; (2) individual father-teacher meetings; (3) meetings organized by the parents' association; (4) lectures, workshops or conferences; and (5) parties, cultural and sport activities organized at school. For dimension two, it was hypothesized that fathers face difficulties to participate in school activities due to some of the following reasons stated in the revised literature: (1) their work schedule; (2) the school schedule; (3) having to take care of small children, elderly relatives, etc.; (4) transport; (5) not having interest in participating, (6) feeling not have been invited to participate; (7) feeling uncomfortable at school, and (8) having had negative experiences in their children's school or even personal ones as students.

To gather information, a questionnaire by Christenson, Lam, and Sinclair on school-family partnership adapted by Martínez-González (1992) was distributed to the respondents. The questionnaire consisted of closed questions, to be answered to on a 5-point Likert scale with the terms representing the range in the dimension under study. Cronbach's alpha reliability measure for the issues analyzed in dimension one was .865 (5 items) for teachers and .778 (5 items) for fathers. Regarding dimension two, the values were .831 for teachers (8 items) and .646 (8 items) for fathers. The data were analyzed using descriptive measures and t test comparisons between fathers and teachers. The latter took into account the figure which results from subtracting the fathers' mean from that of the teachers' for the issues considered in the study.

Sample Population

In selecting the study sample, variables suggested by the international literature as might be affecting fathers' involvement at school were taken into consideration. Such variables include the following:

1. The school level of the children; this study focuses on compulsory secondary school at grades 2 and 4 considering that at those levels children have more risk to fail academically;
2. The school typology: state (42.3%), private (21.5%) and semistate schools (36.3%);

3. The geographical area where the schools were placed; in this study, a region in the north of the Spanish peninsula (Asturias) (56.8%) and also the Canary islands, placed in the south, off the coast of Africa (43.3%). These regions where chosen because of their distance and cultural differences, which might be associated to different educative perspectives, needs and traditions; and

4. The family urban (41.3%) or rural (58.8%) area of residence.

Thus, these variables constituted the basis for the initial selection of the schools and the fathers' sample, which ensured the desired diversity of the participants target group.

The final sample comprised 400 fathers and 400 teachers of compulsory secondary school children who volunteered to participate in the study. Taking into account variables related to fathers' sociodemographic characteristics *as literacy, employment, age, and family typology,* the distribution of the sample was: 36.8% had primary school studies, 37.5% high school education or technical/vocational school and 25.8% reached university studies. According to employment, 93.2% were working, 4.8% pensioners and 2% unemployed. None of them identified themselves as in charge of doing housework. Their average *age* was 45.29 years all (*SD* = 5.4). Most of them (93%) were *married*, while only 5.7% were divorced, 0.3% single fathers and 1% non married couples ("the fact couples"). Regarding *teachers*, 41.5% were males and 58.5% females, who taught in the second (57.3%) and the fourth (42.8%) year of compulsory secondary school. Their teaching experience ranged from 1-11 years (44.5%), 12-22 years (32.3%), 23-33 years (16.5%) and 34-44 years (6.7%). Their average age was 40.91 years old (*SD* = 9.10). In this study, their teaching areas were classified into humanities (55.8%) and sciences (44.3%). Most of them taught in government (44.2%) and private (21.5%) schools, while only a few (36.3%) did so in semigovernment ones.

The following section of the paper presents the comparative findings between fathers and teachers in the issues analyzed in the two dimensions investigated in the study.

Results

Typology of Activities Fathers Attend at School. The variables included in this dimension are related to fathers' participation in school in both academic and extracurricular activities. Due to the value parents usually give to school achievement, it was hypothesized that both fathers and teachers would agree in considering that the former attend meetings for parents as a group or individual parent-teacher interviews regarding academic matters of their children more frequently than any other activities (workshops, conferences, parents' association meetings or sport events). Attending those meetings related to academic matters, would help fathers to be more aware of issues concerning their children's progress at school so as to support them accordingly.

The results obtained about the frequency with which fathers attend *parents' association meetings and conferences or workshops* at school indicate they admit their implication is rare (fathers' $M = 1.96$; $SD = 1.25$). Although the teachers mostly coincide with this (teachers' $M = 2.27$; $SD = 1.27$), there are significant statistical differences which suggest that *fathers consider their participation in meetings organized by the parents' association* ($t(398) = 3.66$; $p = .000$) and in *workshops and conferences* ($t(399) = 2.85$; $p = .005$) is even *lower than teachers think*. This might mean that teachers have a more positive perception of fathers' involvement than fathers themselves have; maybe because they expect them to be involved in these activities related to schooling; or maybe because teachers associate fathers' involvement with that of the mothers, who usually do so more frequently; thus, generalizing the same behavior for fathers, as suggested by Barnes (2009). This finding regarding lack of involvement is supported by the fact that both fathers and teachers have the same perception that only "some times" *fathers participate in general meetings for parents as a group* (fathers' $M = 3.30$, $SD = 1.48$; teachers' $M = 3.27$, $SD = 1.32$) ($t(399) = -.270$; $p = .787$). The same applies to their involvement in *parent-teacher individual meetings* (fathers' $M = 3.20$, $SD = 1.38$; teachers' $M = 3.11$, $SD = 1.21$) ($t(399) = -1.08$; $p = .277$). In these two issues no significant statistical differences between fathers and teachers were found. These results are coherent with the common teachers' comment that parents in general and fathers in particular, attend school meetings only from time to time.

When analyzing fathers' participation in *parties and sport activities*, the results also indicate that they themselves consider they do so only a few times (fathers' $M = 2.66$; $SD = 1.42$). Teachers think more or less the same (teachers' $M = 2.33$; $SD = 1.27$). Significant statistical differences ($t(399) = -4.18$; $p = .000$) indicate that teachers perceive fathers' participation in these activities to be lower than fathers do. Probably parties and sport activities are more commonly organized by the school in collaboration with parents than academic meetings and thus fathers feel more responsive to them. Also, it is possible that these activities are performed in times which are more suitable for fathers, such as after school, weekends or special holidays, facilitating then fathers' participation. If this organization and time schedule for parties and sport activities support such participation, the same criteria could be applied regarding academic activities for parents to be developed at school.

The results obtained in the issues analyzed in this dimension indicate that fathers and teachers coincide when considering that the former seldom attend meetings regarding academic issues involving their children. However, they differ substantially regarding fathers' participation in parties and sport events because fathers' perceive their participation to a higher degree than teachers' do. They also differ when focusing on conferences, workshops and meetings organized by the parents' association, because fathers admit they participate on them less often than teachers' think. These results might mean that fathers should be more aware of and worried about their children's academic progress. In addition, the results suggest that both fathers and teachers should improve their communication in order to better adjust their respective expectations for the benefit of their collaboration and the children's education.

Difficulties Fathers Face to Participate in School Activities. The analysis performed in this study on several barriers that might prevent fathers from attending school activities (time schedules, transport, having to look after family members, interest in participating and previous experiences at school), show that their *work schedule* (fathers' $M = 3.79$, $SD = 1.40$) makes it very difficult for them to be involved. This perception is also shared by the teachers (teachers' $M = 3.46$, $SD = .50$), but in a significant statistical lower degree ($t(399) = -4.35$; $p = .000$). This might mean that teachers consider fathers could organize their time better in order to be able to attend school activities. On the other hand, when considering the extend to which *school timetable* could represent a difficulty for fathers, they agree it is so (fathers' $M = 2.88$, $SD = 1.41$). But in a lower degree than their own work schedule does. Teachers also admit this difficulty for fathers (teachers' mean = 2.32, $SD = .47$), although in a statistically significant lower degree ($t(399) = -7.07$; $p = .000$); thus, maybe insisting in the idea that fathers could organize their time in a way which allows their participation. From these results, deeper understanding and communication between teachers and fathers could be recommended. This could help them to adjust their respective working agendas in a way which facilitates their partnership. *Transport difficulties* could be also sometimes an obstacle to approach the school; however, in this study, both fathers (fathers' $M = 1.54$, $SD = 1$) and teachers (teachers' $M = 1.62$, $SD = .58$) share the idea that this barrier appears rarely. No significant statistical differences were found between them in this regard ($t(399) = 1.51$; $p = .131$). This result was expected considering that at present most Spanish fathers have a car, that public transport is well developed in Spain and that most families enroll their children in schools placed close to their houses or work places.

Another difficulty for fathers to attend the school activities could be associated with the fathers need to assume *home responsibilities or having to care for other family members* as small children or elderly relatives. In this study, fathers report that this is not the case for many of them (fathers' M = 1.93, SD = 1.27). Teachers, however, differ significantly from the fathers on this matter ($t(399)$ = 9.11; p = .000). Teachers perceive that fathers have home responsibilities (teachers' M = 2.53, SD = .50) at a higher extent than fathers themselves admit. This interesting result might mean that teachers try to somehow understand and justify fathers' lack of involvement at school-based activities because these fathers' have home responsibilities.

To participate in school activities, fathers might need to feel they are approached by the school in a personal way so that they are aware their contribution would be valued (Green, 2003). In this study it was found that both teachers and fathers know *the schools invite the latter to participate* (fathers' M = 2.14, SD = 1.39; teachers' M = 1.69, SD = .61). But, fathers are significantly less aware than teachers regarding school requests for the fathers to participate in school activities ($t(399)$ = −5.85; p = .000). Thus, more personal approaches to fathers might help them to feel more motivated to attend school activities and to organize their time to do so. When fathers do not attend, teachers might think they are *not interested*. In this study, the results obtained from the teachers' perspective confirm so (teachers' M = 2.92, SD = .41). However, fathers differ significantly with this interpretation ($t(399)$ = 17.82; p = .000), pointing out that is not the case at all (fathers' M = 1.81, SD = 1.16). From this comparative result, it might be suggested there are other important reasons fathers have for not participating in school activities. For example, a primary reason is that teachers and fathers do not appear to clearly communicate. The two come from different perspectives of the child and need to carefully listen to the others' perspective. Such attentive listening would help both of them understand each other clearly, that way preventing misunderstandings.

Among these reasons, *feeling uncomfortable at school* could have prevented fathers' participation. In this study, both fathers (fathers' M = 1.44, SD = .93) and teachers (teachers' M = 1.62, SD = .51) consider this is not the case, although teachers tend to admit so to a significantly higher degree than fathers do ($t(399)$ = 3.28; p = .001). The same result was obtained when considering the fact that fathers might have had *bad experiences at their children's school or when being students themselves* (fathers' M = 1.43, SD = .91; teachers' M = 1.75, SD = .49) ($t(399)$ = 6.26; p = .000). Both of them think this is not a barrier that prevents fathers in this study from attending school activities; although teachers perceive it could affect the latter more than the fathers themselves think. If this is so, teachers could act and communicate with fathers in a more friendly way, which would help them to feel accepted and motivated to approach the school. When doing so, teachers need to put their social skills into practice.

Discussion

The findings obtained in this study seem to prove that fathers' involvement at school is rare, even when considering activities related to the academic or developmental spheres of their children. This may be due to work and school schedules or to attitudes associated to gender distribution of family and home responsibilities (McBride et al., 2001). Klein (2008) obtained similar results in a study where the fathers, on average, did not visit the schools very often. But they all considered themselves highly "engaged" in their children's education by helping them to maintain daily schedules to build self-discipline to be engaged in their learning and schooling. As proposed by Ho Sui-Chu and Willms (1996), it seems convenient to analyze fathers' involvement at home in addition to analyzing their "school involvement." According to these authors, school-related activities at home had stronger relationship with academic achievement than parents' participation in school. The need to investigate into this area, also called "curriculum of the home," was also remarked by Walberg (1984), Redding (2000) and Marjoribanks (2004). How to recognize or measure this curriculum is an interesting field for future studies on fathers. In doing so, Martínez-González and Corral-Blanco (1991) and Redding (2000) suggest some of the following practices:

1. father/child relationship, such as daily conversation about everyday events; expressions of affection; discussion of books, newspapers, magazines, television programs; visits to libraries, museums, zoos, historical sites, cultural activities and encouragement to try new words, to enlarge vocabulary and alike;

2. family life routine, such as daily activities including time to eat, sleep, play, work, study and read quietly and family interest in hobbies, games and activities of educational value; and

3. family expectations and supervision, such as priority given to schoolwork and reading over television and recreation, parental expectation that children do their best, concern for correct and effective use of language, parental monitoring of children's peer group and parental knowledge of the child's progress in school and personal growth. As Martínez-González and Corral-Blanco (1991) and Redding (2000) stated, all these could take place in most homes, regardless the parents' literacy or socioeconomic status, providing parents are given some guidance.

A possible strategy to cope with time difficulties to attend school activities is promoting the use of information and communication technologies. Such utilization could help fathers to communicate with teachers (through SMS, chat, e-mail, videoconferences, etc.) from any place and at any time. Using these resources requires, of course, appropriate technology equipment and abilities to use them. If some fathers were not able to, maybe the schools could take this diversity into account in order to approach them accordingly.

An interesting finding from this study indicates that fathers perceive significantly more than teachers do that they have not been invited to participate in the school. Teachers tend to disagree completely with this, maybe because they usually send information notes to all families. Nevertheless, it could happen that when parents receive these notes, they do not necessarily identify themselves with the issues to be discussed; or maybe they consider their particular and personal contribution is not expected. As noted by Klein (2008), this could especially apply to some immigrant families, who may not feel comfortable enough at school. The findings of the present study suggest the convenience to improve the style these notes are written when addressed to fathers of compulsory secondary school students. They could be made more personal, a suggestion also remarked by Klein (2008) and Green (2003). Since most parents have cell phones, a telephone call or text message may be more personal. By doing so, all fathers could feel that their specific, unique and personal contribution is expected and valued.

SUGGESTIONS FOR PRACTICE

In this study's findings, both fathers and teachers consider work and school schedules as obstacles for fathers to attend the school. Teachers believe that fathers could organize their time better to be able to do so. If schools look forward to promoting partnerships with fathers, teachers should be more sensible to fathers' perception on the matter. For example, teachers should organize meetings for the fathers' convenience, such as after school hours or distributing them along different periods during the day or the week. This probably demands more flexibility on the part of the teachers when assigning a timetable to those activities. Also, such practices require teachers' positive attitude towards staying at school longer that usual in the afternoon, when fathers are more likely to come. Accordingly, fathers should recognize these teachers' efforts.

The significant statistical differences found between fathers' and teachers' perceptions on the issues analyzed show they do not communicate frequently enough as to be able to adjust their respective expectations about fathers' involvement at school. Thus, as also stated by

Hiatt-Michael (2001, 2010), opportunities to increase their communication and partnerships might be developed.

Also, deeper discussions on gender issues regarding fathers' involvement at compulsory secondary school and in their children's education should be promoted. Both teachers and fathers may need to be more aware of their important contribution not just at school but also at home. McBride et al. (2001) claimed that the variety of educational and workplace backgrounds fathers have might bring about an interesting pool of potential of ideas, actions and resources to be positively used in collaboration with schools for the benefit of children's education.

In addition, attention must also be directed to both identification of classroom teachers' knowledge, skills, and dispositions related to working with fathers. There is little or no preservice and in-service training for teachers on this matter in Spain and elsewhere. In spite of the positive effects that building partnership might have upon children and schools, some initiatives to implement parents' participation at schools have failed. The causes for that are, among other factors, important attitudinal differences between parents in general and fathers in particular, and teachers (Villas-Boas, 2005). According to Epstein (2003) as well as Van Voorhis and Sheldon (2004), these attitudinal differences may be contributed, in part, to the fact that teachers, principals and administrators are still not sufficiently prepared to understand and conduct effective programmes to involve family and community. Consequently, educational policymakers should address this issue. Compulsory schools as well as universities should include teacher preparation to communicate and work with fathers. Also, policymakers and compulsory schools should support educational policies and initiatives to both stimulate research and to train teachers for partnership as a means to contribute to school efficacy and quality in education.

ACKNOWLEDGMENT

This research was supported by funding from the Spanish Ministry of Science and Innovation (project SEJ2007-67082) to the third author. We thank the families and the schools for their kind cooperation and ongoing support during the data collection.

REFERENCES

Appl, D. J., Brown, S., & Stone, M. (2008). A father's interactions with his toddler: Personal and professional lessons for early childhood educators. *Early Childhood Education Journal, 36*, 127-134.

Barnes, C. M. (2009). *Some relationships among father involvement and the literacy interests of young children with disabilities* (Master's thesis) University of Tennessee. Retrieved from http://trace.tennessee.edu/utk_gradthes/16

Bazarra, L., Casanova, O., & Ugarte, J. G. (2007). *Profesores, alumnos, familias* [Teachers, students, families]. Madrid, Spain: Narcea.

Comellas, M. J. (2009). *Familia y escuela: Compartir la educación* [Family and school: Sharing education]. Barcelona, Spain: Graó.

Council of Europe. (2006). Recommendation Rec(2006)19 of the Committee of Ministers to Member States on Policy to Support Positive Parenting (Adopted by the Committee of Ministers on 13 December 2006 at the 983rd meeting of the Ministers' Deputies).

Day, M. (Ed.). (2006). Committee of Experts on Children and Families (CS-EF), Council of Europe *Parenting in contemporary Europe: A positive approach*. Lisbon (Portugal), Conference of European Ministers Responsible for Family Affairs, "Changes in Parenting: Children Today, Parents Tomorrow."

Epstein, J. L. (2003). No contest: Why preservice and inservice education are needed for effective programmes of school, family, and community partnerships. In S. Castelli, M. Mendel, & B. Ravn (Eds.), *School, family and community partnership in a world of differences and changes* (pp. 190-208). Gdansk, Poland: University of Gdansk.

Epstein, J. L. (2011). *School, family, and community partnerships: Preparing educators and improving schools*. Boulder, CO: Westview Press.

Forest, C., & García-Bacete, F. J. (2006). *Comunicación cooperativa entre la familia y la escuela* [Cooperative communication between family and school]. Valencia, Spain: Nau Llibres.

Franco-Martínez, R. (1989). *Claves para la participación en los centros escolares* [Keys for participation at schools]. Madrid, Spain: Escuela española.

García-Bacete, F., & Martínez-González, R.-A. (2006). (Eds.). Editorial: La relación entre los centros escolares, las familias y los entornos comunitarios como factor de calidad de la educación de menores y adultos [Editorial: School-Family-Community partnerships as quality factor in children's and adults' education]. *Cultura y Educación* [Número Monográfico: Familias, Escuela y Comunidad, Factores de Calidad Educativa] [Special issue: Families, Schools and Communities, Factors of Educational Quality], *18*(3-4), 213-218.

Green, S. (2003). Reaching out to fathers: An examination of staff efforts that lead to greater father involvement in early childhood programs. *Early Childhood Research & Practice, 5*(2). Retrieved from http://ecrp.uiuc.edu/v5n2/green.html

Gregorio-García, A. (1990). *La participación de los padres en los centros educativos* [Parents' participation at schools]. Bilbao, Spain: Deusto.

Hiatt-Michael, D. B. (Ed.). (2001). Home-school communication. In *Promising practices for family involvement in schools* (pp. 39-57). Greenwich, CT: Information Age.

Hiatt-Michael. D. B. (Ed.). (2010). Communication practices that bridge home with school. In *Promising practices to support family involvement in schools* (pp. 25-56). Charlotte, NC: Information Age.

Ho Sui-Chu, E., & Willms, J. D. (1996). Effects of parental involvement on eighth-grade achievement. *Sociology of Education, 69*(2), 126-141.

Karther, D. (2002). Fathers with low literacy and their young children. *Reading Teacher, 56,* 184-193.

Klein, A. (2008). From Mao to Memphis: Chinese immigrant fathers' involvement with their children's education. *The School Community Journal, 18*(2), 91-117.

Kñallinsky, E. (1999). *La participación educativa: Familia y escuela* [Participation in education: Family and school]. Las Palmas de Gran Canaria, Spain: Servicio de Publicaciones de la Universidad de las Palmas de Gran Canaria.

Lamb, M. E. (Ed.). (2004). *The role of the father in child development.* Hoboken, NJ: Wiley.

López, V. (2007). An exploratory study of Mexican-origin fathers' involvement in their child's education: The role of linguistic acculturation. *The School Community Journal, 17*(1) 61-76.

López-Larrosa, S. (2009). *La relación familia-escuela* [Family-school partnership]. Madrid, Spain: CCS.

López-López, M. T. (2006). *La familia en el proceso educativo* [The family in the educational process]. Madrid, Spain: Ediciones Cinca.

López-López, M. T. (2008). *Familia, escuela y sociedad: Responsabilidades compartidas en la educación* [Family, school and society: Shared responsibilities in education]. Madrid, Spain: Ediciones Cinca.

Marjoribanks, K. (2004). Families, schools, individual characteristics and young adults' outcomes: Social and cultural group differences [Special issue]. *International Journal of Educational Research, 41*(1), 10-23.

Martínez-González, R. -A. (1992). *Diagnóstico de necesidades en la cooperación entre familia y centro escolar* [Needs assessment regarding family-school partnership] (Research report). Asturias, Spain: Oviedo University and Washington, DC: Department of Education, Office of Educational Research and Improvement.

Martínez-González, R. -A. & Corral-Blanco, N. (1991). Parents and children: Academic values and school achievement [Special issue: Parents and teachers as collaborative partners]. *International Journal of Educational Research, 15* (2), 163-169.

Martínez-González, R. -A., Pereira-González, M., Rodríguez-Díez, B., Peña del Agua, A., Martínez-Alvarez, R., García-González, M.P., ... Casielles-Muñoz, V. (2000). Dinamización de las relaciones familia-centro escolar a través de la formación del profesorado en este campo de actuación [Encouraging family–school partnership through teachers' training]. *Revista Española de Orientacion y Psicopedagogia, 11*(19), 107-120.

Martínez-González, R. -A., Rodríguez-Ruiz, B., Pérez-Herrero, M. H., & Torío-López, S. (Eds). (2005). *Family–school–community partnerships merging into social development.* Oviedo, Spain: SM Publishing Group.

McBride, B., Rane, T. R., & Bae, J. H. (2001). Intervening with teachers to encourage father/male involvement in early childhood programs. *Early Childhood Research Quarterly, 16,* 77-93.

McBride, B. A., Brown, G. L., Bost, K. K., Shin, N., Vaughn, B., & Korth, B. (2005). Paternal identity, maternal gatekeeping, and father involvement. *Family Relations, 54,* 360-372.

Musitu, G., & Cava, M. J. (2001). *La familia y la educación* [Family and education]. Barcelona, Spain: Octaedro.

Ortiz, R. W., & Stile, S. (2002). Project dads: Training fathers in early literacy skills through community-university partnerships. *The School Community Journal,* *12*, 91-106. Retrieved from http://www.adi.org/journal/ss02/Ortiz%20&% 20Stile.pdf

Real Decreto 55/2005, 21 de Enero. Enseñanza Universitaria de Grado en Magisterio de Educación Infantil y Enseñanza Universitaria Grado en Magisterio de Educación Primaria [Royal Regulation 55/2005, January 21. Policy on Curriculum for Higher Education Degree on Infant Education Teachers and Policy on Curriculum for Higher Education Degree on Primary Education Teachers].

Real Decreto 1393/2007, 29 de Octubre. Ordenación de las enseñanzas universitarias oficiales de Máster que habiliten para el ejercicio de las profesiones de Profesor de Educación Secundaria Obligatoria y Bachillerato, Formación Profesional y Enseñanzas de Idiomas. [Royal Regulation 1393/2007, October, 29. Policy on Curriculum for Higher Education Master on Compulsory Secondary School Teachers, High School, Vocational School and Language Teaching].

Redding, S. (2000). *Parents and learning.* Geneva: UNESCO. International Bureau of Education in collaboration with The *International Academy of Education, 2.* Retrieved from http://www.ibe.unesco.org

Redding, S. (2005). Improving student learning outcomes through school initiatives to engage parents. In R. A. Martínez-González, B. Rodríguez-Ruiz, H. Pérez-Herrero, & S. Torío-López (Eds.), *Family–school–community partnerships merging into social development* (pp. 477-501). Oviedo, Spain: SM Editorial Group.

Symeou, L. (2007). Cultural capital and family involvement in children's education: Tales from two primary schools in Cyprus. *British Journal of Sociology of Education, 28,* 473-487.

Van Voorhis, F., & Sheldon, S. (2004). Principals' roles in the development of U.S. programs of school, family, and community partnerships. In R. A. Martínez-González & S. Paik (Guest Eds.), International perspectives on families, schools, and communities: Educational implications for partnership [Special issue]. *International Journal of Educational Research, 41*(1), 55-70.

Villalta, M., Tschorne, P., & Torrente, M. (1989). *Los padres en la escuela* [The parents at the school]. Barcelona, Spain: Laia.

Villas-Boas, M. A. (2005). The mismatch between results on parental involvement and teachers' attitudes: Is convergence ahead? *Aula Abierta, 85,* 205-224.

Walberg, H. (1984). Improving the productivity of America's schools. *Educational Leadership, 41*(8), 19-27.

CHAPTER 6

A CROSS-CULTURAL PERSPECTIVE ON FATHER INVOLVEMENT IN EARLY CHILDHOOD EDUCATION

Turkey and the United States

Elif Karsli and Martha Allexsaht-Snider

INTRODUCTION

Knowledge about the changing roles for fathers around the world is highlighted in the educational, demographic, sociological, and psychological literature. However, much of this research has been conducted within the context of the United States and other economically developed countries. Therefore, the ideas related to fatherhood are described from this body of research. This research has limited the conceptual framework of fatherhood. Interdisciplinary knowledge drawing on the disciplines of psychology, sociology, and anthropology, and situated cross-cultural research can provide a better way to understand the phenomenon of fatherhood as it is enacted in different settings around the world, across generations, and in diverse multicultural contexts.

Promising Practices for Fathers' Involvement in Children's Education
pp. 95–112
Copyright © 2012 by Information Age Publishing

In the past decades, the research literature on fathers was dominated by the psychological literature with comparative accounts of paternal behavior and maternal behavior. Along with the fatherhood research in different disciplines, recently father involvement has been the focus of educational research. In the United States, early childhood has been the context for father involvement research for more than 2 decades, and these various studies point out that father involvement in early childhood settings produces positive outcomes for families and children (Berger, 1998; McBride & Rane, 1997; Palm & Fagan, 2008; Rimm-Kaufman & Zhang, 2005). In Turkey, research on father involvement, that is not mainly in the context of schooling but instead is situated in the early childhood period, has gained momentum in the last 10 years. The few studies to date have focused on generational issues related to father involvement as well as father involvement levels in children's lives and in children's play and its relationships with different variables such as social class, gender, and age (Çelik, 2007; Evans, 1997; Gursimsek, Kefi, & Girgin, 2007; Ivrendi & Isikoglu, 2010; Ögut, 1998; Ünlü, 2010).

Through introducing a new facet of fatherhood focused on father involvement in early childhood education, research from the two countries opens up a new space for educational researchers to promote and encourage the idea of fathers being welcomed in early childhood settings. In light of these studies, father involvement in schools is situated in the complex, dynamic relationships in the society and addresses different elements such as school policies, teachers, and mothers' beliefs and attitudes, fathers' demographic backgrounds, and, most importantly, the cultural contexts of families. Diverse families' funds-of-knowledge (Moll, Amanti, & Gonzalez, 2005), histories, and cultural practices (Gutierrez & Rogoff, 2003) shape the ways that they relate to school. This perspective motivated us to analyze father involvement in early childhood settings in two different contexts: Turkey and the United States. Obviously, Turkey and the United States have different historical and cultural backgrounds and economic conditions, as well as different histories of early childhood education, as will be discussed later in the chapter. We expected that cross-cultural research on father involvement from these two countries could provide us with a way to better understand each context and could also contribute to the exchange of dynamic and meaningful new ways of thinking. Therefore, in this chapter and in the small-scale study it incorporates, we address these questions:

- What are the father involvement levels of fathers of young children from Turkey and the United States?
- What are kindergarten teachers' ideas about father involvement in schools?

- What are the types and frequency of fathers' communication with teachers?

- In general, how can this cross-cultural analysis assist us in seeing something new about fathers' involvement and roles in their young children's learning in Turkey and the United States?

THEORETICAL LENS:
FATHER INVOLVEMENT AS *CULTURAL PRACTICES*

Through a socioculturally sensitive perspective, this study draws on the concept of cultural practices, which derives from the work of Moll et al. (2005) and Gutierrez and Rogoff (2003). The concepts of fatherhood and father involvement are addressed as being situated in the cultural practices of fathers from particular communities. Recognizing these two concepts as cultural practices opens up the possibility to grasp unique historical and cultural characteristics of two countries as well as their similarities stemming from global social, economic, and political changes.

The notion of cultural practices locates the everyday, patterned activities of individuals within their complex historical contexts. Dantas and Manyak (2010) define these practices as the way individuals believe, value, think, behave, speak, feel, and interact. Personal and cultural histories of individuals shape these ways of participation in social life. According to this perspective, in the present study, fathers' involvement in their children's lives, and their interactional patterns with teachers, are considered as cultural practices. From the perspective of teachers, their conceptualization of father involvement is also in relation with teachers' own cultural practices.

Cultural practices reflect both similarities and differences within and across cultural groups. People in the same cultural groups have shared meanings. However, experiences of individuals as agents of the particular culture vary (Dantas & Manyak, 2010). Gutierrez and Rogoff (2003) shed light on the meaning of investigating practices of individuals from different cultural groups. They argue that categorization of individuals into cultural groups and attribution of differences to ethnic group membership can cause overgeneralizations that view groups as homogenous with fixed characteristics. While acknowledging the caution provided by Gutierrez and Rogoff, we believe that it is important to interpret individuals' (such as fathers') practices within the histories of their engagement in cultural practices. This approach provides a dynamic view of cultural practices within and across groups.

Following the above theoretical perspective, we assume that fathers will vary in their beliefs related to fatherhood and involvement. We view

Turkish and American fathers as heterogeneous groups by situating them into the larger social, cultural, and political contexts unique to each country. Socioeconomic structures of the two contexts, the historical views on fatherhood, possible meanings of father involvement and the educational histories and characteristics of early childhood education are discussed accordingly. Practical considerations for father involvement in the two countries is built on the Moll and Greenberg's (1990) idea of creating new zones of possibilities, which can offer additional, valuable opportunities for fathers, teachers, and children inside and outside of early childhood classrooms.

THE CONTEXTS OF TURKEY AND THE UNITED STATES

The perspectives on father involvement from different parts of the world show that the concept of fatherhood cannot be meaningful when it is isolated from societal relationships, economic opportunities, and cultural practices. This broad perspective situating views on fatherhood in a notion of cultural practices leads to our investigation of the factors surrounding the context of fatherhood and father involvement in Turkey and the United States. Turkey is located at a crossroads where two continents, Europe and Asia meet. This special location gives Turkish culture a unique feature: it is a mix of Eastern and Western values. Yet, in terms of religion, Turkey is less diverse than the United States. Ninety-eight percent of the Turkey's population is Muslim. Islamic tradition, which values respect for and obedience to elders and traditional gender roles, is influential over the society on father roles. However, it should be noted that in Turkey, there is a strict separation of religion and the state and education is secular (McMullen et al., 2005).

In the past, in traditional Turkish extended families, which had patriarchal characteristics, fathers were viewed as authority figures (Kagitcibasi, 1996). However, the "Value of Children in Turkish Culture" study (Kagitcibasi & Ataca, 2005) that lasted 3 decades, identified changes in the Turkish family structure in terms of a decrease in patriarchal characteristics and an increase in the psychological value of the child, which is defined as "psychological benefits of having children, such as the joy, fun, companionship, pride, and the sense of accomplishment parents gain from having children" (p. 319). This new perspective resulted in a change of the social expectations for the father in the family and fathers' roles in general. Industrialization, urbanization, economic changes, and an increase in the women's participation in labor are the main reasons given for these changes in Turkey. These same global conjunctures are considered as the reasons for changes in fathers' roles in the United States

(Fagan & Palm, 2004). However, the degree of these global changes is different in Turkey and the United States. Turkey is behind the United States in terms of the industrialization, economic growth, as well as human development indexes regarding education, income, and gender equality (International Human Development Index, 2011).

The United States has a longer history in early childhood education compared to Turkey. Starting from the 19th century, the progressive child-study movement, which focuses on child-centered education, has been the main influence in the U.S. early childhood education. The quality of early childhood education opportunities, such as class size and teacher educational background, varies depending on the location in the United States, socioeconomic status, and educational background of families, and language spoken at home (Fromberg, 2006). In the area of father involvement, there are many recognized scientific research studies (Berger, 1998; McBride & Rane, 1997; Palm & Fagan, 2008; Rimm-Kaufman & Zhang, 2005) as well as father involvement initiatives across the country (e.g., National Fatherhood Initiative, 2010; United States Department of Health and Human Services' Head Start and Early Head Start Father Involvement Initiatives, 2011).

Unfortunately, the rate of enrollment in early childhood education in Turkey is low compared to the United States and the European countries. Since Turkey started European Union full membership negotiations in 2005, policy initiatives in early childhood education have increased. Public and private kindergartens, child-care centers, and elementary schools have been providing early childhood education on a small scale in Turkey for many years. However, in many cities, compulsory early childhood education for 5-year-old children has started only recently, and it is estimated that compulsory, free early childhood education will only become available for all 5-year-olds in public schools in 2013. Unlike the United States, in Turkey there is single national early childhood education curriculum implemented in the whole country. The western influence is evident in the fundamental goals and principles of the Turkish Educational Constitution.

> Turkish early childhood teachers' beliefs are closer to the more child-centered or DAP (developmentally appropriate practices) end of the continuum, considering the emphases on active, hands-on learning, dramatic play, activities that respond to the needs and interests of the individual child and also the whole group. (Erdiller & McMullen, 2003, p. 91)

The child-centeredness evident in policy is balanced in practice with traditional ideals of respect for and obedience to elders, which are important cultural values in Turkey (McMullen et al., 2005).

As would be expected, since early childhood education is a new area in the context of Turkey, teachers and parents are all in the adaptation process. Even so, there are a few but effective national and local initiatives targeting fathers' involvement in early childhood education.

FATHER INVOLVEMENT INITIATIVES: IMPLEMENTATIONS IN TURKEY AND THE UNITED STATES

Turkey

One of the most important initiatives related to father involvement is governed by the Mother Child Education Foundation (ACEV), which is a nongovernmental organization developing and implementing programs for early childhood education and adult education, and aiming to empower and improve the quality of life for beneficiaries through education and training (www.acev.org/?lang=en). ACEV has led several successful campaigns around the country through the effective use of media, support from international organizations, and local companies. In particular, the campaign "7 is too late!," to raise the awareness of early childhood education, has been very successful. Under the ACEV family education program, the Father Support Program was specifically designed for fathers and reached 32,000 fathers and children. This program is based on scientific research and aims to contribute to child development by supporting fathers. Fathers from all education levels are incorporated in this program. Primary schools and public education centers have made this program available to fathers. The program includes group meetings, participatory and face-to-face educational techniques, and interactive learning experiences through different activities over a period of 10-12 weeks. A broad range of topics is included, such as parenting styles, understanding the child, children and play, physical and sexual development, life difficulties, and fathers' roles.

The Mother Child Education Foundation's Father Education Program is an example of a program implemented on a national level in Turkey. There are also local implementations targeting fathers in different cities in Turkey. An effective and creative example, which also had a place in the media, has been implemented by the Guidance and Psychological Research Center under the Ministry of Education. "Father Education Seminars" are designed and made available for fathers at traditional "*coffeehouses*." Actually, in Turkey, traditional coffeehouses are social meeting places where only males attend for having conversations with their male peers during their free time. These places are mostly located in rural areas but are also found in urban areas. Rather than inviting fathers to other places such as schools, or various public spaces, the implementation in coffeehouses makes these educational seminars available in places where fathers are daily attending. It has been reported that fathers show great interest in these seminars.

Along with the small educational programs designed by schools or by some researchers to evaluate the effectiveness of fathers' educational programs influences on fathering behaviors (Aydin, 2003; Kocayoruk & Sumer, 2009), special programs have been designed for in-service teachers. Recently, the president of the Turkish Ministry Education reported that through seminars for teachers, they aim to support fathers so that they can become "caring and respectful of children's rights and have democratic relationships with their children." Information about all these programs on the social media, newspapers, and television channels contribute to the rising awareness about father involvement in children's lives in Turkey.

The United States

There has been research on father involvement in early childhood programs in the United States and there are specific programs for fathers in some early childhood programs. Fagan and Palm (2004) reported on four of these early childhood programs specifically designed for fathers: The Fairfax San Anselmo Children's Center, San Francisco Bay Area Male Involvement Network, The Dad's Project, and Head Start. The design of these programs highlights the positive impacts of father involvement in early childhood programs and includes enjoyable activities for fathers' participation. Fagan and Palm (2004) argue the importance of designing programs targeting the needs of fathers in their specific contexts. In the United States, one fatherhood initiative that targets incarcerated fathers and their children is governed by the federal prison system. The National Resource Center on Children and Families of the Incarcerated at the Family and Corrections Network is also working as a complement to these programs. This initiative is an important one because of the significant number of fathers who are in prison in the United States. In their study, in a federal prison in a Northeastern urban community, Smith and Morote (2011) point to the effectiveness of parenting programs targeting incarcerated fathers and show that special programs for these fathers have power to contribute to parent-child interactions, and in particular to the discipline dimension of those interactions. Focusing on our local context, in Georgia, a fatherhood initiative is led by the Georgia Fatherhood Program (fatherhoodgeorgia.gov), which has a general aim of *helping children by helping their parents*. This program is available for low income, non-custodial, nonsupporting young fathers. Those fathers are supported not just in the area of fatherhood but in terms of life management and survival skills as well as job placement opportunities.

A SMALL-SCALE STUDY ON FATHER INVOLVEMENT: URBAN WESTERN TURKEY AND RURAL/SUBURBAN SOUTHEASTERN UNITED STATES

Purpose and Design

Turkish researcher Kagitcibasi (1996), who has conducted many recognized studies both in the context of the United States and Turkey, points out that cross-cultural research provides new insights and perspectives on cultural practices, which is father involvement in our case. We believe that there are wide variations in the interactions and involvement practices of fathers across cultures and in particular settings within cultures or countries. With a goal of investigating commonalities and differences in practices of father involvement in early childhood education, we conducted a study in two environments that are familiar to each of us as researchers. The study considered how changing roles for fathers might influence fathers' involvement levels in their children's lives and different enactments of teacher-father partnerships in specific contexts located in Turkey and the United States. The characteristics of teacher-father interactions, teachers' ideas of partnerships, and fathers' involvement in children's lives were examined through surveys with fathers and parallel surveys and logs documenting interactions with the fathers completed by teachers. In this exploratory study, we recruited one elementary school from a rural/suburban area in the southeastern US and also two schools from two cities in urban Western Turkey. The research sample included a total of 70 fathers of kindergarten children from Turkey (37) and the United States (33) who were invited to answer the "Inventory of Father Involvement" instrument, developed by Hawkins et al. (2002), which measures different forms of father involvement in children's lives. Turkish translation and adaptation of the instrument were completed by Ünlü (2010). In addition to this instrument, demographic information from fathers was collected, including information on the primary male caregiver of children, children's gender and fathers' work hours. Gender and fathers' work hours were included in the analysis because of the different results related to these variables in the father involvement literature (Coley & Morris, 2002; Evans, 1997; Pleck, 1997; Ünlü, 2010). A total of 13 teachers of targeted fathers' children were invited to complete "Family Involvement Logs" developed by Rimm-Kaufman & Zhang (2005) to record frequency and characteristics of father-school communication during one month. All these teachers were also invited to answer open-ended questions about father-school partnership in early childhood education.

The Context of the Study

Drawing on the concept of cultural practices through a socioculturally sensitive perspective, we assume that parental functioning is complexity determined. Then, a wide range of determinants in different sociocultural environments affect the fathers' involvement in their children's lives as well as their involvement in schools. Moreover, since this study is a cross-cultural one, data on larger communities surrounding the research contexts play a prominent role in understanding father involvement. According to the Turkish and American national demographic survey results, both in Turkey and the United States, the contexts surrounding our target schools, have some different as well as some similar background characteristics. According to the Turkish Statistical Institute (2010) and American Community Survey results (2009), in general, income level is higher in the United States compared to Turkey; and on average, males in Turkey have a lower educational level than males in America. In Turkey, a majority of males have less than a high school degree (Ministry of National Education of Turkey, 2011), whereas in the United States a majority of males has a high school degree (U.S Census Bureau Statistical Abstract of the United States, 2009) . When we compare the contexts surrounding our target schools, males have a higher unemployment rate (around 6%) and children have a lower participation ratio (61%) in kindergarten in the Turkish context (Turkish Statistical Institute, 2010). In our context in the United States, the male unemployment rate is 4% and all children attend kindergarten, since it is compulsory (American Community Survey, 2009). When we compare the divorce rate of males, the United States has a higher divorce rate in males (around 11%) (Statistical Abstract, 2009) compared to Turkey (less than 1%) (Turkish Statistical Institute, 2010). In addition to these trends, in Georgia in around 5% of households, grandfathers are living with children and many of them are responsible for childcare (American Community Survey, 2009).

Results

Father Involvement Levels in a Sample of Turkish and American Fathers. A multiple regression analysis was conducted with a set level of significance of .05, to explain involvement levels (measured by the Inven-

**Table 6.1.   Multiple Regression Analysis
on Father Involvement Levels in Children's Lives**

	B	SE	β	Sig.
Constant	135.75	6.97	....	0.001
Ethnic background	10.06	3.49	−.33	.005*
Work hour	−.21	.11	−.21	.06
Gender	−2.9	3.2	−.88	.38

Note: $N = 70.$ $R^2 = .22.$ *$p < .05.$

tory of Father Involvement, Hawkins et al., 2002) of fathers whose children were attending kindergarten by their ethnic background (Turkish, American), fathers' weekly work hours, and children's gender. In this analysis, dummy coding was used to include the categorical variables gender and ethnicity in the linear regression (Pedhazur, 2010). In the overall results of the multiple regression analysis, a significant result appeared for the full model $F(4, 69) = 6.29$, $p = .001$. R^2 was .222. $Y = 135.756 + 10.067$(Ethnic Background) $- 2.10$ (Work Hour) $- 2.915$ (Child Gender). Only ethnicity of fathers was found as a statistically significant predictor, $p = .005$, showing that in this sample, father involvement levels of American fathers were higher than for Turkish fathers.

Father-Teacher Communication in Early Childhood Education. One of the goals of this study was to describe the type, frequency, and content of the communication of fathers with teachers. A total of 13 Turkish (6) and American (7) teachers completed "Family-School Communication Logs" for the participant fathers during 1 month (Rimm-Kaufman & Zhang, 2005). Table 6.2 and Table 6.3 show the pattern of father-teacher communications. These patterns depict clear similarities for Turkish and American fathers, as well as some differences. Findings show that the same ratio of participants, around one third of Turkish fathers and around one third of American fathers (grandfathers included), had communicated with their children's teacher in 1 month. Another similar pattern for these two contexts is that communication was composed of individual contacts and was mostly started by fathers. However, in the U.S. sample we see that grandfathers are also communicating with teachers. It should be noted that these grandfathers are those who are the primary caregivers of the children.

Table 6.3 shows that fathers from the two countries mostly preferred face-to-face communication, which is considered to be short contacts (less than 10 minutes.) While in the U.S. sample, we can see e-mail as an alternative communication tool. Turkish fathers preferred phone calls, which is still more common than e-mail, especially in the school context in Tur-

Table 6.2. Type and Frequency of Fathers' Involvement at School

During 1 Month	Number of Fathers Involving	Other Male	Number of Total Contacts	Initiated by	Group Contact or Individual Contact
Turkish Fathers	15	Only fathers	21	10 by teacher 11 by fathers	20 individual contact 1 group contact during school activity
American Fathers	8	3 grand-fathers	19	5 by teacher 14 by fathers	13 individual contact 6 group contact during school activity

Table 6.3. Communication Between Teachers and Fathers

During 1 Month	Type of Communication	Duration	Topic	General Impressions of Teachers About This Communication
Turkish Fathers	• 15 face-to-face contacts • 6 contacts by phone	• 8 contacts are more than 10 minutes	• 19 contacts are about child • 1 contact is about family • 1 contact is about participation	• Just 1 contact was rated as neutral Overall, all other contacts are positive
American Fathers	• 12 face-to-face • contacts • 4 contacts by letters • 3 contacts by e-mail	• Just 3 contacts are more than 10 minutes	• 12 contacts are about child • 2 contacts are about family • 5 contacts are about participation in school activities	• Just 1 contact was rated as negative • Overall, all other contacts are positive

key. Across cultures, the topic of communication is mostly about the child. However, there are varieties in the topics related to the child. Turkish fathers communicated about the child's health, the child's adjustment to school, and financial issues related to school. American fathers communicated about the child's education, transportation changes, and reasons for absences. Differently from Turkish fathers, American fathers also communicated about participation in school activities such as field days, field trips, and having lunch at school.

Turkish and American Teachers' Beliefs About Father Involvement. Turkish and American teachers were invited to answer open-ended questions developed by researchers about their beliefs on father involvement in early childhood education. Questions included their ideas related to fathers' participation levels, the importance of father involvement, and how to support fathers in the process. Constant-comparative analysis, an inductive analysis approach used in grounded theory to identify broad themes and patterns (Charmaz, 2006), was performed on the written answers of Turkish (6) and American teachers (7). Linking back to the theoretical lenses of the study, which view teachers' ideas in relation to their professional and cultural practices, we try to conceptualize the variety that we found in teachers' answers and try to look for commonalities in their perspectives. A step-by-step approach was followed, including first, a comparison within the single teacher's text and then, comparison between the texts within the same group of teachers, such as in the group of Turkish and in American teachers. Lastly, cross-comparison of texts from different groups was completed (Boeije, 2002). The major categories in teachers' answers, in relation with the questions asked, were found to be the benefits of involvement, conditions of father involvement, and fathers' motives of involvement. Under these categories, different themes emerged for Turkish and American teachers.

Under the category of benefits of father involvement, two themes emerged in this sample of Turkish and American teachers.

Academic Benefits of Father Involvement. American teachers proposed that father involvement increases children's academic achievement, by articulating that father involvement supports children to perform better, to succeed, and to achieve at school.

Social Benefits of Father Involvement. Turkish teachers mainly pointed to the social benefits of father involvement by articulating that father involvement supports children to love their school more, to adjust to school more, and to enjoy being at school more.

Under the category of conditions of father involvement, two different themes and one same theme emerged for American and Turkish teachers.

School as Responsible for Father Involvement. American teachers claimed that they do not have specific activities targeting fathers and that there is a low level of participation. However, they claim that schools have the primary responsibility for father participation and that schools could implement different activities. In Turkey, fathers are responsible for father involvement in schools. Moreover, all of them added that effective father involvement could be possible if only fathers would be eager to participate. They emphasize that just the teacher and school effort cannot make this process successful.

Diversity in Fathers. A few Turkish and American teachers claim that involvement levels differ from father to father. In the two contexts, there are fathers who are engaged in school and communicate with teachers more, especially when compared to other fathers.

Under the category of fathers' motives of involvement, two different themes emerged for Turkish and American teachers.

Essential Communication. Turkish teachers claimed that fathers mostly communicate with them when it is "necessary" such as in regard to health problems, discipline problems, and financial issues. This situation is evident also in the results of the communication logs for Turkish fathers.

Volunteering. American teachers pointed out that fathers communicate with them and have a tendency to participate if they planned to engage in "fun" activities such as games at school, celebration of birthdays, field trips, and field days.

DISCUSSION

Although the sample size of this study is small and the sample is not generalizable to the broader Turkish and American population, the results are in line with previous research about father involvement from both Turkey and the United States. Moreover, the demographic information presented by participants reflects the general contexts in which the study was conducted, such as the inclusion of single fathers, stepfathers, and grandparents as the primary caregivers in the sample of American fathers. The fact that fathers' work hours was not a significant predictor of fathers' involvement levels in their children's lives is consistent with the recent research conducted in Turkey by Ünlü (2010). In the literature, the studies on the relationship between children's gender and father involvement levels are ambiguous. The present study found no statistically significant relationship between children's gender and their fathers' involvement levels both for Turkish and American fathers (in line with Coley & Morris, 2002; Evans, 1997; Ünlü, 2010). The results of the study found that the father involvement levels of Turkish fathers are lower than the American fathers. This might be because of the more traditional gender roles existing in Turkish culture or the slower process of the father involvement initiatives taking place in Turkey. In addition to these factors, as stated by Ünlü (2010), who completed the adaptation of the instrument to Turkish fathers for her own study, the nature of the scale developed in the United States may not allow culturally appropriate evaluations for father involvement in the context of Turkey. This possibility suggests a need for cross-cultural researchers to develop interviews with parents and teachers in Turkey and then to develop scales possibly more appropriately adapted to the cultural practices of Turkish fathers.

The claim of one American teacher that "Those who are involved in their children's lives at all are interested in their child's schooling" is an important result of this study. Fathers who had high scores on their father involvement inventory were those who had been involved in communication with teachers and involved in activities at kindergarten during the 1-month logging documentation. Focusing on the teacher-father partnership, it is logical to interpret that American fathers are more involved in school activities compared to Turkish fathers. When we analyze the Turkish teachers' answers, we see that the notion of involving fathers in schools is newly emerging. Turkish teachers and fathers are talking about the adaptation and adjustment processes of children to school, which is an expected result in this context since early childhood schooling is newly developing in Turkey.

Both Turkish and American teachers' answers show the lack of practical father involvement strategies in early childhood education. While American teachers claim that activities just for fathers could be effective, Turkish teachers argue that, because of the traditional gender roles in their context, it is not convenient for them as female teachers to conduct activities just for fathers.

The study reminds us of the requirement of new lenses for thinking about families and the diverse predictors affecting father-teacher partnership cross-culturally. Growth of single-parent families, due to the high level of separations and divorces, and changes in the fathers' traditional roles are evident in the study and suggest the need for an expanded conceptualization of family to include single fathers' and grandfathers' involvement in children's lives (Dantas & Manyak, 2010). As communicated by Turkish teachers, after the completion of the father involvement inventory, Turkish fathers reacted to the research by pointing out that schools are always targeting mothers. They claimed that a variety of activities, as they are asked about in the inventory, could be conducted with their children at home. In response to this perspective shared by fathers, one Turkish school decided to develop a father education program in the school after the study. These reactions of Turkish fathers and teachers to the research may indicate their readiness for a transformation stemming from global changes in paternal roles.

CREATING NEW ZONES FOR FATHERS

Low father involvement levels in both the United States and Turkish contexts render schools responsible to catch up to global changes and to generate local programs for fathers. The lack of practical father involvement strategies in Turkish and American teachers' answers implies the need for culturally sensitive teacher education programs that emphasize the importance of fathers. To illustrate, in some settings in Turkey, rather than just targeting fathers, teachers should work on effective involvement activities targeted for mothers and fathers. However, low father involvement can also be used as an opportunity, as illustrated by a story of a Turkish teacher. In class, they had just one father involved in class activities. During this time, the father engaged in caring for children, helping them to eat and get dressed. In this school, the availability of one father who engaged in traditionally cross-gender roles is becoming a role model for children and parents. He is helping to change the notion of traditional gender roles in the context of Turkey.

Drawing on the notion of creating zones of possibilities (Moll & Greenberg, 1990), most importantly, creating new zones for fathers in the early childhood settings could only be possible through social sharing of knowledge between schools and fathers. The answer to what might be effective father involvement strategies lies within the ideas of fathers who have unique personal histories, values, and family dynamics. Personal household histories of male primary caregivers such as fathers, stepfathers, single fathers, or grandfathers across cultures should be communicated with teachers for development of effective father involvement practices both in school and in children's lives. The exchange of funds of knowledge may open a path to teachers to involve fathers through their own meaningful involvement types, which could be as a storyteller, cook, musician, scientist, handyman in class, or a participant in the activities that extend beyond the classroom and into the home.

At the same time as educators were taking a context-specific, local "funds of knowledge" approach to engaging fathers, they could examine, along with parents, national and innovative initiatives for involving fathers such as were discussed in our initial review of literature. They should consider the implications of this approach for local application in particular schools and communities. For example, Father Education Seminars, such as those implemented by Guidance and Psychological Research Center in traditional coffeehouses in Turkey, could be adapted and used by groups of teachers and fathers in early childhood settings in different communities. In the southeastern U.S. context, Waffle House–type diners would be a parallel setting that might provide a comfortable context for fathers and grandfathers involved as caregivers to have breakfast conversations with teachers and administrators about educational roles that fathers might play at home and at school. National and local fatherhood initiatives such as those targeted at incarcerated fathers and low-income noncustodial fathers would be valuable examples for early childhood educators in some U.S. contexts to examine for application in their settings, as many communities have significant numbers of families demonstrating these trends. In the Turkish context, initiatives targeting fathers absent due to work abroad (e.g., What is in Germany, Dad? by CihanBeyli National Education Directorate project awarded by The Scientific and Technological Research Council of Turkey), or in distant regions of Turkey might draw on these and other U.S. initiatives focused on parents in the armed forces (e.g., Attorney General of Texas', 2011 HEROES: Help Establishing Responsive Orders and Ensuring Support for Children in Military Families Program; Sesame Workshop for Military Parents, 2010) for inspiration.

The kinds of volunteering activities that U.S. teachers identified as engaging a number of fathers seems a promising direction for educators in many contexts from Turkey to the southeastern United States to consider as ways to welcome fathers at school and then build opportunities for learning together with teachers and children. If educators and fathers in many schools begin to actively seek resources and opportunities for creatively reaching out to fathers such as those outlined above, children around the world could have a caring, involved paternal presence in schools and in their lives, fathers could enjoy their school involvement and their intimate, reciprocal attachment to their children, and mothers, whose work status is similar to fathers in the 21st century, could be empowered by sharing the responsibility for their growing child.

REFERENCES

Attorney General of Texas. (2011). HEROS: Help Establishing Responsive Orders and Ensuring Support for Children in Military Families. Retrieved from https://www.oag.state.tx.us/cs/ofi/index.shtml#heroes

Aydın, A. (2003). *The effect of father involvement training on the fathers' involvement level and perceptions of their fathering roles.* Unpublished master's thesis, Middle East Technical University, Ankara: Turkey.

Berger, E. H. (1998). Don't shut fathers out. *Early Childhood Education Journal 26*, 57-61.

Boeije, H. (2002). A purposeful approach to the constant-comparative method in the analysis of qualitative interviews. *Quality & Quantity, 36*, 391-409.

Çelik, S. B. (2007). Family function levels of Turkish fathers with children aged between 0-6. *Social Behavior and Personality: An International Journal, 35*(4), 429-442.

Charmaz, K. C. (2006). *Constructing grounded theory: A practical guide through qualitative analysis.* Thousand Oaks, CA: SAGE.

Coley, R. L., & Morris, J. E. (2002). Comparing father and mother reports of father involvement among low?income minority families. *Journal of Marriage and Family, 64*(4), 982-997.

Dantas, M. L., & Manyak, P. C. (2010). *Home-school connections in a multicultural society: Learning from and with culturally and linguistically diverse families.* New York, NY: Taylor & Francis.

Erdiller, Z. B., & McMullen, M. B. (2003). Turkish teachers' beliefs about developmentally appropriate practices in early childhood education. *Hacettepe University Journal of Education, 25*, 84-93.

Evans, C. (1997). *Turkish fathers' attitudes to and involvement in their fathering role: A low socio-economic sample* (Unpublished master's thesis). Boğaziçi University, Istanbul, Turkey.

Fagan, J., & Palm, G. (2004). *Fathers and early childhood programs.* Clifton, Park, NY: Thomson Delmar Learning Press.

Fromberg, D. P. (2006). Kindergarten education and early childhood teacher education in the United States: Status at the start of the 21st century. *Journal of Early Childhood Teacher Education, 27*, 65-85.

Gutierrez, K. D., & Rogoff, B. (2003). Cultural ways of learning: Individual traits or repertories of practice. *Educational Researcher, 32*(5), 19-25.

Gursimsek, I., Kefi, S., & Girgin, G. (2007). Investigation of variables related with father involvement in early childhood education. *Hacettepe University Journal of Education, 33*, 141-153.

Hawkins, A. J., Bradford, K. P., Palkovitz, R., Christiansen, S. L., Day, R. D., & Call, V. R. A. (2002). The inventory of father involvement: A pilot study of a new measure of father involvement. *The Journal of Men's Studies, 10*(2), 183-196.

International Human Development Index. (2011). Country profiles and international human development indicators. Retrieved from http://hdr.undp.org/en/data/profiles/

Ivrendi, A., & Isikoglu, N. (2010). A Turkish view on fathers' involvement in children's play. *Early Childhood Education Journal, 37*, 519-526.

Kagitcibasi C. (1996). *Family and human development across cultures: A view from the other side.* Mahwah, NJ: Psychology Press.

Kagitcibasi, C., & Ataca, B. (2005). Value of children and family change: A three?decade portrait from Turkey. *Applied Psychology, 54*(3), 317-337.

Kocayoruk, E., & Sumer, Z. H. (2009). The effects of father involvement training on family functioning and adolescents' peer relations. *Journal of Theory and Practice in Education, 5*(1), 3-17.

McBride, B. A., & Rane, T. R. (1997). Father/male involvement in early childhood education programs: Issues and challenges. *Early Childhood Education Journal, 25*, 11-15.

McMullen, M., Elicker, J., Wang, J., Erdiller, Z., Lee, S-M., Lin, C-H., & Sun, P-Y. (2005). Comparing beliefs about appropriate practice among early childhood education and care professionals from the U.S., China, Taiwan, Korea and Turkey. *Early Childhood Research Quarterly, 20*(4), 451-464.

Moll, L., Amanti, C., & Gonzales, N. (2005). *Funds-of-knowledge: Theorizing practices in households and classrooms.* Mahwah, NJ: Erlbaum.

Moll, L. C., & Greenberg, J. B. (1990). Creating zones of possibilities: Combining social contexts for instruction. In L. Moll (Ed.), *Vygotsky and education: Instructional implications and applications of sociocultural psychology* (pp. 319-348). Cambridge, MA: Cambridge University Press.

National Fatherhood Initiative. (2010). Retrieved January 5, 2012, from http://www.fatherhood.org/organizations/programs/father-source

Office, American Community Survey. (2009). Retrieved from http://www.census.gov/acs/www/

Office, CihanBeyli National Education Directorate. (n.d.). What's in Germany, Dad? Project. Retrieved from http://cihanbeyli.meb.gov.tr/proje.html

Office, Ministry of National Education of Turkey. (2011). National education statistics. Retrieved from http://www.meb.gov.tr/english/indexeng.htm

Office, Turkish Statistical Institute. (2010). Retrieved from http://www.tuik.gov.tr

Öğüt, Ü. (1998). *Father involvement with respect to the age and gender of preschool children and the employment status of the mother in a sample of upper and middle socioeconomic status Turkish fathers* (Unpublished master's thesis). Boğaziçi University, Istanbul, Turkey.

Palm, G., & Fagan, J. (2008). Father involvement in early childhood programs: Review of the literature. *Early Child Development and Care, 178,* 745-759.

Pedhazur, E. (1997). *Multiple regression in behavioral research: Explanation and prediction.* Orlando, FL: Harcout Brace.

Pleck, J. H. (1997). Paternal involvement: Levels, sources and consequences. In M. E. Lamb (Ed.), *The role of the father in child development* (3rd ed., pp.66-104). New York, NY: Wiley.

Rimm-Kauffman, S. E., & Zhang, Y. (2005). Father-school communication in preschool & kindergarten. *School Psychology Review, 34,* 287-308.

Sesame Workshop (2010). Talk, listen, connect: Helping military families during difficult transitions. Retrieved from http://www.sesameworkshop.org/initiatives/emotion/tlc/deployments

Smith, M., & Morote, E. S. (2011). *Perceptions of parenting practices of incarcerated fathers who have received parent training and those who have not in a federal prison in a Northeastern urban community in the USA.* Paper presented at the biennial meeting of the European Research Network About Parents in Education, Milano, Italy.

United States Department of Health and Human Services. (2011). Father involvement in Head Start and Early Head Start. Retrieved from http://fatherhood.hhs.gov/Parenting/hs.shtml

U.S. Census Bureau. (2009). Statistical abstract main page. Retrieved from http://www.census.gov/compendia/statab

Ünlü, S. (2010). *Being fathered and being a father: Examination of the general pattern of Turkish fathers' and their own fathers' involvement level for children between the ages of 0-8* (Unpublished master's thesis). Middle East Technical University, Ankara, Turkey.

CHAPTER 7

FATHER AND PARENT INVOLVEMENT ACROSS AFRICA

A Time of Transition

Diana B. Hiatt-Michael, G. Ugo Nwokeji, and Cheri Scripter

VALUE OF EDUCATION AS A PASSAGE TO A BETTER LIFE

An Afar boy, age 9, living in rural northeastern Ethiopia, traveled with his father to the city to purchase a new camel. The boy had not attended school because, as most sons in his area, he was expected to assist with herding and family work. In order to legalize the purchase of the camel, the father had to pay a scribe to record the transaction. Impressed by the transaction, the son asked why did his father pay the scribe. "He has learned to read and write," replied his father. The son did not get paid for his labor at home and, thus, asked his father if he might study to become a scribe. That day, his father made arrangements for his son to stay with a relative in the town in order to learn to read and write. The father expressed pleasure at his son's interest. This young man rewarded his father, securing a top ranking in his class and, thus, received scholarships for high school and college. (E9, Hiatt-Michael, 2012)

Promising Practices for Fathers' Involvement in Children's Education
pp. 113–127

This remarkable life story from a high poverty country describes African fathers' highest hopes for their children. Although sons receive preference if choices need to be made, African fathers generally value education for sons and daughters. African fathers desire that their children should lead a better life and perceive education, especially education in a boarding or mixed-ethnicity school, as the road to that better life (Consortium for Research on Education, Access Transition & Equity, 2011; Hiatt-Michael, 2005; 2012). In Enkorika, Kenya, a young father moved his family to the city so his four children would receive an education and a better life. He worked any job, heartened that his children were attending school (E7, Hiatt-Michael, 2012). A Uganda parent in rural area shared "I want an education for my children. That is the only way he can lead a better life. I walk to work so that I can pay school fees" (E6, Hiatt-Michael, 2012).

During February and March, 2012, the primary author conducted in-depth interviews with 13 educators from eight different African countries (Hiatt-Michael, 2012). These educators were selected because they possessed a doctorate or masters degree and represented firsthand knowledge of diverse sections of Africa—namely Ghana, Uganda, Nigeria, Namibia, South Africa, Kenya, Ethiopia, and Egypt. These interviewees are identified throughout the chapter as E1–E13. The interviewees responded to four open-ended questions with a series of prompts. The first question addressed their overall perceptions of father involvement in Africa, followed by questions that focused on concepts of responsibility, accessibility, and engagement as related to African fathers (Cabrera, Tamis-LeMonda, Bradley, Hofferth, & Lamb, 2000). The transcribed interviews were qualitatively analyzed by trained coders. The findings are presented as supporting evidence throughout this chapter. This data offered insights into particular ways that fathers are involved in their children's education within recent and contemporary Africa.

These in-depth interviews with educators across Africa revealed the high importance placed on education by fathers, as well as mothers, as a passport to a better life than the one experienced by their parents. All respondents shared that African fathers' first responsibility is to feed the family and, secondly, to educate the children. Five respondents specifically remarked how this high value on education resulted in fathers' willingness to walk to work, take two jobs, or do without personal conveniences. Two other respondents noted that, in order to pay for their child's education, fathers sell clothes, jewelry, and even family land. Three respondents remarked how a father's dedication to education extends to fathers who may move to distant cities or to other countries. Two respondents described how various associations of African groups in America help support education in their native African town. These groups send funds to renovate school buildings, pay for schools fees and scholarships for children, new libraries, and educational activities.

Interviewees indicated that fathers who are present in the home tend to assume the dominant role and be the family member that is the director of the family. They shared the perception of wa Thiong'o (2010) who described African fathers as a strong, more emotionally distant figure. E11 (Hiatt-Michael, 2012) recalled that:

> My father provided for our schooling and expected us to go to school. He was a disciplinary figure who gave us praise very rarely. However, when I did well at school he presented me with a radio or camera, something very special. My mother took care of problems at the elementary, level but, at the high school level, my father handled such matters.

African fathers serve as invaluable resources for social skills and networking. E1 (Hiatt-Michael, 2012) explained that:

> Fathers in Ghana educate their boys in the ways to deal with others. My father taught me the way a man behaves in a social situation, such as a man must dine with his colleagues before he begins talks about serious affairs or business. He introduced me to people who could help me in school. Other fathers would do the same.

E3 (Hiatt-Michael, 2012) informs that: "Fathers expect their children to be polite. My father knew the local people. If I needed something, such as at school, he told me how to do it and what to say."

Five interviewees, those involved in rural areas of Africa, noted that in rural two-parent families, fathers tended to be more accessible to their sons than daughters. The fathers spent time teaching trades or aspects of the traditions and culture. Mothers tended to be more accessible to their daughters because they were sharing chores and other activities. However, an African female educator from an economically advantaged urban home in Nigeria, E10 shared her perception about her accessibility to her father:

> My father was at work most of the day. At night he might ask about my schooling like how I was doing. My mother took care of homework supervision and meeting with teachers. To my father, my ranking in school was very important. Students are ranked from highest to lowest in every school. Fathers boasted to others about their children's ranking. If I ranked high, my father reminded me that I would get a scholarship and I could attend a university. If I did less than he expected, I did not receive a Christmas or a birthday present.

The interview data offered insights into particular ways that fathers engage in their children's education within contemporary Africa. As previously noted, the working father assumes the strong, seemingly distant, authority role. One interviewee described that the mother supervises homework but she relies on the words "your father will expect it to be done when he [your father] gets home" to motivate the child to quickly complete the homework (E2, Hiatt-Michael, 2012). In addition to homework, the data supported that the fathers share their expectations for the future careers of their sons and daughters. For example, the father is the family member that establishes higher education and career expectations. To elaborate, E12 (Hiatt-Michael, 2012) commented, "My father encouraged me [a daughter] to obtain a masters' degree and attend the university in America, not my mother. She would have been happy to have me attend college and get married in Egypt."

In Africa, cars are considered a luxury and bus fare is less important than paying for a child's schooling (E5, Hiatt-Michael, 2012). Fathers walk to their place of employment because they prefer to spend their earnings on a child's education than bus fare. These fathers, who could otherwise afford bus fare or some personal items, express their engagement in their children's schooling by walking to work or doing without personal comforts. In this daily action, these fathers express their commitment to their children's education. Children witness what their parents must do in order to send them to school. As children observe their fathers' commitment to their ability to attend school, African children acquire a deep understanding of their fathers' strong expectations for education and their academic achievement.

TRADITIONAL ROLE OF AFRICAN FATHERS

Although Africa is diverse in geography, ethnicities, and European colonial experience, common themes emerged from these interviews with educators as representatives of different African areas as well as the literature (Hiatt-Michael, 2012). While we do not subscribe to Diop's (1989) idea of a cultural unity, there are enough similarities among the cultures of Sub-Sahara Africa to warrant at least qualified generalizations. To understand the role of fathers in Africa, comment must be made regarding heritage, patriarchy, and councils of elders. Across Africa, countries are comprised of various ethnic groups. The basis of African society is a long history of belongingness to a clan (B. Annan, personal communication, February 22, 2012; D. Anajemba, personal communication, February 20, 2012; N. Asika, 1984, personal communication, June, 2001; Colley, 2005; Diop, 1989; Hiatt-Michael, 2012; Scanlon, 1964). These ethnic groups are generally patriarchal with councils of elders that guide and support the extended family life of the group. These councils maintain the cultural ethos of each group, supporting all members; their goal is to care for every member. If a child is orphaned, family members are expected to take care of the orphaned child (Madhavan, Townsend, & Garey, 2008). A Uganda father (E10, Hiatt-Michael, 2012) shared that "My older brother died and I became responsible for my sister-in-law and her children. I call her my 'stepwife' and her children 'our children' although they live in another city." This father financially provides for the education of his dead brother's children. If families live apart from one another, they are expected to travel great distances to attend fathers meetings (E2 & E3, Hiatt-Michael, 2012). Even if Africans move to another country, fathers, as well as mothers, continue a sense of the clan (E1, Hiatt-Michael, 2012). They return to visit and to be buried in their family's native town.

In the traditional African family, the fathers assumed a primary role in their child's education, especially that of the boys (Scanlon, 1964; Venter, 2012). The father's task was to educate his son to assume all his responsibilities as an adult within the family, the village and his clan (Hipple, 2008). Fathers, following the elders' wise council, educated and inducted their sons into adulthood through their support of the clan's values, rules, rewards, and punishments. Many ethnic groups had a formal ritual for induction into adulthood, such as the Maasai's Enkipaat (precircumcision ceremony) and Emuratare (circumcision ceremony) (Maasai Association, 2012).

The African father's, as well as mother's, approach to teaching is the oral tradition (Hipple, 2008; Smith, 1940). Adhering to this oral tradition of teaching, the African father has the responsibility to pass on cultural values and norms, knowledge of the environment, and trade skills (all respondents, Hiatt-Michael, 2012). Marah (2006) indicates that oral teaching may assume many forms of instruction such as stories, tales, songs, and demonstration. For example, in rural Uganda, E6 shared that a father would tell his children stories that would help sharpen their minds. "He told me a couple of them that he remembered. They were like fables that taught a lesson and had a riddle component to them, so you would have to think to figure out the answer" (E6, Hiatt-Michael, 2012).

Researchers have supported the strong role of the African father in the emotional and social education of their children (Hewlitt, 1991; Hewlett & Lamb, 2005). Hewlitt has studied the Aka pygmies for many years, hunter-gatherers in the Central African Republic. Among the Akas, fathers were observed to be the primary source of emotional support to their infant, devoting 47% of their day either holding or attending to their infant children. Describing his role as a father, one Aka man explained, "We, Aka look after our children with love from the minute they are born to when they are much older.... With us, even if the child is older, if he is unhappy, I'll look after him, I will cuddle him" (Hewlitt, 1991, pp. 93-94).

Hewlitt and Lamb (2005) conclude that the nature of the hunter-gatherer social work interaction between mothers and fathers fostered the most intimate relationships between parents. Parents' caring social/emotional interactions provided their offspring with the opportunity to develop in a supportive and caring environment The authors note that the Efe in Uganda and other hunter-gatherers had similar frequent father-child relationships as the Akas throughout the day and throughout the child's upbringing. Konner (2010) connects such strong father support to significant development of these children's emotional brains and to the positive emotional development of children across their childhood. His reasoning suggests that African fathers played a major role in their emotional development and educational goals that relate to social/emotional development. As the foregoing suggests, African fathers' involvement in the education of their children, particularly sons, though changing, has remained strong over time.

TRANSITION FROM FATHERS' ROLE IN TRADITIONAL EDUCATION TO THEIR EMERGING ROLE IN SCHOOLS

Missionaries and later European colonial governments introduced the school and the importance of Western education to the education of children (Gallego & Woodbury, 2010). These groups placed increased emphasis on the importance of school and education to develop children's skills for a different way of thinking and new careers. The press for children to attend school is altering the role of the African father as primary educator (Hiatt-Michael, 2012; Hipple, 2008). Adding to this change is the migration of African families from rural areas to urban ones (United Nations Children's Fund [UNICEF], 2011). This immigration is occurring because of famine and poverty in rural areas and increasing development of industrial, service and telecommunication position in growing urban areas (Bigombe & Khadiagala, 2004).

In Kenya's Enkorika village, fathers needed their sons and daughters to assist in family support and work on their land and homes (E7, Hiatt-Michael, 2012). Because of this family need, the fathers sent no one to school. However, the local chief, assumed the role of "truant" officer and met with each father. He negotiated with each family which child should attend school. This chief believed that at least one member of every family should go to school and become educated. He informed the fathers that the children would support the family after the children completed schooling. His goal was that the selected children would share the benefits of schooling with other siblings and then more children would attend school.

From serving as the child's primary educator, especially for sons, African fathers' role in education is altered in the process of rural to urban social change. The father departs the household for work in another location and the children remain at home. If a child is to be educated, either the mother or other family members assumes the responsibility or the family considers sending one or more children to a government or private school. Thus, the role of the urban African father has changed from the primary educational authority to the family member whose primary role is to provide for the financial support for the children's education (Quarcoo, 2008).

In most places, African schooling has been fee based (Education and Training Unit for Democracy and Development, 2012). Thus, fathers—and/or mothers if the father is unavailable, uninterested or otherwise indisposed—are responsible to pay for his children's schooling costs, costs that the government imposes. Parents' costs for government or private schools include fees or tuition, student uniforms, books and school supplies. These school supplies include classroom needs such as the teacher's chalk and other items for instruction. In poverty areas, such educational costs often consume 25% of a family's income (UNICEF, 2012). Global efforts are underway to help abolish primary school tuition fees throughout Africa; however, the cost of schooling is still prohibitive for millions of children and their families (Selby, 2005; World Bank, 2009). Additionally, schools that are tuition free usually require students to pay for compulsory uniforms, textbooks, and other miscellaneous classroom fees (El, Hiatt-Michael, 2012).

Consequently, many parents do not have sufficient family income to send any child or only one child to school. Thus, many children across African nations are not enrolled in school. UNICEF (2010b) reports that over 44 million children in Africa are not enrolled in school, either in primary or secondary education programs. The lowest rates of primary school participation are in poverty areas of sub-Saharan Africa, in which the United Nations reports that only 65% of primary-school-aged children are enrolled in school (UNICEF, 2010b, p. 18). As a representative example, UNICEF (2009) cites The Republic of Niger—a western Africa country. In Niger, 54% children enroll in a primary school and, of those that enroll, only 67% of these children continue to the final level of primary school. At the secondary level, 13% of the boys are enrolled compared to 8% of the girls. This gender difference in school enrollment exists at both the primary and secondary levels and across Africa (UNICEF, 2010b). Furthermore, UNICEF (2010b) indicates that children in rural areas are less likely to be enrolled in school than those in urban areas; children from the poorest households are far more likely to be out of school than those whose parents possess greater financial resources.

In sub-Saharan Africa, fathers who are either unavailable or unemployed are often unable to send their children to school. A high school student in Namibia explains:

> "The thing that my father isn't with me ... is affecting me badly ... because this is the time that I need him more than ever, 'cause of my examination fees." A teenage boy in the same study remarked, "My problem is I do not have a father because I only saw him when I was 8 and he gave me [$300]....
> If he was here I would have gone to school and everyday I would have something to eat and not have stayed in the streets." (UNICEF, 2010a, pp. 41-42)

African children whose father is not known or absent have the least opportunity for any education. Responding to the importance that African men record their names on a child's birth certificate, Davies (2008) refers to comments by Kudzai Makombe from the UN Development Fund for Women:

> Emotional, along with financial support is vital.... It's not just about the cash. If the child loses contact with the father it also loses all the social capital and networks that the father has available to help the child develop ...
> [i.e.] education contact. The value of these is inestimable.... Many men can play the role of father to a child [and assume] financial responsibility to care for children.

Some parts of Africa, namely the east and north, including the northern rural areas of Ghana and Nigeria are Muslim (E1, E7, & E8, Hiatt-Michael, 2012). School attendance is lowest in these areas. Fathers express concern that their children will not receive teaching from the Muslim faith but from the Christian faith. These fathers are reluctant to send their children to government schools. For example, Kenyan teachers in the bush schools may teach stories from the Christian Bible (E7, Hiatt-Michael, 2012).

Several African countries are working toward a support for school fees so that primary education is public (World Bank, 2009). Reduced fees have increased attendance in Ghana (UNICEF, 2007). In 2007, South Africa passed a no fee exemption policy to assist fathers in high poverty areas, approximately 40% of the populations (Consortium for Research on Education, Access Transition & Equity, 2009). Since the 1950s, the central and regional governments of Nigeria have gone back and forth in the provision for tuition-free elementary education. Many states in the south of the country, including all in the oil-rich Niger Delta, have within the last 8 years or so resumed offering free tuition for elementary-level state schools. This free tuition supports parents, such as fathers who cannot pay fees for their children to attend school (E2, E13, Hiatt-

Michael, 2012). However, in South Africa the school determines which families are considered low income and which children may qualify for a grant for tuition. Local politics may determine which fathers receive the no-fee exemption, as funds are limited (E13, Hiatt-Michael, 2012). In Nigeria, many schools have entrance tests, and fathers can assist their children so that their children score high on these tests and obtain scholarships (E3, Hiatt-Michael, 2012).

AFRICAN SOCIAL PROBLEMS AFFECTING FATHERS' ROLE IN SCHOOLING

Across Africa, millions of children do not have father engagement in their education. These are the orphans, living on the streets or in orphanages. These children have become orphans because of loss of parents due to AIDS, HIV, famine, or war (Hoeffler, 2008; Queiroz, 2006). The HIV/AIDS epidemic dramatically increased the numbers of children without surviving parents in Africa, the major cause of children without fathers (AVERT, 2010). This situation is stronger in sub-Saharan areas with South Africa experiencing the highest numbers of orphans created by HIV/AIDS related parent deaths (Organization for Economic Co-Operation and Development, 2012; United States of America International Development, 2011).

These children are missing connections to an extended family or the area is so poor that no male adult is able to assume their care. They may roam the streets such as in Cairo, Egypt, or be placed in an orphanage in Uganda (Fleishman, 2011; Orphanage.org, 2012). Orphanages are usually directed by females because women are expected by the culture to be the primary caretakers of the children, leaving these orphaned children without male interaction and father figures (E6 & E10, Hiatt-Michael, 2012).

Because in parts of Africa, fathers and father figures are absent due to the HIV/AIDS epidemic, community groups like the *African Fathers Initiative* are urging schools to teach safe sex and prepare students to care for younger siblings, ill family members and older relatives. The community-built African Fathers Initiative (2012) starts with the endorsement "for every African child—a committed and responsible father." Mentoring programs also encourage African men to "become more intentional about reaching into their communities to guide children in need."

PARENT PARTICIPATION AND EQUAL ACCESS TO SCHOOLING IN RURAL AND URBAN SOUTH AFRICA

A research study, completed in 2008 in rural South Africa, revealed that for 272 children, 76% received paternal support at some point in their life, 62% had received support for more than half their life, and 41% for their whole life (Madhavan et al, 2008). Furthermore, 24% had never received any support from their fathers and, of those, 13% had never had any connection with their fathers, and only 7% always had some connection to their fathers but had never received any paternal support from them. Factors that limited father involvement included unemployment, migratory work patterns, and cultural norms.

Consortium for Research on Education, Access Transition & Equity (2011) studied parents participation and meaningful access to schools in South Africa. This study focused on concerns that promote "silent exclusion" of children from schooling and equitability of education between rural and urban areas. Two diverse sites for their study—the rural area of Dutywa in Eastern Cape and the urbanized, industrial area of Ekurhuleni South district of Gauteng were selected as sample areas to compare the same factors. School records noted that in Dutywa 20% of the children live with both parents, and 41% with mother or father. In Ekuruleni, 44% live with two parents and 31% live with father or mother. Others live in a sibling head of household or part of an extended family with an adult. In Dutywa, 24% of parents were employed compared to 57% in Ekurhuleni. Most parents in both regions had a grade 10 or lower level of education attainment.

Researchers administered a questionnaire to 87 Dutywa parents and 108 Ekurhuleni parents, either dual or single family households. The sex of the reporting parent was not noted. The interesting finding was that 57% of Dutywa parents indicated that they supervised their children's homework every day compared to 43% of Ekurhuleni parents. Parents at both sites reported that chose their children's school on the basis of proximity, not quality. Although Dutywa parents referred to the local school as "theirs," meaning belonging to the community, only 50% of these parents felt satisfaction with the child's school. Almost 70% of Ekuhuleni South parents reported satisfaction with their child's school but called it by its name, considering the school as a government controlled, not a community, entity. Parents from both localities expressed concerns about high school fees, secondly the cost of uniforms. Parents at both sites value schools that teach English and ones that include White children.

Researchers in this study noted that parents must place feeding their children before education. The authors commented that: "Most Dutywa [Eastern Cape] parents tended to treat schooling as secondary to the daily struggle of existence, summed in the phrase 'You don't eat school'" (Consortium for Research on Education, Access Transition & Equity, 2011).

HOPE FOR THE FUTURE

Hooker (1975) solemnly noted "that one who possesses a diploma, can bargain, whereas those without certificates have no cards to play." In the case of contemporary Africa, that means that millions cannot compete in the local as well as the global economy. The current situation in Africa is changing from a primarily rural-based economy to an industrial/telecommunications based population. For example, in Nigeria four major industries have shifted the population from 94% rural living in rural areas in 1963 to 50% currently dwelling in urban centers (Asika, 1984; UNICEF, 2011). Across Africa, rural areas house from the low of 38% in South Africa to 83% in Ethiopia (United Nations Department of Economic and Social Affairs, 2011). The recent uprisings in northern African countries, famine in midcontinent sections, and HIV-AIDS in sub-Saharan Africa have affected children's access to fathers and father figures. In addition, the strong patriarchal culture has less influence on youth growing up as orphans or living in poverty in urban or rural areas.

The United Nations Children's Fund's (2012) second Millennial Developmental Goal (MDG) is that all children should achieve a primary education by 2015. This has become a daunting and seemingly unrealistic expectation in Africa as sub-Saharan Africa houses millions of children out of school. Inequality of education in many areas thwarts progress toward universal education. Father involvement and support of this goal is essential for its achievement. McCullum (2005) questions the possibility of that target date, suggesting that 2050 is a better target for most African countries. He argues that a realistic goal is essential so that every father's child "achieve the dignity and equality that Nelson Mandela so eloquently advocates and for the path away from poverty." In order to reach the second MGD, the West African nation of Ghana inaugurated a school feeding program at the primary school level and a fee-free policy providing direct funding to all public basic schools based on enrollment (Sabates, Akyeampong, Westbrook, & Hunt, 2010). This program assists fathers and other family heads to send their children to school and, thus, increase school attendance and reduce the number of school. This free-fee policy removes the parents' cost burden to enroll their children in school and attracts many children to enroll, including those who previously dropped out because of the high fees.

Hosegood and Madhavan (2010) suggest better data collection on father involvement in households and the role many men play as social fathers. They indicate that surveys should include more specific questions that focus on father involvement with children and the role males play to other children in the society at large. Because of the focus on maternal engagement in surveys, these researchers believe that the many activities that fathers and other males may perform for their children and other children in the society are not recognized.

The African Fathers Initiative (2012) is a bold and brave start toward engaging fathers in their children's education. This initiative is modeled after a United States of America initiative begun in later 1990s. The African group sponsors a comprehensive website that promotes information and activities regarding fathers that will connect associations, agencies, research groups, services, and governments in Africa. They noted that groups are working toward sponsoring father recognition events, similar to ones in America. For example, school children may write an essay to nominate their father for father of the year. In 2008, Fathers' Day was instituted and is celebrated annually. This group intends that their efforts will promote local activities to strengthen the connections between men and their children. The website announces policies and initiatives to encourage father-child relationships, especially regarding health and schooling.

An Internet search reveals numerous social agencies to assist school-age children and their families. World Food Program (2012) is supporting fortified lunches for school children and sending home rations to other family members. World Vision International (2012), founded in America in 1977, is an example that promotes schooling for African children. A contributor may adopt a child and assist a father by sending money for the child's schooling fees. In addition, young men can volunteer to serve as an intern, working in schools in Africa. A more recent group, begun in 2007, Building Schools for Africa (2012) has funded 37 schools. Room to Read (2012), founded in 2007, has worked with fathers in schools, families, and government to help build hundreds of libraries in South Africa and Zambia. This group is currently sponsoring "local language publishing" for indigenous stories that can be shared from father to child. These sample programs are conduits to support Africa fathers in their quest to assist their children to meet their 21st century educational aspirations.

REFERENCES

African Fathers Initiative. (2012). Retrieved from http://www.africanfathers.org

Asika, N. (1984). *A Delphi study of managers' identification of managerial competencies for management education in Nigerian universities* (Unpublished doctoral dissertation). Pepperdine University, Malibu, CA.

AVERT. (2010). *Worldwide HIV and AIDS statistics*. Retrieved from avert.org /worldstats.html

Bigombe, B., & Khadiagala, G. M. (2004). *Major trends affecting families in Sub-Saharan Africa*. Retrieved from http://www.un.org/esa/socdev/family /Publications/mtbigombe.pdf

Building Schools for Africa. (2012). *Building schools for Africa* Retrieved from http:/ /www.schoolsforafrica.co.uk/content/view/3/3/

Cabrera, N. J., Tamis-Lemonda, C. S., Bradley, R. H., Hofferth, S., & Lamb, M. (2000). Fatherhood in the Twenty-first century. *Child Development, 71*(1), 127-136.

Colley, B. (2005). Community and parental involvement in Gambia, West Africa. In D. B. Hiatt-Michael (Ed.), *Promising practices for family involvement in schooling across the continents* (pp. 31-42). Greenwich, CT: Information Age.

Consortium for Research on Education, Access Transition & Equity. (2009, August). *'No fee' schools in South Africa*. Retrieved from http://www.create-rpc .org/pdf_documents/Policy_Brief_7.pdf

Consortium for Research on Education, Access Transition & Equity. (2011, May). *Parental participation and meaningful access in South African schools*. Retrieved from www.create-rpc.org/pdf.../South_Africa_Policy_Brief_4.pdf

Davies, T. (2008). Re: Botswana: Campaign calls on fathers to register their names. Retrieved from http://allafrica.com/stories/200806170214.html

Diop, C. A. (1989). *The cultural unity of Black Africa*. London, England: Karnark House.

Education and Training Unit for Democracy and Development. (2012). *Education policy: School fees*. Retrieved from http://www.etu/org.za/toolbox/docs /government/schoolfees.html

Fleishman, J. (2011, November 27). For a boy on the streets of Cairo, revolution is his only hope. *Los Angeles Times*. Retrieved from http://articles.latimes.com/ 2011/nov/27/world/la-fg-egypt-homeless-boy-20111128

Gallego, F. S., & Woodberry, R. (2010). Christian missionaries and education in former African colonies: How competition mattered. *Journal of African Economies*. Retrieved from http://jae.oxfordjournals.org/content/

Hewlitt, B. S. (1991).*The nature and context of Aka Pygmy paternal infant care*. Ann Arbor, MI: University of Michigan Press.

Hewlitt, B. S., & Lamb, M. E. (Eds.). (2005). *Hunter-gatherer childhoods: Evolutionary, developmental and cultural*. New Brunswick, NJ: Transaction.

Hiatt-Michael, D. B. (Ed.). (2005). Global overview of family-school involvement. In *Promising practices for family involvement in schooling across the continents* (pp. 1-11). Greenwich, CT: Information Age.

Hiatt-Michael, D. B. (2012). [Interviews with African educators on father involvement]. Unpublished raw data. Pepperdine University, Malibu, CA.

Hipple, A. (2008). Coming of age rituals in Africa: Tradition and change. *Prudence International Magazine, 4*(1). Retrieved from http://www.annikahipple.com/ writing-samples/coming-of-age-rituals-in-africa-

Hoeffler, A. (2008). Dealing with the consequences of violent conflicts in Africa. Retrieved from tradition-change/Center for the Study of African Economies. Oxford University. http://users.ox.ac.uk

Hooker, J. R. (1975). *Henry Sylvester Williams: Imperial pan-Africanist*. London, England: Rex Collins.

Hosegood, V., & Madhavan, S. (2012). *Data availability on men's involvement in families in sub-Saharan Africa to inform family-centred programmes for children affected by HIV and AIDS*. Retrieved from http://www.jiasociety.org/content/13/S2/S5

Konner, M. J. (2010). *The evolution of fatherhood: Relationships, emotion, mind.* Cambridge, MA: The Belknap Press of Harvard University Press.

Maasai Association. (2012). Retrieved from http://www.maasai-association.org

Madhavan, S., Townsend, N. W., & Garey, A. (2008). Absent breadwinners': Father-child connections and paternal support in rural South Africa. *Journal of Southern African Studies, 34*(3), 647-663.

Marah, J. K. (2006, June). The virtues and challenges in traditional African education. *The Journal of Pan African Studies, 1*(4), 5-25.

McCullum, H. (2005) *Education in Africa: Colonialism and the millennium developmental goals.* Retrieved from http://www.newsfromafrica.org/newsfromafrica /articles/art_9909.html

Organization for Economic Co-Operation and Development. (2012). *African outlook 2010.* Retrieved from http://www.un.org/esa/dsd/resources/res_pdfs /publications/sdt_afri/AEO2010_part1_p76.pdf

Orphanage.org. (2012). *Free links and websites for orphans.* Retrieved from http:// www.orphanage.org/#africa/

Quarcoo, T. (2008). Ghana: The father in contemporary Ghanian household. *African Fathers Initiative.* Retrieved from http://www.africanfathers.org

Queiroz, M. D. (2006, December 13). A continent of orphans. *Inter Press Service News Agency.* Retrieved from http://ipsnews.net/news.asp?idnews=35827

Room to Read. (2102). *Fostering a habit of reading, one library at a time.* Retrieved from http://www.roomtoread.org/page.aspx?pid=462

Sabates, R., Akyeampong, K., Westbrook, J., & Hunt, F. (2010). *School drop out: Patterns, causes, changes and policies.* Retrieved from http://unesdoc.unesco.org/ images/0019/001907/190771e.pdf

Scanlon, D. (1964). *Traditions in African education.* New York, NY: Teachers College Press: Columbia University.

Selby, K. (2005). South Africa education: The growing impact of parental choice. In D. B. Hiatt-Michael (Ed.), *Promising practices for family involvement in schooling across the continents* (pp. 43-50). Greenwich, CT: Information Age.

Smith, E. W. (1940). The function of folk-tales. *Journal of the African Royal Society, 36*(C), 64-83.

United Nations Children's Fund. (2007). *Achieving universal primary education in Ghana by 2015: A reality or dream?* Retrieved from http://www.unicef.org /videoaudio/PDFs/Achieving_Universal_Primary_Education_in_Ghana_by _2015.pdf

United Nations Children's Fund. (2009). *At a glance: Niger.* Retrieved from http:// www.unicef.org/infobycountry/niger_statistics.html

United Nations Children's Fund. (2010a). *Children and adolescents in Namibia.* Retrieved from www.unicef.org/sitan/files/SitAn_Namibia_2010.pdf

United Nations Children's Fund. (2010b). *Progress for children: Achieving the MGDs with equity.* Retrieved from http://www.unicef.org/protection/Progress_for_ Children-No.9_EN_081710.pdf

United Nations Children's Fund. (2011). *Adolescents, youth and international migration: Figures and facts.* Retrieved from www.unicef.org/socialpolicy/index _43139.html

United Nations Children's Fund. (2012). *The state of the world's children 2012: Children in an urban world—Key fats*. Retrieved from http://www.unicef.org/ceecis/media 19314.html

United Nations Department of Economic and Social Affairs. (2011). *World Urbanization Prospects*. Retrieved from http://esa.un.org/unpd/wup/unup/index.asp?panel=1

United States of America International Development. (2011). *HIV/AIDS health profile: Sub-Saharan Africa*. Retrieved from http://www.usaid.gov/our_work/global_health/aids/Countries/africa/hiv_summary_africa.pdf

Venter, N. V. L. (2012). The need for unique parental involvement programmes in rural multi-grade schools in South Africa: Principals views and opinions. In M. Pieri, A. Pepe, & L. Addimando (Eds.), *Home, school and community: A partnership for a happy life?* (pp. 121-122). Milan, Italy: EMIL.

wa Thiong'o, N. (2012). *Dreams in a time of war: A childhood memoir*. New York, NY: Pantheon Books.

World Bank. (2009). *Abolishing school fees in Africa: Lessons from Ethiopia, Ghana, Kenya, Malawi, and Mozambique*. Retrieved from http://www.unicef.org/publications/files/Aboloshing_School_Fees_in_Africa.pdf

World Food Programme. (2012). *School meals*. Retrieved from www.wfp.org/school-Meals

World Vision International. (2012). *Our work*. Retrieved from http://www.worldvision.org/our-work/international-work?lpos=top_drp_OurWork_International

CHAPTER 8

EDUCATION
AND FATHERHOOD
IN ARGENTINA

Ana Inés Heras

PATRIARCHAL AND GENDER-BALANCED PERSPECTIVES
IN LATIN AMERICA: A DYNAMIC TENSION

Scholars have documented that Latin American countries have been, and
still are, patriarchal societies (Jelin, 2005; Olavarría, 2003; Rivera & Ceciliano, 2004). Jelin (2005), for example, noted that the

> father (*pater familiae*) used to have the right to decide over his family mem-
> bers' lives. It was the father who must be obeyed, and later in life [for mar-
> ried women], the husband. Women were not considered full citizens, nor
> did they have any legal independence, and they were instead defined as
> dependent and in need of tutelage and therefore, incapable of conducting
> public activities on their own. (p. 6, author's translation)

In contemporary Argentina, different layers of context shape educational practices and fathers' involvement in their child's education. Historical normative frameworks, face-to-face daily interactions, organization
of household chores, and present public policy are among the most
important ones. These contexts need to be understood before any educa-

Promising Practices for Fathers' Involvement in Children's Education
pp. 129–145

tional reform regarding father involvement in education can be implemented. Bogino Larrambebere's (2011) concept of *emergent* social practices is useful to compare fathers' new behavior with those that have been traditionally or historically accepted ways of doing things. This framework has been selected as a means to comment on recent change in the roles fathers seem willing to undertake.

This chapter will first examine fatherhood as a cultural practice within historically changing contexts by interrogating what kinds of meanings (social discourses, see Angenot, 1999) about male and female relationships have been at stake. Second, a summary of programs and research will identify emergent practices and discourses on fatherhood in present Argentina. Third, the results of two studies[1] will be presented in order to support the claim that fatherhood is a culturally oriented and situated practice that is subject to tension beyond the bounds of its definition. I will conclude by reflecting on the ways in which I see change in the roles of Argentine fathers as dynamic, specifically concerning the responsibilities of fathers in domestic duties, the education of children and gender inequities within the culture.

HISTORICAL CONTEXTS OF LATIN AMERICAN FATHERHOOD

Patriarchal practices, beliefs and orientations in Latin America originally related to Catholic norms and expectations (Faur, 2004, 2006; Jelin, 2005), a result of Spain's and Portugal's colonization of the continent. During several centuries (16th to mid 19th), religion and tradition were the normative frames at play. Both provided discretional power to specific groups (Halperin Donghi, 1972, 1980; Widuczynski, 1992). It was during the mid 19th century that civil law gained place in Latin America, and these laws supported differential power relations between the two sexes. Thus, the legal framework as well as customary cultural practices and discourses, continued to support a patriarchal view. A male-oriented, authoritarian perspective, by which nondemocratic practices were accepted, continues as valid today.[2]

While predominant in Latin America, patriarchal ideologies and practices have been contested at different moments. In Argentina, at the time the National State was consolidated circa 1880, several political groups, such as anarchists, socialists and libertarians, openly challenged sexist practices (e.g., they supported both men and women in public political and community participation). Between 1890 and 1930, they publicly expressed their ideas about the capacity of men and women to access money, to work, to become fathers and mothers with equal rights, and to make informed decisions on public matters. In particular, they promoted different ways of being a family and of conceiving fatherhood and motherhood altogether (Suriano, 2001). These ideas also translated into the ways in which they viewed education, a practice not only restricted to school but to everyday interactions in the family and at the community level. These political groups also defined education as a tool for critically examining and transforming reality, not as a set of norms and values to be uncritically accepted, which defied the dominant discourse at that time. As a stance, this perspective clearly challenged what was accepted at the time.

These groups were active in participating at the community level by supporting alternative educational settings or by participating as members of parent associations in public schools (Carli, 1991). For example, the anarchist political position in Argentina was that the way in which women and men practiced day-to-day, face-to-face interactions was indeed a powerful educational experience for their children, and for that reason, some groups developed communal systems to organize everyday living responsibilities that included childcare, food, and health. Educational historians have identified that educational norms and regulations prescribed between 1880-1930 by the newly created Argentinean State established clearly what parents could or could not do in regard to schools and community-based educational settings. The interpretation they offer is that progressive, nonsexist perspectives were quite influential in Argentina (De Luca, 1991) and that groups in power wanted to limit their effect. As result, these orientations were crudely repressed in 1930 when a military regime took over, labeling them as *revolutionary and foreign*.[3]

During subsequent decades, authoritarian practices and discourses were held as hegemonic. They found their place in state-run official discourse once again. Thus, a traditional patriarchal view about family, parenthood, and what was considered *natural* for women and men, gained support. Nonetheless, several concurrent processes were at play, such as changes in the economy that included modifications in the work force (e.g., women entered the work force, generated income, and started to examine their role in society more fully). These innovations played an important part in a transformation that took place from 1930-1960 over education, parenting and family, and women's right to vote.

In reviewing the literature that summarizes other Latin American countries, similar patterns emerge (Batres, 2006; Camacho, 2005; Gargallo, 2004) yet it seems that there are some key aspects that distinguish Argentina. Fuller (2007) for example points out that for Argentina in particular, the extended presence of psychoanalysis after 1950 was key in opening up reflection on parenting and on "natural" ways of conceiving woman- and manhood, especially in regard to caretaking family practices, education and the expression of public affection.

Jelin (2005) has pointed out that concurrently there were several international laws, treaties and agreements to which the majority of Latin American countries adhered; these normative frameworks had the value of local law and in turn, challenged patriarchal ideologies. Such was the case for Argentina as well. To be highlighted as seemingly contradictory is the fact that the Argentinean State adhered to the Convention on the Elimination of All Forms of Discrimination against Women even during the military de facto regime (it was adopted in 1979 by the UN General Assembly[4]). Recent changes in public policies[5] (Faur, 2006; Programa Naciones Unidas para el Desarrollo, 2008, 2011), including marriage for people of the same sex (a law passed in July, 2010), provided additional questioning of what counts as *parenting* (mother and fatherhood) in 21st century Argentina.

As a corollary of what has been presented in this section, I argue that Argentina has historically been a terrain of contested ideological positions toward what counts as fatherhood, what is to be considered natural for women and men, and whether fathers should be involved in daily child-related activities at home or at school.

EMERGING SOCIAL PATTERNS REGARDING FATHERHOOD

In the last 2 decades a consistent pattern toward balancing women and men in the public and domestic spheres in Latin America has emerged, a pattern that has played out in favor of the engagement of fathers in their children's education (Bogino Larrambebere, 2011; Olavarría, 2003; Proyecto América Latina Genera, 2007). However, research is scarce documenting what counts as fatherhood and how it relates to day-to-day educational practices. What has been studied mostly focuses on curriculum change at schools in favor of nonsexist education or the participation of men in favor of gender-balanced educational, cultural and policy change at large.

As an example I present an examination of the compilation of recent conference papers, delivered at the historic 2011 Ibero American Conference on Masculinity and Equity: Research and Activism, held in Barcelona, Spain. The main goals of this conference were: to disseminate research on *masculinities* being conducted in Spain and Latin America; to analyze and debate public policy regarding the inclusion of men in pursuing gender equity; to establish links between research, practice and intervention through an international Spain-Latin America network; and to make visible public policy that currently is addressing the inclusion of men in the pursuit of gender equity. It is noteworthy that there were no presentations addressing fatherhood and education as a day-to-day, interactional practice, or the effects of father involvement in schools. At the same time, however, this topic was indirectly addressed as one of the most important ones in establishing a sustainable agenda for egalitarian gender relations. A close examination of the papers presented shows an identification of emergent perspectives in different social domains (e.g., the work force, the household, education). For example, it is reported that as women have more fully accessed the work force and schooling and have started to gain some independence in Latin America and Spain, intrafamily relations have started to change as the result of the greater presence of the father within the home, school and community. These data constitute indirect evidence of some transformations of fatherhood. Some presentations and papers reported policy changes that allowed men to play a more present role in being fathers, such as legislation that provides men with leaves from work when their children are born.[6] However, to date, there are no areas of public policy reinforcing the presence of men in *schools* specifically or favoring a more balanced gendered perspective on *domestic* responsibilities as an item of policy or of research agendas. Therefore, as a primary conclusion of this review, it becomes evident that is necessary to further discuss what questions may provide a framework to construct research agendas more aligned with documenting the changes that seem to be taking place on multiple levels in Latin America.

EDUCATIONAL PRACTICES THAT REDEFINE FATHERHOOD IN ARGENTINA

Three Contemporary Programs

In this section, I will review three contemporary programs in Argentina that reveal emergent social practices by fathers. These educational experiences occurred during the last two decades. I will also discuss data from two research studies commented below (namely, *Exploratory study on the capacity of women and men of diverse socioeconomic groups to access justice as rightful subjects and learning and creativity in self-managed, diverse groups* (see Note 1 for some details on these). Both the programs and the studies provide evidence revealing that patriarchal and egalitarian perspectives are still at play in a dynamic and tense relationship. However, specific groups today (e.g., *groups autogestionados*, self-managed groups) seem to be breaking ground in egalitarian ways of conceiving parenthood. This trend seems to be influencing the ways in which fathers see themselves and act toward their children's education. These preliminary findings may indicate that specific groups are creating dramatically different notions of family and thus, of fatherhood, which needs to be interpreted as a political decision (Arendt, 1997).

Educational Rural Centers[7]

These educational centers were established in 1988 in the Province of Buenos Aires, in rural areas of the Argentinean Pampas. Their mission was to provide good quality education for all rural families, for whom accessing middle- and high-school quality education was a challenge. These schools are comanaged between the state and the families of each local community where the schools are located. They constitute a unique educational context for rural families as a whole, since it is not only the students who access education, but adults do so as well by participating in school management. In these schools, the pedagogical authority is the principal, yet s/he works collaboratively with adults representing families at each local family association. It is fathers and mothers who participate in these family associations; thus the experience provides first-hand involvement for parents who want to make decisions over their children's education. Research on these educational centers (e.g., Ferraris & Baccalini, 2001; Heras & Burin, 2002) has shown that it is their unique pedagogical and management strategies that provide opportunities for developing participatory frameworks that simultaneously address students and their families. These schools provide learning opportunities where teachers, principals, local workers, families, and local institutions integrate educational councils. As a public and state funded educational strategy, it has been innovative; the fact that the number of schools under this policy grew from 10 (in 1988) to 34 (in 2011) seems to show a consistent pattern toward a sustainable project. Even though *father* involvement in education was not specifically studied at these educational centers, some indirect results suggest that it provides an atmosphere of democratic family-teacher-student-community involvement, which allows greater father participation.

Mothers and Fathers as Caregivers

This was an initiative taken up by the National Ministry of Health during the 1990s, and initially, it involved only women. It was designed as a state-supported program to establish a structure by which caregiving services were provided for families who lacked the economic resources to hire caretaking services for their children, a practice commonly held in Argentinean middle-class families. While this program was discontinued in 2001, it provided a model for other caretaking public services in designing new lines of public policy. What was distinctive about this program was that when it was implemented, it was only geared toward women's participation. However, male community participants asked to be a part of it, suggesting that the program would be better implemented if they could act as caregivers, equal to women. The National Ministry of Health agreed to this request and the program included men, and therefore, it changed its name from *Mothers as Caregivers* to *Fathers and Mothers as Caregivers*. Given that this program was implemented from 1997 to 2000, it could be considered groundbreaking, since at the time, there were no other state-funded lines of work that included men in similar roles. No research or program evaluation was conducted, so the results of its actions remain unexplored.

Families in Support of State-Funded Public Schools (Buenos Aires)

This is a self-organized group of families who send their children to state, public-funded schools in the city of Buenos Aires. The group was funded in 2009 when the city government implemented changes in public policy that were detrimental to state-funded schools. For example, state-funded schools suffered severe budget cuts, while private schools had their state-funded resources increased. Additionally, the government decided to close state-funded teacher-education programs for continuing teacher education. A group of families decided to participate by demanding changes in the orientation of public policy and government accountability with the goal of quality state-funded education for all. Since its foundation, it has been observed that mothers as well as fathers have participated and continue to participate (see Heras Monner Sans, 2012a, for an analysis of families' agency toward meaningful educational policy). Since this is a group directly involved with schooling processes, K-12, it is important to highlight efforts to create gender-balanced participation because typically at these school levels, it is mothers who participate.

In addition to the three programs reviewed in the prior sections, I conducted an exploratory study and present a summary of the results on the capacity of women and men of diverse socioeconomic groups to access justice as rightful subjects (Heras Monner Sans, 2010), and on a study currently being conducted on learning and creativity in self-managed, diverse groups in which self-managed groups learn about how to do their work (Heras Monner Sans, 2012b).

Fatherhood and Gender Relations: Emergent Patterns

The focus of the first study was on gender relationships in different geographical areas of Argentina. For this study, people of different socio-economic strata were interviewed.[8] Results seem to indicate that while a patriarchal perspective is still very strong, an egalitarian tendency is emerging. For example:

> Sometimes, my wife travels for work and I am the one who takes care of my kids for 1 or 2 weeks. Some people comment when they see me around, for example, "oh, you're baby sitting today" and I respond (bluntly) that I am not *sitting* but performing my role, (which is) being a father. It seems as if people think that, as a man, I am not supposed to take care of my sons. (Father of two children, professional entrepreneur)

The quote above illustrates the belief, still very much instilled in Argentina, that when a man is taking care of his children, he is replacing momentarily the one who is the real caregiver, namely, the mother (and other female family members).

This person adds:

> A while ago, my wife practiced sports, she was a soccer player, and we used to participate in regular community meetings (for neighborhood matters). The meetings were scheduled on a different weekday at one point and my wife stopped participating because the meetings conflicted with her soccer practice day. People started asking and making negative comments such as "what, is she playing soccer and you are washing dishes at home?" In the context of increasingly negative comments, we decided to make a flyer with pictures of me washing dishes and my wife in her soccer practice outfit. The caption read: "all of us can do it! Women, it is fun to practice sports! Men, it is great to wash dishes or do chores at home! Movement For Gender Equity." We distributed the flyer via email and it was provocative to see the reactions.

From his experience, many individuals do not easily tolerate that women and men have an equal right to sports and recreation, and thus other persons' reactions toward his flyer with the pictures. His final reflections point to the fact that, even though some changes are at play, these changes are not sufficient in terms of gender balance. As noted from the following, the accepted societal changes do not seem to cover all areas of domestic chores and responsibilities:

> At the same time, I think it is true that more and more men take care of domestic chores or play a role as a father different than how it used to be. Some of them even see cooking as a viable activity, perhaps, in part,

inspired by a burgeoning gourmet trend here in Argentina. I find it more difficult to consider that things would change to the extent that men would start doing *all* the work implied in care taking, such as washing, ironing, cleaning, mending clothes and the like. (Father)

Other testimonies showed that for women to reconcile work in the public sphere (e.g., if they run and win office at the House of Representatives) with what is still expected from women at home is almost impossible:

It is a very hard sacrifice to have run for the House since the interpersonal relationships in the family have changed very much and it has not been easy for me to adapt, as a woman. I have managed to organize the domestic chores differently, but my relationship with my husband and kids has been strained. This happened in spite of us agreeing that it would be good for me to run for office, and we were all very happy when I got in. It is accepted by society that men can be out of the house, and that house chores or family chores are not their responsibility; it is not the same with women. Mother-hood is based on the whole idea that we'll be at home, or taking responsibility for domestic chores and family relationships. Fatherhood is not based on the same assumption. (Woman, mother of two children, elected for the House of Representatives of the City of Buenos Aires)

Our study highlighted several different day-to-day strategies that women and men are using to support change in regard to sharing more fully what it takes to support their households in egalitarian ways (where both act as caregivers and as providers as well). However, these strategies seem to be contradictory since they show that women still cannot rely on their partners in the same way as perhaps their partners are relying on them. One of the strategies we identified was that women made detailed lists for men:

Because of my work schedule, I sometimes stay out of the house for very many hours, so I worry and make "What To Do Lists," very detailed, and stick them on the fridge. If I don't do it, my husband does not remember what to do and when, every step of the way. For example, when they come home after school, there are several things to pay attention to, such as homework, or whether there are any communications from school to respond to.... And even if I do make the list, it may be the case that still he does not read it all or does not pay enough attention to the details. It seems as if it is not part of fatherhood. (Mother of two children, working professional woman)

Thus, it seems, a research agenda that wants to specifically understand the changes currently taking place should look carefully at microinteractions because interview data is revealing that it is in these contexts where gender balance is negotiated, enacted and (potentially) challenged and/or transformed.

Summarizing Results From Self-Managed Groups

I am currently conducting a study on the ways in which several self-managed (*autogestionados*) groups learn about how to do their work. Even though our study is not focusing on families or fatherhood,[9] we have once and again found indirect evidence that is pointing to the creative ways in which these groups, as collective endeavors, are questioning traditional gender relationships and presenting opportunities for men to be present as fathers in their children's day-to-day education.

The practices more commonly observed and reported also in interviews are:

- Extending a leave or permission for a leave when a child is born in their family. A member of a cooperative of workers stated in an interview: "Our cooperative has decided to provide men with a paternity leave of 30 days when a baby is born in the family."

- Providing equal opportunities for both men and women to take care of their family members for health and educational reasons. According to interview data, this is because "(our cooperative) puts male and female figures both as role models, in equal rights, and therefore supports concrete organizational structures to allow that both can take care of domestic, day-to-day chores."

- Allowing children to accompany their fathers to work, if it is necessary, and designing on-site, spontaneous caretaking activities, when needed.

- Making agreements and revising them when necessary about work-schedule, hours at work, or on-site/out-of-site work activities (a more flexible approach toward work responsibilities which are redistributed among coworkers and coassociates, since in these collective self-managed groups all participants share the same associate, cooperative status).

- Discussing gender relationships openly, identifying patterns which urgently need to be changed, such as violence against women or children. Interview data surfaces statements such as:

  > We are trying to have our sons and daughters see that males can do work at home as well as outside (the household), and thus we are educating the young in seeing concretely that if both men and

women are equal in this way, sexist ideologies that support the idea that there are certain chores only for women can be overturned.

- Designing and implementing workshops on themes related to gender relationships, policies and politics, as a way to deepen participants' understanding on the ways the larger context is influencing their views and actions. For example, women who participate as workers in a cooperative also voluntarily participate in conducting Gender Relationships Workshops. They also document the local changes (at the community level) of these actions. They have participated in 2010 and 2011 in National Women's Conferences, showing the day-to-day results of their work. They are finding two concrete changes to be very important: (1) the decrease of domestic violence against women and children; (2) the acknowledgement by men that women also may have free time to conduct cultural, artistic or sports-related activities.[10]

To date there is no study that has specifically addressed father involvement in education for participants in these kinds of self-managed programs.

SUMMARY

As I have shown in prior sections of this chapter, there is no doubt that more open discussion and interrogation of maleness and fatherhood in the public sphere is taking place currently in Argentina and in Latin America. Some examples in Latin America include research on what counts as responsible fatherhood in Central America (Proyecto América Latina Genera for example), and designing state funded programs that acknowledge the value of providing opportunities for women and men to equally participate in caregiving programs designed for children whose families need help in accessing child-care in Argentina. Also, laws have emerged acknowledging different family styles and public policies supporting the presence of fathers at birth (during labor and in the first four weeks of the baby). Castro García and Pazos Morán (2011) have stated that, like other cultural changes, transformations regarding equal gender rights should be a public policy matter, open for discussion and supported by state laws, funding and media discourse. These changes should include providing opportunities to publicly discuss a totally different framework concerning who takes care of children or the elderly in families, why and how (Equipo Latinoamericano de Justicia y Género, 2011; Seiz, 2011). Since 2005, an initiative called Equal and Non Transferrable

Rights for Birth and Adoption Platform (PPIINA, 2011) is seeking to create a worldwide network to participate in the public sphere so that these issues become international public policy themes of different countries' agendas. Therefore, the patriarchal trend is being currently questioned; nonetheless, the tension between what was in place and what emerges is still at play at the larger society level.

Second, and from the perspective presented in this chapter (i.e., fatherhood as a socially constructed notion) I suggest that school experiences where father and mother participation is balanced constitute an *emergent* pattern as well (see for example the programs and experiences reviewed in the prior section). Involvement in education, at least at the level of participation in management or voluntary association structures, is becoming more of a father *and* mother caring practice. It would be important to pursue research to further investigate whether this participation, in day-to-day involvement and interactions, supports democratic gender-balanced sharing, or whether within these structures, any patterns of male domination are still prevalent. Closer study would be needed to determine whether father involvement in education might still reproduce patriarchal practices or offer opportunities for dynamic transformation.

Thirdly, and in terms of a research agenda, a line of inquiry focusing on emergent change also needs to explore tensions *within* the household in light of the results shared for the current research studies (i.e., the exploratory study on gender relations and the study on self managed groups). It seems important because, even though both partners seem to *want* to work toward egalitarian ways of doing things, still it is not easy to agree on *how* exactly to do it. Conflict surfaces about *how to do things* and about *what counts as fatherhood* in particular (e.g., feeding children with fast food is seen as not healthy, and it is challenged by mothers who want to share domestic responsibilities with their partners). Therefore, a worthwhile line of research would be to study day-to-day household interactions from an ethnographic perspective to document how this emergent pattern is being constructed by members of families who are trying to create gendered-balanced relationships. Additionally, this type of research would prove useful in identifying specific *father-guided* educational patterns.

I conclude by stressing that change in the roles of Argentina's fathers is dynamic and related to the interaction between two seemingly contradictory trends being a constitutive part of Argentina's history (i.e., patriarchal and egalitarian perspectives). The contested terrain seems to be located in gender inequities within the culture. In turn, and specifically related to fatherhood and education, there seems to be an ongoing debate about the responsibilities of fathers in domestic duties, the education of children and their involvement in schooling, and their participation in social change in regards to gender equity.

NOTES

1. One of these studies *(Exploratory Study on the Capacity of Women and Men of Diverse Socioeconomic Groups to Access Justice as Rightful Subjects)* was conducted during 2009-2010. The study was based on interviews and focus groups, as well as on a review of literature concerning gender relationships in Argentina. Twenty-three focus groups in three different regions of Argentina (North West, Center rural area and the City of Buenos Aires) were undertaken. Fifteen in-depth interviews were conducted as well. Additionally, as the study evolved, specific-topic interviews were held with professionals who worked in key roles (e.g., Gender Relations Area in the Secretary of Rural Affairs). A complete technical report was written and presented to the Equipo Lationamericano de Justicia y Género, the non-governmental organization who financed the study. The other study *(Learning and Creativity in Self-Managed, Diverse Groups)* focuses on the ways self-managed groups *(autogestionados)* learn how to do their work collectively, and on the ways in which they perceive difference among group members. Several published papers and chapters in Spanish and English have been recently published; see for example Heras Monner Sans 2012 cited in the reference list. All translations of interview excerpts provided in this chapter are mine.

2. Literature and film have presented several examples of how patriarchal relationships have been enacted in most Latin American countries. See for example Vargas Llosa's novel *La fiesta del Chivo* or Marcela Serrano's *Nosotras que nos queremos tanto*. See also *Las mujeres verdaderas tienen curvas*, a film by Patricia Cardoso.

3. These adjectives were used to characterize anarchist, libertarian, and socialist views by nationalist, traditional views.

4. See http://www.un.org/womenwatch/daw/cedaw/

5. For example, the national law supporting responsible procreation and sexual health, passed in 2002; the national law prescribing Comprehensive sex education at all levels of mandatory schooling, passed in 2006; the national law regulating media and mass communication programs, passed in 2009.

6. Changes in normative aspects ruling gender relations in favor of more democratic, less patriarchal standards are very recent in Latin America. For example, Jelin (2005) shows that shared parental custody was as recent as 1985 in Argentina, shared administrative household responsibilities have been very recently acknowledged in Brazil (by 2001), and divorce was established by law in 2004 in Chile.

7. These educational centers are called Centros Educativos para la Producción Total in Spanish. They are rural schools and are part of a community-school-family partnership initiative, which started in the 1990s with a few schools. Currently there are 34 schools (called "educational centers"). See http://www.facept.org.ar/intitucion/ListadoCEPTs.html

8. For this study, all interviews were audiotaped and transcribed. Coding of data was then undertaken to surface issues regarding: democracy and

women participation; access to information on health issues, specifically on sexual and reproductive health; domestic work and specifically the care of children and the elderly; social and economic women's rights and violence against women in face-to-face interactions. Participants in the 23 focus groups shared socioeconomic and cultural characteristics; we interviewed men and women from different socioeconomic and cultural groups in three different regions of Argentina. The issues discussed in these groups followed a protocol. For the rest of the interviews a similar procedure was followed. However, the topics discussed were specific according to the vantage point of the interviewees (e.g., nongovernmental organizations participants; public servants; professionals in key roles of the administration, etc.).

9. See Note 1 for information on the main theme of the study. Data reported in this section came out of a larger data set. The study on *autogestionados* (self-managed egalitarian groups) was designed in two phases. Phase 1 was exploratory, mostly interview based, looking at several different groups that qualified for the criteria originally set by the study and to decide about participation in the ethnographic phase (Phase 2). The criteria were that they saw themselves as self-managed, egalitarian groups; that they had been together as a group for 3 years; that their members acknowledged difference among themselves, which they saw as a challenge to work on, which led to interesting interactions among them; and that they were willing to reflect on their experiences in an action-participatory research study. Phase 2 (currently taking place) entails carrying out ethnographies in several self-managed groups with clear objectives for data sets. For example, it includes participant and nonparticipant observation, interviews, discussion groups, e-mail, and virtual forum interactions, and focus groups. Since the design is based on action-research and participatory frameworks, the research team has invited members of the self-managed groups to be a part of a larger research team in order to discuss ongoing analysis of these groups. Research methods and data collection techniques are not exactly the same for all ethnographic-based studies because each group organizes itself differently. Data transcribed for this section are part of follow-up interviews designed to explore issues on gender relationships more specifically. All translations are mine since original data are in Spanish.

10. Free recreational time for women has been found to be a very crucial yet problematic issue according to research on gender relations in Latin American countries, see Equipo Latinoamericano de Justicia y Género, 2011, as one example.

ACKNOWLEDGMENTS

I would like to thank my soul sister Faviana (Dr. Hirsch Dubin) for her unconditional help. I would also like to thank all the men, women, and children with whom I have worked in the studies cited in this chapter. They have helped me understand once again why research is important, and what can our studies modestly contribute to make meaningful change possible. Last yet not least, to David, Javier, and Matías: gracias!

REFERENCES

Angenot, M. (1999). *Interdiscursividades De hegemonías y disidencias* [Interdiscourse: About hegemony and dissidence]. Córdoba, Argentina: Universidad Nacional de Córdoba.

Arendt, H. (1997). ¿Qué es política? [What is politics?]. Barcelona, Spain: Ediciones Paidós.

Batres, K. (2006, December). El terremoto silencioso [The silent earthquake]. *Revista Violeta: Por Una Cultura de Equidad, 12*(3), 6-7.

Bogino Larrambebere, E. (2011, October). Modelos emergentes de paternidad. Análisis de las políticas públicas y nuevas paternidades [Emergent models of fatherhood: An analysis of public policies and new fatherhood models]. Paper presented at CIME (Congreso Iberoamericano de Masculinidades y Equidad. Investigación y Activismo [*IberoAmerican Conference on Masculinity and Equity: Research and Activism*], Barcelona, Spain. Retrieved from http://www.cime2011 .org/home/panel1.html

Camacho, F. (2005, June). Ser hombre es suficiente [Being a man is enough]. *Revista Violeta: Por Una Cultura de Equidad, 6*(2), 8-9.

Cardoso, P. (Director). (2002). *Las mujeres verdaderas tienen curvas* [Real women have curves; motion picture]. United States.

Carli, S. (1991). Infancia y sociedad. La mediación de las asociaciones, Centros y Sociedades Populares de Educación [Childhood and society: Mediating processes undertaken by associations, centers and popular educational societies). In A. Puiggróss (Ed.), *Historia de la Educación Argentina II. Sociedad civil y estado en los orígenes del sistema educativo argentino* (pp. 13-46). Buenos Aires, Argentina: Galerna.

Castro García, C., & Pazos Morán, M. (2011, October). *Hombres, cuidado e igualdad de género. Fundamentos para la equiparación efectiva entre los permisos de padres y madres* (Men, Caring and Gender Equity: Foundations for Effective Egalitarian Rights for Fathers and Mothers). Paper presented at Congreso Iberoamericano de Masculinidades y Equidad. Investigación y Activismo [IberoAmerican Conference on Masculinity and Equity: Research and Activism], Barcelona, Spain. Retrieved from http://www.cime2011.org/home/ panel1/cime2011_P1_PPiiNA.pdf

De Luca, A. (1991). Consejos escolares de distrito: Subordinación o participación popular (District educational boards: Subordination or popular participation). In A. Puiggróss (Ed.), *Historia de la educación Argentina II: Sociedad civil y estado en los orígenes del sistema educativo argentino* (pp. 47-69). Buenos Aires, Argentina: Galerna.

Equipo Latinoamericano de Justicia y Género. (2011). *De eso no se habla. El cuidado en la agenda. Estudio de opinión sobre la organización del cuidado* [The unspoken: Care-taking as an item on the agenda: a research study on care-taking organizational strategies]. Buenos Aires, Argentina: Equipo Latinoamericano de Justicia y Género.

Faur, E. (2004). Masculinidad y desarrollo social. Las relaciones de género desde la perspectiva de los hombres [Masculinities and social development: Gender relations from a masculine point of view.] Bogotá, Colombia: UNICEF y Arango Editores.

Faur, E. (2006). Género, masculinidades y políticas de conciliación familia-trabajo [Gender, masculinities and public policies on family and work]. *Nómadas, 24,* 130-141.

Ferraris, S., & Bacalini, G. (2001). Estrategias educativas para el desarrollo local en el medio rural [Educational strategies for local development in rural areas]. In D. Burin & A. I. Heras (Eds.), *Desarrollo local, una respuesta a escala humana.* Buenos Aires, Argentina: Ediciones CICCUS

Fuller, N. (2007). Comentario sobre los trabajos de Catalina Wainerman y de Maria Coleta Oliveira [Comments on the work of Wainerman and Oliveira]. In M. A. Gutiérrez (Ed.), *Género, familias y trabajo: rupturas y continuidades. Desafíos para la investigación política* [Gender, families and work: Ruptures and continuities, challenges on policy research]. Buenos Aires, Argentina: CLACSO, Latinamerican Council in Social Sciences.

Gargallo, F. (2004). *Las ideas feministas latinoamericanas* [Feminist ideas in Latin America]. Retrieved from http://www.nodo50.org/herstory/textos/Ideas%20feministas%20en%20%20latinoamerica.pdf

Halperin Donghi, T. (1972). *Revolución y guerra* [Revolution and war]. Buenos Aires, Argentina: Siglo XXI.

Halperin Donghi, T. (1980). *Historia Argentina, Tomo 3* [Artentinean history, Vol. 3]. Buenos Aires, Argentina: Paidós.

Heras, A. I., & Burin, D. (2002, October). *Preparing for local development in rural contexts. An analysis of pedagogical and management tools in Rural Schools in Buenos Aires Province.* Paper presented at the Education and Work Symposium, VII Conference in Humanities and the Social Sciences, National University of Jujuy, Jujuy, Province of Jujuy, Argentina.

Heras Monner Sans, A. I. (2010). Informe Técnico: "Estudio exploratorio sobre la capacidad de varones y mujeres de grupos socioeconómicos diversos para constituirse como sujetos de derechos y acceder a la justicia" [Exploratory study on the capacity of women and men of diverse socioeconomic groups to access justice as rightful subject (Unpublished technical report). Equipo Latinoamericano de Justicia y Género, Buenos Aires, Argentina.

Heras Monner Sans, A. I. (2012a). Struggle for agency in contemporary Argentinean schools. In D. R. Cole (Ed.), *Surviving economic crises through education* (pp. 133-148). New York, NY: Peter Lang.

Heras Monner Sans, A. I. (2012b). *(Aprendizaje y creación en proyectos de autonomía* (PICT ANPCyT 0696) [Learning and creativity in self-managed groups]. Unpublished raw data.

Jelin, E. (2005, June). *Latinamerican families and global transformation. Towards a New Public Policy Agenda.* Paper presented at the CEPAL (Latin American Economic Committee) expert seminar "Policies towards families: Social protection and inclusion," Santiago de Chile, Chile.

Olavarría, J. (2003). Studies on masculinities in latin america: A point of view. *Social and Political Annuary for Latin America and the Caribbean, 6,* 91-98.

Programa Naciones Unidas para el Desarrollo. (2008). *Desafíos para la igualdad de género en la Argentina (Challenges for gender equity in Argentina)* Buenos Aires, Argentina: PNUD.

Programa Naciones Unidas para el Desarrollo. (2011). *Aportes para el desarrollo humano en Argentina. 2011: Género en cifras* [Towards human development in Argentina, 2011: Gender relationships in numbers]. Buenos Aires, Argentina: PNUD.

Proyecto América Latina Genera. (2007, Julio). *Masculinidades y paternidad responsable* [Masculinities and responsible fatherhood]. Retrieved from http:// www.americalatinagenera.org/es/index.php?option=com_docman&task =doc_download&gid=1504

PPIINA. (2011). *Equal and Non-Transferrable Rights for Birth and Adoption platform.* Retrieved from http://www.igualeseintransferibles.org/

Rivera, R., & Ceciliano, Y. (2004). *Culture, masculinity and fatherhood: Social representations by men in Costa Rica.* San José, Costa Rica. FLACSO.

Seiz, M. (2011, October). *Hacia una creciente implicación masculine en los cuidados en América Latina?* [Towards a growing implication for males in care-giving domestic tasks in Latin America]. Paper presented at Congreso Iberoamericano de Masculinidades y Equidad. Investigación y Activismo [IberoAmerican Conference on Masculinity and Equity: Research and Activism), Barcelona, Spain. Retrieved from http://www.cime2011.org/home/panel1.html

Serrano, M. (1991). *Nosotras, que nos queremos tanto* [We love each other so much]. Buenos Aires, Argentina: Planeta Editorial.

Suriano, J. (2001). *Anarquistas. Cultura y política libertarian en Buenos Aires 1890-1910* [Anarchists: Libertarian culture and politics in Buenos Aires 1890-1910]. Buenos Aires, Argentina: Manantial.

Vargas Llosa, M. (2006). *La fiesta del Chivo* [The Feast of the Goat]. Madrid, España: Alfaguara Editorial.

Widuczynski, I. (1992). El sistema de hacienda. ¿Matriz de la sociedad latinoamericana? [Haciendas as a way to conceptualize Latin American social relationships]. In P. Funes (Ed.), *América Latina: Planteos, problemas y preguntas* (pp. 75-88). Buenos Aires, Argentina: M. Suárez.

CHAPTER 9

FATHER INVOLVEMENT IN SOUTH KOREA

Ann Y. Kim and Hsiu-Zu Ho

Once my kids have a dream, I want to financially support them. Aside from excelling academically, backing them up when they find something that they want to do with a vision or a dream, that's the kind of father I want to be. It's difficult. (A. Y. Kim, personal communication, December, 2011)

The above quote reflects one of the diverse perspectives of fathers in contemporary South Korean[1] society, that range from fathers who think their only role is to financially support their families to those who attempt to be involved in various aspects of their children's lives. This father has two toddlers and although he expressed his idea regarding the kind of father he wants to be, during an interview for the present study he also seemed nervous about its responsibilities. Traditionally influenced by Confucian teachings, the roles and relationships among family members are being redefined during recent decades due to socioeconomic, political, and cultural changes. Currently the shape of Korean families is being transformed with respect to the time of family formation, structure, and size; and such changes play a role in redefining parenting roles and responsibilities.

One significant factor that is relevant to changes in contemporary Korean families is the increase in women's economic participation. Many more women living in Korean society today are going to college and pursuing careers. In a report regarding the workforce in 2010, of women who are over 15 years old, 49% were working (Ministry of Gender Equality and Family, 2011). Along with the increase in women's economic participation, Korean society is experiencing an extremely low birthrate. Along with Taiwan and Japan, Korea has one of the lowest birthrates in the world; a growth rate of 1.22 in 2010 (Statistics Korea, 2011a). Yang and Rosenblatt (2008) postulate some reasons for this decrease in childbirth. Mothers may perceive the expectations placed on them to raise the child as one-sided and difficult to manage when they have careers. Married couples may also decide to not have children or delay having children because of the economic burden of raising a child.

Changes in Korean families with respect to time of family formation, structure, and size have taken place in the last few decades. In 2008, the average age for first time marriage was 31.4 years for men and 28.3 years for women (Statistics Korea, 2009). This statistic has shifted since a decade prior when the average ages were 28.6 and 25.7 for men and women. Women are delaying childbirth: the age at which women are having their first child has changed from 27.7 years in 2000 to 30.1 years in 2010 (Statistics Korea, 2011b). The divorce rate in Korea is increasing as well. In 2010, among the married population 9.5 couples out of 1000 couples ended in divorce. Furthermore in the same year the ratio of couples who married to the couples who divorced was 3:1 (326,100 couples married while 116,900 couples divorced).

A relatively new phenomenon that may change the face of Korea in years to come is a surge of foreigners marrying Korean nationals, referred to as *keul-hon-ee-min-ja* (*marriage immigrants*). The families that are made up by these marriages are referred to as multicultural families. To date, there are approximately 131,000 marriage immigrants and the gender distribution is 9.6 male marriage immigrants for every 100 female marriage immigrants (Ministry of Tourism, 2009); that is, marriage immigrants are predominantly female. This is one faction of society where the birthrate is increasing. In 2009, there were a total of 24,745 multiethnic children in Korea, a 32% increase from 2008 (Ministry of Tourism, 2009). Of these children 90% had mothers who were not Korean nationals. A significant majority (81%) of these marriage immigrants entered the country after 2000 and growth of this subpopulation is expected to continue. These marriage immigrants are mostly from other Asian countries such as China, Vietnam, and the Philippines with the majority living in the Seoul metropolitan area and other urban areas (Ministry of Tourism, 2009).

In a report on multicultural families by the Ministry of Health and Welfare (2009) there were clear differences in education levels among the *marriage immigrants* as well. Nearly 94% of those who immigrated from North America, Australia, and Western Europe had a college degree or more, whereas over 60% of those from Cambodia or Vietnam had less than a middle school education (Ministry of Health and Welfare, 2009). Often in these multicultural families, there was an educational gap between the partners; that is, slightly over half (51%) of the women who had less than an elementary school education were married to men with more than high school educations (Ministry of Health and Welfare, 2009). Moreover these multicultural families tend to have lower socioeconomic status. Little is known about the levels of father involvement and expectations of fathers in these multicultural families.

RESEARCH ON FATHER INVOLVEMENT IN KOREAN FAMILIES

This chapter views father involvement from a social constructivist framework and asserts father behavior to be "shaped by social networks within a local culture" (Roggman, Fitzgerald, Bradley, & Raikes, 2002). In other words, fathering consists of a negotiation of roles within the familial structure that are shaped by a range of sociocultural factors (Marsiglio, Amato, Day, & Lamb, 2000). How fatherhood is understood across cultures has changed over time along with changes in ideologies, embedded in its own cultural contexts (Cabrera, Tamis-LeMonda, Bradley, Hofferth, & Lamb, 2000). In efforts to further understand father involvement in relation to its contexts, Coleman's social capital theory is particularly relevant to the study examined in this chapter because it allows for each individual father to define his own involvement within social, cultural, and economical contexts. Social capital theory allows researchers to draw connections among the different fathers with respect to their financial, human, and social capital, all three of which have been influenced by their unique history, community, and culture.

Father involvement in Korea has been limited in scope due to low societal expectation for fathers to be involved and demanding working conditions that did not make it feasible. In a report by the Organisation for Economic Co-Operation and Development (OECD) in 2008, Korea's laborers worked on average 2,357 hours per year (45.3 hours per week in a 52-week work year, as cited by Olson, 2008). With Korean fathers expected to be the sole breadwinner of the family (Chae & Lee, 2011), the laborers referred to by the OECD statistic are primarily fathers and the statistic reflects the lack of time fathers have for participating in their children's education. Despite these working conditions, there has been recent change in societal expectations for father involvement at all ages of child development.

Past studies on father involvement with Korean children has primarily focused on social and emotional development (i.e., Belsky & Park, 2000; Chae & Lee, 2011; Cho & Yoon, 2005; Y. H. Lee, 1992; Youn & Chung, 1997). For example in their study on the role fathers play in the development of social competence of preschool children (5.5 years), Chae and Lee (2011) found that fathers' parenting behavior played a mediating role between sons' social competence and fathers' retrospective memories of their own upbringing; such a relationship was not found for fathers with daughters. Compared to fathers with sons, fathers with daughters reported significantly higher scores on responsiveness and intimacy, which was positively related to daughters' social competence. In a different study on social and emotional development in young adults, S.-I. Kim and Rohner (2003) examined the role of perceived parental acceptance on empathy in university students. Sons who perceived having more accepting fathers during childhood rated themselves as being more empathetic; and this relationship was not found among daughters. Moreover, Kim and Rohner (2003) did not find any difference in reported empathy levels between sons and daughters who reported perceived paternal rejection. While these studies focused on children's social/emotional development, future studies may also examine the relationship of social/emotional behaviors on aspects of schooling, such as school adjustment and engagement.

The increase in divorce rate in Korean society has led to research on social development and academic pursuit of children in divorced families. For example, in a study examining self-esteem and internalizing problems (withdrawal, somatic complaints, and anxiety/depression) in divorced and nondivorced families, Chung and Emery (2007) found that although the majority of adolescents who lived in divorced families did not report severe maladjustment, they reported lower self-esteem and a greater number of internalizing problems. In a different study, Shin, Choi, Kim, and Kim (2010) examined adolescent resilience in three different types of divorced families; those lead by fathers, by mothers, or by grandparents. Shin and colleagues (2010) found that for adolescents living with their fathers, having higher self-esteem was a significant predictor of their having better adjustment. With regards to academic pursuits, H. Park (2008) compared the academic aspirations of adolescents from single-parent households, distinguishing between divorce or death of one parent. H. Park (2008) found that students from divorced families had the lowest educational aspirations and greatest educational disengagement, compared to their peers from two-parent households as well as peers from widowed-parent households. These three studies on divorced families contribute to the understanding of the importance of fathers on children's social, emotional and cognitive development.

Another unique phenomenon in Korean society is the *kirogi* (Korean term for *wild goose*, migratory birds) family or *kirogi* parent. The term refers to families that live in different countries for the sake of the children's education, particularly to English-speaking countries in efforts to obtain English language skills for the children (H. Lee, 2010). Typically these families take on the form of the mother moving overseas with the children and the father staying in Korea to make money to support the family financially (H. Lee, 2010). J. Kim (2010) studied lower- and middle class *kirogi* families who live in Singapore. The father of one of the families works 12-hour days at a small restaurant the family owns in Korea and only has 2 days off each month. Effort to provide a stable living situation for the family members overseas is likely to be a challenge for these fathers' active involvement in their child's education. In a different study, Y.-J. Lee and Koo (2006) found fathers, who remained in Korea, and may have not been aware of the particulars regarding the educational advantages of the United States, to have negative perceptions of the Korean educational environment. This study brings attention to the fact that some fathers are willing to sacrifice living with their families in order to ensure educational success of their children. Reflecting women's increased economic participation, Kang's (2010) *kirogi* families were five stay-at-home fathers who remained with their children in Singapore while their wives worked in Korea. Some negative effects of *kirogi* families have been reported in the media, such as its contribution to divorce, adulterous relationships, fathers committing suicide, and adjustment difficulties upon return to Korea (H. Lee, 2010). However, there is little research on how this type of family structure influences father involvement and its subsequent effects on child cognitive and social development.

THE PRESENT STUDY: VOICES OF KOREAN FATHERS

Using a social constructivist framework, a review of the literature indicated a greater lack of research on father involvement in education compared to social and emotional development in the majority Korean population. Additionally, the limited research on father involvement in education appears to have mainly focused on at-risk populations or distinct populations such as divorced and *kirogi* families. In efforts to understand how Korean fathers perceive their paternal role and expectations of involvement in their children's education, a qualitative study utilizing Coleman's social capital theory (Coleman, 1988) was conducted on 13 Korean fathers working in Seoul. Coleman's theory (1988) separates a father's roles into three distinct categories: (1) Financial capital which refers to the income and monetary capital the father can provide for the child; (2) Human capital which refers the characteristics the father has to further the child's development; and (3) Social capital which refers to the relationship the father has with the child that facilitates the transference of human capital.

Fathers ranged in age (35 to 52 years old) and the age of their children (1 to 21 years old). Eleven of the 13 had bachelor's degrees; three worked in blue-collar positions while the remaining fathers had white-collar corporate positions. All were married with one father a widower. Each father was asked individually about his paternal role with regards to their child's education, how involved they are, and how much they wanted to be involved. Using a semistructured interview format, fathers were asked nine main questions, with some more specific to education (i.e., What is a father's role in his child's education? Who communicates with the school?) and others more contextual (i.e., Are there any policies that hinder or encourage father involvement?). The questions were intended to guide, rather than place limitations on the interview. The interviews were digitally recorded and subsequently transcribed by a Korean-English bilingual researcher and then analyzed for themes.

In order to methodologically identify and categorize themes, Attride-Stirling's (2001) *thematic networks* were used to connect themes from the interviews. Thematic networks suggest a three-level model to organize data collected. The first level is *basic themes*, and they are derived from the texts directly. The second level is the *organizing theme*, and they incorporate the contextual background to enhance the meanings of the basic themes. The *organizing theme* connects the *basic themes*. The third level is the *global theme*, and Attride-Stirling (2001) describes it as the final tenet that "encompasses the principal metaphors in the data as a whole." Responses that were vocalized by two or more fathers were considered a *theme*. Once themes were established, they were translated into English and discussed with a research team to confirm that the higher level themes were found.

Using the Attride-Stirling method of analysis, the following global themes emerged that reflected Coleman's three categories of capital: financial, human, and social (Coleman, 1988).

1. Fathers' perceived burden to provide financial capital influence their educational involvement.

While seven remaining fathers did not make comments directly related to financially supporting the family and its effects, 6 of the 13 fathers expressed the burden of having to financially support their family. They further elaborated on how it interfered with their direct involvement in their child's education and how it was the means to providing educational opportunities, such as cram schools. The following quote from one father of a 9-year-old son and a 6-year-old daughter illustrates how busy fathers feel: "I feel like there are few opportunities to get close to the children. Yes, too busy. Both are busy, the kids are busy and I'm busy. " In this family, the father perceived both himself and his children as being too busy to establish a relationship.

However, being busy was necessary because the fathers wanted to have the financial means to support their family; and furthermore, invest in their children's education. One of the fathers who has two young sons stated,

> I feel kind of funny constantly talking about money but it's really difficult to raise a child in this country without having a dual income.... Right now there's nothing I can do with my kids that doesn't require money. They are 1 and 3 years old.

His words make it clear that financial stability is at the forefront of his mind. He is the same father quoted in the beginning of the chapter who verbalized the importance of having enough financial resources in order to help his sons become successful in whatever they chose.

While most of the fathers acknowledged that grandparents were minimally involved in aspects of their grandchildren's lives, one father provided a different perspective. He shared, "They [grandparents] are a significant help, because, and I mentioned this before, there is a funny expression these days, 'the education of children is dependent on the financial resources of their grandfather.'" This suggests that while grandparents are less involved in the day-to-day matters they may still be highly involved by providing financial resources toward the grandchild's education.

2. Fathers experience confusion regarding their roles, and this confusion likely limits their human capital.

In this second theme, fathers seemed to feel lost and confused about how to pursue a relationship with their children, and this attitude limited their human capital. They experienced conflicting thoughts surrounding their authority.

> Fathers used to have a place, back then it was having authority. Now they say to be like friends. Because of that, there is talk about spending more time with children and being more involved but like I said, it is confusing to know it means that the distance between father and son should be like friends or like junior/senior classmen because there is a distance there. I know there is a shared space between father and son but I'm confused if there is supposed to be separate space and the father's role being separate.

Another father described how he felt that he was providing a type of accommodating customer service to keep the relations positive between him and his kids because he practically only sees them on the weekends. These quotes show that Korean fathers are trying to move away from the traditional father image but are left without any direction regarding the alternative.

Not all of the fathers experienced role confusion. There were two fathers who spoke confidently about not wanting to be involved with the everyday lives of their children and appeared to be comfortable in their limited father roles. Future efforts to encourage father involvement in their child's education should also take these fathers' attitudes toward involvement into consideration because the needs of these fathers may be different from those who are experiencing role confusion.

3.   Feelings of alienation overpower fathers' desire to provide social capital for their child's education.

Most of the fathers expressed wanting to be more involved with their children's education. However, many fathers found reasons for their lack of involvement. For example, two fathers with daughters respectively said, "I want to be involved but I think my kids won't like it." and "I want to be actively involved, but maybe it's because they are going through puberty but they talk to their mom mostly. I think it's that time. " Additionally, two different fathers with young children all under the age of 7 years old also felt that they had little place to be involved because their children were young and the emphasis was on caregiving rather than education. The fathers with older children, in high school or above, also talked about their children being too old to want advice or involvement from their fathers. Another father explicitly named his wife as a deterrent of his involvement.

> So, I feel that I just tell my kids nice things and I don't participate as much as their mother. This is because, and I feel bad saying this, but you know there's that thing called "*skirt wind.*"[2] In other words, you can consider mom's having all the control over education and not liking fathers being involved ... [the kid's] mom, my wife, and I have conversations and she tells me "do you know what kind of time we live in? Take a step back. We have to do this in this situation and that in that situation. We can't let our kid fall behind. We have to do this and we have to do that." All these [rules] are established among the mothers. I think the education [system] does not allow for fathers to be involved. So, even if fathers want to be involved, unless you are highly educated or are of a specialized profession or are extremely proficient in English or Math, then maybe you can contribute there.

In contrast, two fathers denied wanting to be more actively involved with their children. One said he was too busy and the other said that he likes the relationship he has with his adolescent daughter. He further elaborated that his daughter consulted with him on matters such as college and future careers, but the day-to-day matters were not shared.

One interesting distinction found from the interviews was that for many of the fathers, even the father who said he did not want to be more involved with his child, involvement in education was not limited to academic education. Rather, school and academic success was considered the realm of the mothers, and fathers wanted to focus on development of morals and character, manners and etiquette, and becoming a member of society. One father said,

> In my case, I am a step back. I don't do things directly, such as taking my kid to cram school, that's all the mom's job. I'm always thinking about how to raise my child. So, even though I'm not involved directly I try to tell my kid what I expect of him.

A second father commented,

> For me, I try not to give my kids too much stress, and for them to be healthy, have healthy thoughts. I try to tell them about nice things. I don't value academics, put more focus on health thoughts and moral values. I don't want to put stress on them.

Another father remarked that he and his wife disagree on the issue but he is happy with his daughter "just being average" or "not too far behind" others with regards to academics.

CURRENT PRACTICES AND POLICIES IN CONTEMPORARY KOREAN SOCIETY

Government Support of Father Involvement

Recently, the government has taken a more active approach in addressing the country's low birthrate by creating policies that aim to promote paternal involvement with their children. Specifically, the National Assembly of Korea reopened a special committee in June 2011 to focus on issues of low birthrate and the ageing population. The government's initiative is based on research that showed Korean women, especially those who are employed, express greater intentions to have a second child when their husbands contributed to childrearing and household chores (e.g., S.-M. Park, Cho, & Choi, 2010). Policies have been put in place to encourage fathers to become more involved in helping to raise their children. Two main policies are aimed at encouraging father involvement in early childrearing. One policy allows fathers to request up to 3 days of parental leave when their wives are giving birth. The other policy allows for fathers to request up to a year of paid leave to raise their children. Additionally, there are also limited services available for targeted populations, such as counseling services for family members and Korean language and culture classes that teach cooking and traditions offered by the Ministry of Gender Equality and Family for multicultural families.

Corporate Atmosphere and the Government's Response

Although these policies for paternal leave from the workplace are in place to encourage fathers to be more actively involved in raising children, the corporate atmosphere has been found to not be welcoming to the idea. Of those who are eligible to request paternal leave, only 1.9% have done so (N. J. Kim, 2011). Fathers who requested paternal leave are described as being bold. Recent newspaper articles (i.e., N. J. Kim, 2011; S. M. Kim & Gee, 2011) report many fathers being afraid that they will not have a "desk" when they return. Fathers are quoted saying that they know that they will get "funny looks" from coworkers or negative comments such as, "You're the dad, why do you need to stay at home with the kids?" (S. M. Kim & Gee, 2011). The article quoted one father who worked in the financial industry, "Neither my family nor my in-laws know that I am on paternity leave" (translation by author).

In efforts to change negative societal perceptions about paternity leave and further its benefits, the government has recognized private companies that encourage their employees for having children. Specifically, in September of 2011 the Ministry of Labor held an award ceremony for companies that were identified as making efforts in the *Creating a Better World to Raise Children* movement (Shin, 2011). Companies who received the highest awards had implemented practices that included enforcement of paternity leave, allowance for flexible work hours and telecommuting, and even provision of financial benefits for employees who were having a second and third child (Shin, 2011).

Grassroots Movements

In addition to the government and corporate sector, there are many grassroots organizations interested in promoting paternal involvement. For example, *father schools* sponsored by nongovernmental organizations are proliferating in Korea. These schools (of which some are faith based) aim to create a community and resource for fathers and ultimately restore healthy families. The most well-known *father school*, *Duranno*, was started by a church pastor in 1995 in Korea, and currently offers a 2-weekend course consisting of four 5.5-hour classes. The course encourages fathers to reflect on themselves and think about the influence they have on their families, their goals in life, and their male identity. Additionally, the program counsels fathers on their communication with their wives and their children (Duranno Father School, 2011). There are currently 76 chapters in Korea and the program has spread to 43 countries, in 230 cities all over the world.

Elementary schools and private kindergartens around the nation are making efforts to encourage paternal involvement by planning activities for fathers to participate with their children, such as field days (a day of outdoor games, participated by all the students in the school), hiking on the weekend, and going to sporting events. In 2010 one elementary school located in the city of Incheon was recognized for its large number of fathers attending the school field day. In that school, one third of the students' fathers attended. Another elementary school in the city of Busan was also recognized for the establishment of a father-child group who participated in not only school-hosted events and parent education programs but also extracurricular activities, such as camping and attending baseball games in efforts to encourage emotional growth in their children.

In an informal interview, a mother with a high school-aged son expressed that she felt there was a difference in attitude toward father involvement as her child got older (A. Y. Kim, personal communication, November, 2011). In contrast to the elementary schools and kindergartens focused on above, the mother shared that her son's high school administration was not open to fathers participating in the school and was greatly reluctant to open the school's field day to the fathers. She perceived that the school does not want fathers to be involved and that high school is only a place for college preparation.

CONCLUSIONS AND RECOMMENDATIONS

This chapter examines the sociocultural context of Korean society as it relates to the various issues regarding father roles in contemporary Korea. Social changes, such as increase in divorce rates and multicultural families, and economic changes, such as increases in women's economic participation, are influencing time of family formation and family structure, which in turn influence father involvement. The chapter also presents results of a qualitative study on Korean father involvement and discusses current policies and practices in Korean society today.

Based on the findings reported in the chapter, the following are some recommendations from the authors aimed to further promote and support father involvement in children's education in Korea. Since fathers are reporting that they do not feel comfortable asking for paternal leave, it is recommended that government/corporations place into practice the implementation of parental leave policies. This is in hopes that fathers can request parental leaves and not be concerned about being penalized in their job positions.

Additionally, considering that fathers were found to be confused about how to build relationships with their children across developmental stages, extending the development of father involvement programs to middle and high schools to cover topics regarding academic support, communication, and relationship building with their adolescent children is recommended. Development of father-mentor programs in corporations and workplaces are other suggestions, so new fathers can ask questions and discuss with other fathers strategies for future involvement. The study in the chapter also found fathers struggling with determining their parental expectations and roles. Establishment of family education centers focusing on both father-child programs as well as holistic family programs (including mothers) that accommodate fathers' interests and work schedules would be beneficial for the entire family. Finally, promotion of the benefits of father involvement in children's education through media (i.e., textbooks, storybooks, parent magazines, television commercials and advertisements) would encourage as well as help distribute the understanding that father involvement is needed.

Three areas to consider for future research emerged from this study. One area would be to explore the types of involvement that Korean fathers consider realistic, feasible, and compatible with their professional work. A second area would examine the types of support that fathers need from mothers in order to successfully participate in caregiving responsibilities, household duties, and children's education. A third area would focus on ways to improve the implementation of government and corporate policies in order to enhance the engagement of fathers in their children's everyday activities. Research in these specific areas would help to advance the ways that fathers can maximally support the needs of families, and ultimately promote their children's educational success.

NOTES

1. The authors acknowledge North and South Korea as separate countries, which have been split for nearly 60 years. For this chapter we follow the common usage of Korea to refer to South Korea.
2. A colloquial term (similar to the English expression "stir the pot") that has a negative nuance and refers to a mother's behavior, like a strong wind, that attempts to force the attention of school staff toward her child.

REFERENCES

Attride-Stirling, J. (2001). Thematic networks: An analytic tool for qualitative research. *Qualitative Research, 1,* 385-405.

Belsky, J., & Park, S. -Y. (2000). Exploring reciprocal parent and child effects in the case of child inhibition in US and Korean samples. *International Journal of Behavioral Development, 24,* 338-347. doi:10.1080/01650250050118321

Cabrera, N. J., Tamis-LeMonda, C. S., Bradley, R. H., Hofferth, S., & Lamb, M. E. (2000). Fatherhood in the twenty-first century. *Child Development, 71*(1), 127-136.

Chae, J. -Y., & Lee, K. Y. (2011). Impacts of Korean fathers' attachment and parenting behavior on their children's social competence. *Social Behavior and Personality, 39,* 627-644. doi:10.2224/sbp.2011.39.5.627

Cho, S., & Yoon, Y. (2005). Family processes and psychosocial problems of the young Korean gifted. *International Journal for the Advancement of Counseling, 27,* 245-261.

Chung, Y., & Emery, R. (2007). Early adolescents and divorces in South Korea: Risk, resilience and pain. *Journal of Comparative Family Studies, 41*(5), 855-870.

Coleman, J. S. (1988). Social capital in the creation of human capital. *American Journal of Sociology, 94,* S95-S120.

Duranno Father School. (2011). Program introduction. Retrieved from http://www.fatherschool.org/1pro_info/pro1.php

Kang, Y. (2010, June). *"Any one parent will do": Negotiations of fatherhood among South Korean 'Wild Geese' fathers in Singapore.* Paper session presented at the meeting of Dads for Life, Family Research Network, Asia Research Institute and Gender Studies Minor Programme, Faculty of Arts & Social Sciences, National University of Singapore, Singapore.

Kim, J. (2010). 'Downed' and stuck in Singapore: Lower/middle class South Korean wild geese—kirogi. *Research in the Sociology of Education, 17,* 271-311.

Kim, N. J. (2011). *Male paternity leave.* Retrieved from http://pdf.joinsmsn.com/article/pdf_article_prv.asp?id=DY01201104220156

Kim, S. M., & Gee, H. K. (2011). *Paternity leave fathers "happy but anxious".* Retrieved from http://news.chosun.com/site/data/html_dir/2011/02/23/2011022300053.html

Kim, S. -I., & Rohner, R. P. (2003). Perceived parental acceptance and emotional empathy among university students in Korea. *Journal of Cross-Cultural Psychology, 34,* 723-735. doi:10.1177/0022022103257071

Lee, H. (2010). "I am a *kirogi* mother": Education exodus and life transformation among Korean transnational women. *Journal of Language, Identity, and Education, 9,* 250-264. doi:10.1080/15348458.2010.503915

Lee, Y. H. (1992). A case study of an infant's attachment to the father in a strange situation. *Korean Journal of Child Studies, 13,* 5-18.

Lee, Y. -J., & Koo, H. (2006). Wild geese fathers and a globalised family strategy for education in Korea. *IDPR: International Development Planning Review, 28,* 533-553.

Marsiglio, W., Amato, P., Day, R. D., & Lamb, M. E. (2000). Scholarship on fatherhood in the 1990's and beyond. *Journal of Marriage and the Family, 62,* 1173-1191.

Ministry of Gender Equality and Family, Republic of Korea. (2011). *Brochure of Services, Experience the services that makes everyone in my family smile.* Retrieved from www.mogef.go.kr

Ministry of Health and Welfare, Republic of Korea. (2009). *Multicultural family department press release and attachment material.* Retrieved from www.mohw.go.kr

Ministry of Tourism, Republic of Korea. (2009). *Situation of multicultural family children.* Retrieved from www.mct.go.kr

Olson, P. (2008). *The world's hardest working countries.* Retrieved from http://www.forbes.com/2008/05/21/labor-market-workforce-lead-citizen-cx_po_0521countries.html

Park, H. (2008). Effects of single parenthood on educational aspiration and student disengagement in Korea. *Demographic Research, 18,* 377-408.

Park, S. -M., Cho, S. -I., & Choi, M. -K. (2010). The effect of paternal investment on female fertility intention in South Korea. *Evolution and Human Behavior, 31,* 447-452.

Roggman, L. A., Fitzgerald, H. E., Bradley, R. H., & Raikes, H. (2002). Overview of methodological measurement and design issues in studying fathers: An interdisciplinary perspective. In C. S. Tamis-LeMonda & N. Cabrera (Eds.), *Handbook of father involvement: Multidisciplinary perspectives* (pp. 1-30). Hillsdale, NJ: Erlbaum.

Shin, S. S. (2011). *If you have a second child 1,000,000 won reward ... paternity leave, work-from-home policy.* Retrieved from http://pdf.joinsmsn.com/article/pdf_article_prv.asp?id=DY01201009170078

Shin, S. H., Choi, H., Kim, M. J., & Kim, Y. H. (2010). Comparing adolescents' adjustment and family resilience in divorced families depending on the types of primary caregiver. *Journal of Clinical Nursing, 19,* 1695-1706. doi:10.1111/j.1365-2702.2009.03081.x

Statistics Korea. (2009). *Results of 2008 marriage statistics.* Retrieved from http://kostat.go.kr/portal/korea/kor_ko/5/2/index.board?bmode=read&aSeq=64068

Statistics Korea. (2011a). Population and housing census 2010 [Press release]. Retrieved from http://census.go.kr/hcensus/FileDownload.do?file=/2010+%EC%9D%B8%EA%B5%AC%EC%A3%BC%ED%83%9D%EC%B4%9D%EC%A1%B0%EC%82%AC+%EC%A0%84%EC%88%98%EC%A7%91%EA%B3%84(%EA%B0%80%EA%B5%AC%EC%A3%BC%ED%83%9D)+%EA%B2%B0%EA%B3%BC(%EB%B3%B4%EB%8F%84%EC%9E%90%EB%A3%8C).hwp

Statistics Korea. (2011b). Birth Statistics 2010 [Press release]. Retrieved from http://kostat.go.kr/portal/korea/kor_nw/2/1/index.board?bmode=read&aSeq=249892

Yang, S., & Rosenblatt, P. C. (2008). Confucian family values and childless couples in South Korea. *Journal of Family Issues, 29,* 571-591. doi:10.1177/0192513X07309462

Youn, J. J., & Chung, O. B. (1997). Preschool children's social competency and perceived social support. *Korean Journal of Child Studies, 18,* 311-331.

CHAPTER 10

FATHER-DAUGHTER AND FATHER-SON RELATIONSHIPS

Predicting Delinquency and Academic Outcomes for Ethnic Minority Adolescents

Brett Kia-Keating, Maryam Kia-Keating, and Karen Nylund-Gibson

FATHER INVOLVEMENT STUDIES

Children and families living in extreme poverty represent a national crisis in the United States, where more than one out of five children live in families with annual incomes lower than 50% of the federal poverty level (incomes less than $22,055 per year for a family of four; Wight, Chau, & Aratani, 2011). These numbers are exceedingly high in comparison to other developed countries, and perhaps most concerning, have only been increasing; in the past decade alone, more than 3.8 million more children entered into these poverty statistics, representing a 33% increase between 2000 and 2009. There are robust findings demonstrating the inextricable patterns and reciprocal feedback loops occurring between poverty and

Promising Practices for Fathers' Involvement in Children's Education
pp. 161–175

educational and health indicators (Currie, 2005; Lynch, 2003; Seith & Kalof, 2011). Most strikingly, researchers have consistently identified father residential status as a key correlate to childhood poverty risk—in other words, a father's presence is a critical factor in a child's life and both short- and long-term well-being (Cabrera, 2010; Cabrera, Ryan, Mitchell, Shannon, & Tamis-Lemonda, 2008). Considering a child's social ecology, and keeping longitudinal trajectories of risk and resilience in mind, it is especially important to better understand the central role that both residential and nonresidential fathers play in the lives of children in poverty.

Research on fathers has been striking in its demonstration of the important and positive role that fathers can potentially play in the social, emotional, cognitive and psychological development of their children, especially among young children (Bogels & Phares, 2008; Cabrera et al., 2007; Fagan & Iglesias, 1999; Gottman, Katz, & Hooven, 1997). Father involvement predicts a range of long-term outcomes associated with psychological adjustment, educational and occupational success, and overall well-being, including the development of problem-solving skills, intellectual development, ability to empathize with others, and the development of an internal locus of control (Flouri & Buchanan, 2003; Hwang & Lamb, 1997; Marsiglio, Amato, Day, & Lamb, 2000; Sanford et al., 1995). Research has also shown that father involvement may play a protective role in preventing psychopathology (Flouri & Buchanan, 2003) and delinquent behaviors in adolescents (Coley & Medeiros, 2007).

Notably, regardless of the father's presence in the home, research shows that the quality of contact between father and child, and parent-child relational closeness, appear to be more important than the frequency of contact or parent residence (Demuth & Brown, 2004; Nord, Brimhall, & West, 1997). Thus, engaging fathers to improve the quality of their relationships with their children is critical.

AREAS NEEDING RESEARCH ATTENTION

The impact of fathers on child and adolescent development and academic success has been underexplored, particularly when considering the vast array of research on mothers. Even when they do include fathers, researchers tend to overemphasize problematic components of father-child relationships, examining issues such as conflict, negativity, and harsh parenting, to the neglect of more positive factors such as closeness, warmth, and responsiveness. In accordance, prevention and intervention efforts are rarely aimed at fathers. A more nuanced understanding of fathers is important to best inform the development of effective programs to support fathers' roles in academic success.

Comparing father-son and father-daughter relationships provides one avenue to developing a more refined understanding of fathers and child outcomes. Risk and protective factors related to father-child conflict can be different for boys and girls (Crean, 2008). Several studies have demonstrated that father involvement specifically predicts lower aggression and behavior problems among boys (Aldous & Mulligan, 2002; McCabe, Clark, & Barnett, 1999; Vaden-Kiernan, Ialongo, Pearson, Hunter, & Kellam, 1995). Differential longitudinal educational outcomes may also exist given the finding that early father involvement has been shown to be related to later educational attainment in daughters, but not sons (Flouri, 2005). For example, in one nationally representative sample, fathers' engagement in learning activities such as reading and general education, at both early (age 7) and later (age 16) developmental time periods, were predictive of daughters' psychological distress in adulthood (Buchanan, Flouri, & Ten Brinke, 2002; Flouri & Buchanan, 2003). Some research suggests that a father's positive impact on his daughter's academic achievement is mediated by self-esteem (Cooper, 2009). It is important to keep in mind that father-daughter supportive relationships can help to build girls' self-esteem, which subsequently can positively impact daughters' academic outcomes, suggesting that educating fathers on how to strengthen their child's self-esteem may be particularly useful in the case of daughters.

STUDY ON FATHER-CHILD RELATIONSHIPS

Purpose and Design

By examining fathers' roles in the lives of ethnic minority youth living in low-income households, our research fills an important gap in the literature (Cabrera & Garcia Coll, 2004; Marsiglio, Day, & Lamb, 2000). The framework for our study is drawn from a protective and promotive conceptual model (Kia-Keating, Dowdy, Morgan, & Noam, 2011), whereby it is possible to examine both positive and negative features of the father-child relationship rather than taking a deficit-based stance which much of the previous research on ethnic minority fathers tends to rely on (Campos, 2008). More specifically, in the present study we distinguished between the influence of anger/alienation and trust/communication in the father-child relationship, without assuming that one aspect defines the other or that they are predictive of educational outcomes in the same way, while also allowing for these relationships to differ by gender.

We used a subsample drawn from *Welfare, Children, and Families: A Three City Study*, a longitudinal, household-based, stratified random-sample of children and their primary caregivers whose income was 200% below the poverty line. Families were selected from more than 40,000 low income households within Boston, Chicago, and San Antonio (for an overview of the study design see Winston et al., 1999). This study provides longitudinal data so that we can examine primarily African American and Hispanic low income urban young adolescents (ages 10-14) and their fathers across 6 years, in order to look at educational outcomes during an important developmental window. School dropout rates are elevated once adolescents reach high school, and the probability that an adolescent entering the ninth grade will complete high school after 4 years is strikingly low for Hispanic, Black, low income, and urban youth (Abrams & Haney, 2004; Balfanz & Legters, 2004). However, a dearth of research focuses specifically on ethnic minority youth and fathers, rarely considering how factors such as culture, immigration, and education interplay with father engagement (Cabrera & Garcia Coll, 2004; Campos, 2008). Few studies take fathers' beliefs and expectations into account (Saracho & Spodek, 2008). Moreover, although increased involvement is often a general recommendation of the studies that do exist, disentangling the ways in which fathers engage with their children, and identifying characteristics of the father-child relationship that lead to healthy development is often left unclear (Sarkadi, Kiristiansson, Oberklaid, & Bremberg, 2008).

The current investigation examined 920 youth participants between the ages of 10 and 14 at Wave 1. Among this sample 49% were males and 51% females. A majority were categorized in one of two ethnic minority groups: 46% Black and 46% Hispanic. Participants were followed up twice: the second wave of data collection took place 1 year after the baseline interviews, and a third and final wave took place approximately 5 years later. Audio computer-assisted self-interviewing was used to increase the potential for youth participants to provide valid responses to questions about sensitive topics (Turner et al., 1998).

Measures

A subset of items from Armsden and Greenberg's (1987) Inventory of Parent and Peer Attachment were used to assess the affective and cognitive aspects of father-child relationships. Participants rated each of 12 items about their relationships with their fathers from *never true* to *always true*. These items created two subscales: father-child trust/communication and father-child anger/alienation, alternately (for simplification of presentation) referred to respectively as trust and anger (Coley, 2003). Father-child trust represented adolescents' perceptions of the accessibility, warmth, and responsiveness of their fathers, which was comprised of the mean of six items such as: *My father accepts me as I am*; and *I like to get my father's point of view on things I'm concerned about*. Father-child anger represented the adolescents' feelings of alienation from and resentment toward their fathers. The anger score was comprised of the mean of six items such as: *I feel angry with my father*; and *My father doesn't understand what I'm going through these days.*

Recent delinquent behaviors were assessed using 13 items from the National Longitudinal Study of Youth (Borus et al., 1982) and the Youth Deviance Scale (Gold, 1970; Steinberg, Mounts, Lamborn, & Dornbusch, 1991). Participants were asked to rate each item on a 4-point scale (ranging from *never* to *often*), based on the previous 12-month period. Six items captured serious delinquency (such as *how often have you gotten in trouble with the police?* and *how often have you attacked someone with the idea of seriously hurting or killing them?*), six items assessed alcohol and drug use (such as *how often have you gotten drunk?* and *how often have you used hard drugs such as heroin, cocaine, or LSD?*) and one question asked participants how often they had run away from home.

We used three different indicators to look at academic outcomes including grades (*"The last time you got a report card, what were your grades?"*); being held back (*"Have you been held back a year or made to repeat a grade?"*); and current school attendance (*"Are you currently attending any type of school including elementary, junior high, high school, night school, vocational school or college?"*).

Data Analysis Using Longitudinal Mediation Models

Our modeling approach used repeated measures from participants over time. Specifically, we used a longitudinal mediation model within the latent variable framework (also called structural equation modeling). In this framework, we could model the impact of the father-child relationship characteristics on future delinquency and later academic outcomes. An analytic approach that uses data collected over different time points allows for the specification of complex relationships that preserves the temporal impact that they are believed to have. Specifically, we focus on the lasting impact of the father-child relationship on the adolescent's proximal (i.e., delinquency) and more distal outcomes (i.e., academic outcomes). Further, we specified these models separately for girls and boys so we could study how the relationship between the father-child relationship variables and behavioral and educational outcomes are different across gender.

In our analysis, the father-child relationship variables (i.e., trust/communication and anger/alienation) and adolescent's academic outcomes were represented with latent factors (depicted as circles in Figure 10.1). Factor loadings for the three latent factors are presented in Table 10.1, but were not included in Figure 10.1 so that the key relationships among

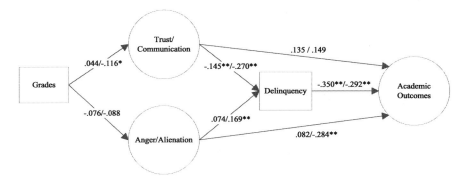

Note: Standardized coefficients for males (*N* = 446) are presented first, followed by females (*N*= 474; e.g., male/female). *p < 0.01. **p < 0.0. Measurement model not presented here; see factor loadings in Table 10.1

Figure 10.1.   Model diagram depicting the pathways tested between father-child relationships, delinquent behaviors, and academic outcomes over time.

Table 10.1.   Factor Loadings for the Latent Variables Trust/Communication, Anger/Alienation, and Grades Presented by Gender

		Factor Loadings	
Factor	*Item Wording*	*Males*	*Females*
Trust/ communication	Child seeks Father's point of view	0.77*	0.80*
	Father accepts child as s/he is	0.72*	0.76*
	Father cares about child's point of view	0.79*	0.84*
	Child tells Father about problems	0.73*	0.76*
	Father gives child a lot of attention	0.81*	0.77*
	Child trusts Father	0.82*	0.84*
Anger/ alienation	Child gets upset more than Father knows	0.55*	0.71*
	Child feels bad discussing problems w/Father	0.50*	0.52*
	Father expects too much from child	0.49*	0.34*
	Child doesn't bother Father with problems	0.48*	0.47*
	Father doesn't understand what child going through	0.45*	0.44*
Grades	Grade point average	0.36*	0.33*
	Repeat	0.49*	0.34*
	In school	0.65*	0.51*

Note: Factor loadings are standardized. *p < .001.

factors and variables are highlighted. The delinquency variable and adolescent prior grades were included as observed variables in the model. Two longitudinal mediation models were fit, one for each gender. The model fit for both genders was adequate. Specifically, the fit statistics for the male sample were: χ^2 (99) = 273.48, p < .001; RMSEA = .063, 90% RMSEA CI [.054-.072], CFI = .904, TLI = .884. The fit statistics for the female sample were: χ^2 (99) = 291.420, p < .001; RMSEA = .064, 90% RMSEA CI [.056-.073], CFI = .911, TLI = .892. We determined that the model fit was adequate enough to interpret the results without further modification.

The mediation model posits that there is both a direct and indirect effect of the father-child relationship on academic outcomes. Specifically, we hypothesized that the father-child relationship will impact the amount of delinquency a student engages in, which in turn, influences the students' academic outcome; and that, over and above the indirect effect, father-child relationship directly impacts academic outcomes, all controlling for student's prior grades. The hypothesized mediational model is depicted in Figure 10.1.

SIGNIFICANT FINDINGS

What We Learned About Father-Daughter Relationships

Daughters' relationships with their father had significant direct and indirect effects on their academics. More specifically, negative father-daughter relationships (i.e., angry) were found to have a significant negative impact on educational outcomes 6 years later. In addition, both positive and negative father-daughter relationships were significantly related to female adolescents' involvement in delinquent activities 1 year later, which subsequently had a significant impact on her academic outcomes 5 years later. These findings demonstrated that negative father-daughter relationships were associated with increased levels of delinquency, followed by a negative impact on academic outcomes. On the other hand, although the direct relationship between positive (i.e., trusting) father-daughter relationships and educational outcomes was not significant, the experience of trust and communication with their fathers decreased a female's likelihood to participate in delinquent behaviors, which ultimately, indirectly positively impacted academic outcomes. These findings in particular highlight fathers' critical role in preventing girls' involvement in delinquent activities and consequently, in indirectly impacting their daughters' educational attainment.

Much research has already focused on negative characteristics of fathers and the potential for increased risk for adolescent girls (Hicks, Dirago, Iacono, & McGue, 2009; Hicks, South, DiRago, Iacono, & McGue, 2009). Our study extends beyond this limited framework to examine the possibility that positive attributes of the father-child relationship might help protect or promote their children's behavioral and educational outcomes. The current findings support past literature demonstrating the importance of positive father characteristics on their daughters' academic success (Lee, Kushner, & Cho, 2007). Drawing from these results, school-based programs focused on building trust and fostering healthy communication between fathers and their daughters could help to prevent female engagement in delinquency and thus, support academic achievement in the long term.

What We Learned About Father-Son Relationships

Our research demonstrated that better father-son trust and communication directly reduced adolescent boys' likelihood to engage in delinquent behaviors. These findings underscore the importance of positive father-son relationship characteristics for healthy and positive youth development. It also suggests that building trust in the father-son relationship can play the role of a developmental asset or promotive factor for male academic achievement (Kia-Keating et al., 2011).

Surprisingly, anger and alienation in father-son relationships did not directly impact male adolescents' likelihoods to engage in delinquent behaviors 1 year later, and it did not directly or indirectly predict their academic outcomes 5 years later. This finding is counter to past literature suggesting a significant relationship between negative father characteristics and involvement in delinquency (Hoeve, Dubas, Gerris, van der Laan, & Smeenk, 2011). It is worth considering whether anger in a father-son relationship might be considered normative in certain contexts, and may neither get in the way of building trust, nor necessarily impact long-term outcomes. Given that the current sample was comprised mostly of fathers living outside the household, it is also possible that given the more limited contact, the anger and alienation that sons experienced had less influence on their behavioral and educational outcomes. Nonetheless, the fact that trust, but not anger, in the father-son relationship was a significant factor in this context and among this population only serves to further highlight how important father-son trust and communication are to target when providing prevention and intervention programs for boys and their fathers.

FAMILY-SCHOOL COMMUNITY PARTNERSHIPS

In large part, the field has typically taken a deficit approach, seeking to decrease problem behaviors and academic failure, without adequately attending to increasing protective or promotive factors and thus, positive outcomes such as academic success and continued academic pursuits. Schools in particular have a distinct opportunity to serve a central role in capitalizing on fathers' potential to impact their children's educational outcomes, while simultaneously addressing mental health and well-being, and positive youth development (Burns et al., 1995; Farmer, Burns, Phillips, Angold, & Costello, 2003). Engaging fathers in the school environment can reduce stigma associated with receiving services directed towards at-risk youth and families.

School-based programs focused on father-child relationships can prevent adolescent involvement in delinquent activities with the potential to not only reduce risky behaviors but also to increase long-term academic success. Programs that focus on family-based models for delinquency or violence prevention hold a lot of promise, particularly for ethnic minority families (e.g., Leidy, Guerra, & Toro, 2010) but they often neglect to mention the particular role of fathers. The research that exists shows that there are often cultural barriers to father engagement in prevention and intervention programs including logistical barriers (e.g., multiple jobs, language barriers; Cabrera & Garcia Coll, 2004; Campos, 2008), as well as traditional belief systems with a limited view on fathers roles (Hossain, Field, Pickens, Malphurs, & Del Valle, 1997).

Utilizing family-school-community partnerships has demonstrated positive results such as increasing school engagement and academic achievement (Spoth, Randall, & Shin, 2008). Given that fathers have the potential to play a critical and unique role in promoting healthy developmental trajectories in their children, family-school-community partnerships can cultivate this potential by attending to the multiple layers of a child's social ecology (Eagle, Dowd-Eagle, & Sheridan, 2008; Esler, Godber, & Christenson, 2008) and, through investing in fathers, ultimately, a broader and more lasting positive impact can occur for individuals, families, schools, and communities.

The first critical step is for schools to build awareness around the importance of father-child relationships. School staff members traditionally receive little to no training on parent involvement, and even less on the critical function that fathers play (Epstein & Sanders, 2006). Utilizing evidence provided by empirical research and the expertise of national organizations such as the National Center on Fathering and the Center for Fathers and Families can help schools provide professional development training for teachers and staff with a focus on better understanding and engaging fathers and help to support healthy father-child relationships (Sander & Sheldon, 2009).

Schools also have the unique opportunity to provide education directly to families and communities. A community public health campaign approach could be applied to the schoolwide community so that families are educated about the central role fathers can play in the healthy development of their children, with the central purpose of enhancing family and school perceptions about fatherhood (Wilcox & Dew, 2008). This strategy has empirical support, whereby fathers' positive perceptions of fatherhood are related to increased father involvement (Ihinger-Tallman, Pasley, & Buehler, 1993). Ultimately, by educating key stakeholders, families and communities are more likely to increase their investment in building and sustaining efforts aimed at improving father-child relationships (Sander & Sheldon, 2009).

Schools should look for ways to incorporate father involvement and father-child relationship building within preexisting successful programs (McBride & Rane, 1996). In addition, schools could make specific efforts to target their curriculum as well as their parent engagement programs to challenge fundamental beliefs and traditional masculine ideologies, a strategy which has been demonstrated to promote fathers' involvement and engagement with their children (Mahalik & Morrison, 2006). Engaging fathers in academic programming is also an important strategy. Fathers' direct involvement in their children's schooling has been found to impact academic outcomes above and beyond what is achieved through mothers' involvement, and has been shown to partially mediate the effects of school-, neighborhood-, and family-level risks and resources on their children's academic achievement (McBride, Schoppe-Sullivan, & Ho, 2005). Finally, father engagement does not solely depend upon the direct outreach to fathers, but through involvement and support from mothers (McBride & Rane, 1996). Since mothers typically perform the role of gatekeeper and liaison between the school and the family, informing mothers of the importance of fathers in the lives of their children has shown to increase father involvement. These strategies could be most effectively put into place through family-school-community partnerships.

Given the diversity of family compositions within school populations, in addition to resident biological fathers, it is important for schools to reach out to nonresident fathers and nonbiologically related father figures. Although research has demonstrated that children living in single parent homes experience negative consequences to their academic achievement and risk for dropout (Pong & Ju, 2000), the majority of these children continue to have an important adult male figure in their lives (Levine, 1993) and have nonresident fathers who are involved (Walter, 2000). Our findings highlight the importance of attending to the role that nonresident fathers play and demonstrate that those father-child relationships have a significant longitudinal impact on behavioral and educational outcomes.

Family-school-community partnerships have the potential to develop programs that take into consideration the complex and interacting systems involved in engaging fathers in order to impact their children's behavioral and educational outcomes, particularly in the context of low income ethnic minority adolescents living in urban settings. Targeting father-daughter and father-son relationships, even in the case of nonresident fathers, has the potential to influence young adolescents' future educational and occupational pursuits, and to ultimately, promote health and reduce disparities in far-reaching and lasting ways (Freudenberg & Ruglis, 2007).

REFERENCES

Abrams, L., & Haney, W. (2004). Accountability and the Grade 9 to 10 transition: the impact on attrition and retention rates. In G. Orfield (Ed.), *Dropouts in America: Confronting the graduation rate crisis* (pp. 181-205). Cambridge, MA: Harvard Education Press.

Aldous, J., & Mulligan, G. (2002). Father's child care and children's behavioral problems. *Journal of Family Issues, 23,* 624-647.

Armsden, G. C., & Greenberg, M. T. (1987). The inventory of parent and peer attachment: Individual differences and their relationship to psychological well-being in adolescence. *Journal of Youth and Adolescence, 16,* 427-454.

Balfanz, R., & Legters, N. E. (2004). Locating the dropout crisis: Which high schools produce the nation's dropouts? In G. Orfield (Ed.), *Dropouts in America: Confronting the graduation rate crisis* (pp. 57-84). Cambridge, MA: Harvard Education Press.

Bogels, S., & Phares, V. (2008). Fathers' role in the etiology, prevention and treatment of child anxiety: A review and new model. *Clinical Psychology Review, 28*(4), 539-558.

Borus, M. E., Carpenter, S. A., Crowley, J. E., Daymont, T., Kim, C., Pollard, T. K., … Santos, R. (1982). *Pathways to the future: Vol. 2. A final report on the National Survey of Youth labor market experience in 1980* (pp. 163-188). Columbus, OH: Center for Human Resource Research, The Ohio State University.

Buchanan, A., Flouri, E., & Ten Brinke, J. (2002). Emotional and behavioural problems in childhood and distress in adult life: Risk and protective factors. *Australian and New Zealand Journal of Psychiatry, 36*(4), 521-527.

Burns, B. J., Costello, E. J., Angold, A., Tweed, D., Stangl, D., Farmer, E. M. Z., & Erkanli, A. (1995). Children's mental health service use across service sectors. *Health Affairs, 14,* 149-159.

Cabrera, N. J. (2010). Father involvement and public policies. In M. E. Lamb (Ed.), *The role of the father in child development* (5th ed.). Hoboken, NJ: Wiley.

Cabrera, N. J., & Garcia Coll, C. (2004). Latino fathers: Uncharted territory in need of much exploration. In M. E. Lamb (Ed.), *The role of the father in child development* (pp. 98-120). Hoboken, NJ: Wiley.

Cabrera, N. J., Ryan, R. M., Mitchell, S. J., Shannon, J. D., & Tamis-Lemonda, C. S. (2008). Low-income, nonresidential father involvement with their toddlers: Variation by fathers' race and ethnicity. *Journal of Family Psychology, 22*(3), 643-647.

Cabrera, N. J., Shannon, J. D., & Tamis-LeMonda, C. (2007). Fathers' influence on their children's cognitive and emotional development: From toddlers to pre-K (Special issue). *Applied Developmental Science, 11*(4), 208-213.

Campos, R. (2008). Considerations for studying father involvement in early childhood among Latino families. *Hispanic Journal of Behavioral Sciences, 30*(2), 133-160.

Coley, R. L. (2003). Daughter-father relationships and adolescent psychosocial functioning in low-income African American families. *Journal of Marriage and Family, 65*(4), 867-875.

Coley, R. L., & Medeiros, B. (2007). Reciprocal longitudinal relations between nonresident father involvement and adolescent delinquency. *Child Development, 78*(1), 132-147.

Cooper, S. M. (2009). Associations between father-daughter relationship quality and the academic engagement of African-American adolescent girls: Self-esteem as a mediator? *Journal of Black Psychology, 35*(4), 495-516.

Crean, H. F. (2008). Conflict in the Latino parent-youth dyad: The role of emotional support from the opposite parent. *Journal of Family Psychology, 22*(3), 484-493.

Currie, J. (2005). Health disparities and gaps in school readiness. *The Future of Children, 15*(1), 117-138.

Demuth, S., & Brown, S. L. (2004). Family structure, family processes, and adolescent delinquency: The significance of parental absence versus parental gender. *Journal of Research in Crime and Delinquency, 41*, 58-81.

Eagle, J. W., Dowd-Eagle, S. E., & Sheridan, S. M. (2008). Best practices in school-community partnerships. In A. Thomas & J. Grimes (Eds.), *Best practices in school psychology* (Vol. 5, pp. 953-967). Bethesda, MD: National Association of School Psychologists.

Epstein, J. L., & Sanders, M. G. (2006). Prospects for change: Preparing educators for school, family, and community partnerships. *Peabody Journal of Education, 81*(2), 81-120.

Esler, A. N., Godber, Y., & Christenson, S. (2008). Best practices in supporting school-family partnerships. In A. Thomas & J. Grimes (Eds.), *Best practices in school psychology* (Vol. 5, pp. 917-936). Bethesda, MD: National Association of School Psychologists.

Fagan, J., & Iglesias, A. (1999). Father involvement program effects on fathers, father figures, and their head start children: A quasi-experimental study. *Early Childhood Research Quarterly, 14*(2), 243-269.

Farmer, E. M. Z., Burns, B. J., Phillips, S. D., Angold, A., & Costello, E. J. (2003). Pathways into and through mental health services for children and adolescents. *Psychiatric Services, 54*, 60-66.

Flouri, E. (2005). *Fathering and child outcomes*. West Sussex, England: Wiley.

Flouri, E., & Buchanan, A. (2003). The role of father involvement in children's later mental health. *Journal of Adolescence, 26*(1), 63-78.

Freudenberg, N., & Ruglis, J. (2007). Reframing school dropout as a public health issue. *Preventing Chronic Disease, 4*(4). Retrieved from http://www.cdc.gov/pcd/issues/2007/oct/07_0063.htm

Gold, M. (1970). Delinquent behavior in an American city. Belmont, CA: Brooks/Cole.

Gottman, J. M., Katz, L. F., & Hooven, C. (1997). *Meta-emotion: How families communicate emotionally*. Hillsdale, NJ: Erlbaum.

Hicks, B. M., Dirago, A. C., Iacono, W. G., & McGue, M. (2009). Gene-environment interplay in internalizing disorders: Consistent findings across six environmental risk factors. *Journal of Child Psychology and Psychiatry and Allied Disciplines, 50*(10), 1309-1317.

Hicks, B. M., South, S. C., DiRago, A. C., Iacono, W. G., & McGue, M. (2009). Environmental adversity and increasing genetic risk for externalizing disorders. *Archives of General Psychiatry, 66*(6), 640-648.

Hoeve, M., Dubas, J. S., Gerris, J. R. M., van der Laan, P. H., & Smeenk, W. (2011). Maternal and paternal parenting styles: Unique and combined links to adolescent and early adult delinquency. *Journal of Adolescence, 34*(5), 813-827.

Hossain, Z., Field, T., Pickens, J., Malphurs, J., & Del Valle, C. (1997). Fathers' caregiving in low-income African-American and Hispanic-American families. *Early Development & Parenting, 6*(2), 73-82.

Hwang, C.-P., & Lamb, M. E. (1997). Father involvement in Sweden: A longitudinal study of its stability and correlates. *International Journal of Behavioral Development, 21*(3), 621-632.

Ihinger-Tallman, M., Pasley, K., & Buehler, C. (1993). Developing a middle-range theory of father involvement post-divorce. *Journal of Family Issues, 14*, 550-571.

Kia-Keating, M., Dowdy, E., Morgan, M. L., & Noam, G. G. (2011). Protecting and promoting: An integrative conceptual model for healthy development of adolescents. *Journal of Adolescent Health, 48*, 220-228.

Lee, S., Kushner, J., & Cho, S. (2007). Effects of parents' gender, child's gender, and parental involvement on the academic achievement of adolescents in single parent families. *Sex Roles, 56*, 149-157.

Leidy, M. S., Guerra, N. G., & Toro, R. I. (2010). A review of family-based programs to prevent youth violence among Latinos. *Hispanic Journal of Behavioral Sciences, 32*(5), 5-36.

Levine, J. A. (1993). Involving fathers in Head Start: A framework for public policy and program development. *Families in Society, 74*(1), 4-19.

Lynch, S. M. (2003). Cohort and life-course patterns in the relationship between education and health: A hierarchical approach. *Demography, 40*(2), 309-331.

Mahalik, J. R., & Morrison, J. A. (2006). A cognitive therapy approach to increasing father involvement by changing restrictive masculine schemas. *Cognitive and Behavioral Practice, 13*(1), 62-70.

Marsiglio, W., Amato, P., Day, R. D., & Lamb, M. E. (2000). Scholarship on father-hood in the 1990s and beyond. *Journal of Marriage & the Family, 62*(4), 1173-1191.

Marsiglio, W., Day, R. D., & Lamb, M. E. (2000). Exploring fatherhood diversity: Implications for conceptualizing father involvement (Special issue). *Marriage & Family Review, 29*(4), 269-293.

McBride, B. A., & Rane, T. R. (1996). Father/male involvement in early childhood programs. *ERIC Digest.* (EDO-PS-96-10)

McBride, B. A., Schoppe-Sullivan, S. J., & Ho, M. (2005). The mediating role of fathers' school involvement on student achievement. *Applied Developmental Psychology, 26,* 201-216.

McCabe, K. M., Clark, R., & Barnett, D. (1999). Family protective factors among urban African-American youth. *Journal of Clinical Child Psychology, 28*(2), 137-150.

Nord, C. W., Brimhall, D., & West, J. (1997). Fathers' involvement in their chil-dren's schools. *U.S. Department of Education, National Center for Education Statis-tics, NCES 98-091*(ED 409 125).

Pong, S. L., & Ju, D. B. (2000). The effects of change in family structure and income on dropping out of middle and high school. *Journal of Family Issues, 21,* 147-169.

Sander, M. G., & Sheldon, S. B. (2009). *Principals matter: A guide to school, family, and community partnerships.* Thousand Oaks, CA: SAGE.

Sanford, M., Szatmari, P., Spinner, M., Munroe-Blum, H., Jamieson, E., Walsh, C., & Jones, D. (1995). Predicting the one-year course of adolescent major depression. *Journal of the American Academy of Child & Adolescent Psychiatry, 34*(12), 1618-1628.

Saracho, O. N., & Spodek, B. (2008). Demythologizing the Mexican American father. *Journal of Hispanic Higher Education, 7*(2), 79-96.

Sarkadi, A., Kiristiansson, R., Oberklaid, F., & Bremberg, S. (2008). Fathers' involvement and children's developmental outcomes: A systematic review of longitudinal studies. *Acta Paediatrica, 97,* 153-158.

Seith, D., & Kalof, C. (2011). Who are America's poor children?: Examining health disparities by race and ethnicity. Retrieved from http://www.nccp.org/publications/pdf/text_1032.pdf

Spoth, R., Randall, G. K., & Shin, C. (2008). Increasing school success through partnership-based family competency training: Experimental study of long-term outcomes. *School Psychology Quarterly, 23*(1), 70-89.

Steinberg, L., Mounts, N. S., Lamborn, S. D., & Dornbusch, S. M. (1991). Author-itative parenting and adolescent adjustment across varied ecological niches. *Journal of Research on Adolescence, 1,* 19-36.

Turner, C. F., Forsyth, B. H., O'Reilly, J., Cooley, P. C., Smith, T. K., Rogers, S. M., & Miller, H. G. (1998). Automated self-interviewing and the survey measure-ment of sensitive behaviors. In M. P. Couper, R. P. Baler, J. Bethlehem, C. Z. Clark, J. Martin, W. L. Nicholls, II, & J. M. O'Reilly (Eds.), *Computer-assisted survey information collection* (pp. 455-473). New York, NY: Wiley.

Vaden-Kiernan, N., Ialongo, N., Pearson, J., Hunter, A., & Kellam, S. (1995). Household family structure and children's aggressive behavior: A longitudinal study of urban elementary school children. *Journal of Abnormal Child Psychology, 23*, 553-568.

Walter, M. (2000). Parental involvement of unwed, nonresident fathers. *Family Matters, 57*, 34-49.

Wight, V. R., Chau, M., & Aratani, Y. (2011). Who are American's poor children?: The official story. Retrieved from http://www.nccp.org/publications/pdf/text_1001.pdf

Wilcox, W. B., & Dew, J. (2008). *Protectors or perpetrators? Fathers, mothers, and child abuse and neglect* (Vol. 7). New York, NY: Institute for American Values, Center for Marriage and Families.

Winston, P., Angel, R. J., Burton, L. M., Chase-Lansdale, P. L., Cherlin, A. J., Moffitt, R. A., & Wilson, W. J. (1999). *Welfare, children and families: A three-city study: Overview and design*. Retrieved from http://web.jhu.edu/threecitystudy/images/overviewanddesign.pdf

LIST OF CONTRIBUTORS

Martha Allexsaht-Snider, Associate Professor, Department of Elementary and Social Studies Education, University of Georgia, Athens, GA, USA. marthaas@uga.edu

Wei-Wen Chen, Assistant Professor, Faculty of Education, University of Macau, Taipa, Macau. weiwen818@gmail.com

Susan S. Chuang, Associate Professor, Department of Family Relations and Applied Nutrition, University of Guelph, Guelph, Ontario, Canada. schuang@uoguelph.ca

Rollande Deslandes, Professor, Department of Education, Universite du Quebec a Trois-Rivieres, Canada and Senior Researcher at the Research and Intervention Center on School Success (CRIRES) at Laval University, Quebec. Rollande.Deslandes@uqtr.ca

Justin J. Hendricks, Doctoral Student, Department of Sociology and Criminology & Law, University of Florida, Gainesville, FL, USA. justinhendricks@ufl.edu

Ana Inés Heras, National Career Track Researcher, IRICE CONICET Argentina and Principal Researcher, Institute for Social Inclusion and Human Development, Buenos Aires, Argentina. herasmonnersans @gmail.com

Diana B. Hiatt-Michael, Professor Emeritus, Pepperdine University, Malibu, CA, USA. dmichael@pepperdine.edu

Hsiu-Zu Ho, Professor, Department of Education, Gevirtz Graduate School of Education, University of California-Santa Barbara, Santa Barbara, CA, USA. ho@education.ucsb.edu

Elif Karsli, Doctoral Student and Fulbright Scholar, Early Childhood Education, University of Georgia, Athens, GA, USA. ekarsli@uga.edu

Brett Kia-Keating, Assistant Researcher and Lecturer, Department of Education, Gevirtz Graduate School of Education, University of California-Santa Barbara, Santa Barbara, CA, USA. Bkiakeating@education.ucsb.edu

Maryam Kia-Keating, Assistant Professor, Department of Counseling, Clinical and School Psychology, Gevirtz Graduate School of Education, University of California-Santa Barbara, Santa Barbara, CA, USA. mkiakeating@education.ucsb.edu

Ann Y. Kim, Doctoral Student, Department of Education, Gevirtz Graduate School of Education, University of California-Santa Barbara, Santa Barbara, CA, USA. akim@education.ucsb.edu

William Marsiglio, Professor, Department of Sociology and Criminology & Law, University of Florida, Gainesville, FL, USA. marsig@ufl.edu

Raquel-Amaya Martínez-González, Faculty of Education, Department of Education Sciences, Oviedo University, Oviedo, Asturias, Spain. raquelamaya@gmail.com

Robert P. Moreno, Associate Professor, Department of Child and Family Studies, Syracuse University, Syracuse, NY, USA. rmoreno@syr.edu

G. Ugo Nwokeji, Associate Professor, Department of African-American Studies, University of California-Berkeley, Berkeley, CA, USA. ugo@berkeley.edu

Karen Nylund-Gibson, Assistant Professor, Department of Education, Gevirtz Graduate School of Education, University of California-Santa Barbara, Santa Barbara, CA, USA. knylund@education.ucsb.edu

María José Rodrigo-López, Faculty of Psychology, Department of Developmental Psychology and Education, La Laguna University, La Laguna, Tenerife, Spain. mjrodri@ull.es

Beatriz Rodríguez-Ruiz, Faculty of Psychology, Department of Developmental Psychology and Education, La Laguna University, La Laguna, Tenerife, Spain. bearodriguezruiz@gmail.com

Cheri Scripter, Administrator, Mount Diablo Unified School District, Concord, CA, USA. cheriscripter@gmail

Connie N. Tran, Doctoral Student, Department of Education, Gevirtz Graduate School of Education, University of California-Santa Barbara, Santa Barbara, CA, USA. ctran@education.ucsb.edu

Chih-Wen Wu, Doctoral Student, Department of Psychology, National Taiwan University, Taipei, Taiwan. d98227102@ntu.edu.tw

Kuang-Hui Yeh, Research Fellow, Institute of Ethnology, Academia Sinica and professor, Department of Psychology, National Taiwan University, Taipei, Taiwan. ykh01@gate.sinica.edu.tw

Made in the USA
Las Vegas, NV
12 May 2021